# Play, Exploration and Learning

A valuable contribution to the evaluation of nursery practice in Britain, this 'natural history' of the activities of children and caring adults presents a comparative study of four types of provision for the under-fives: nursery schools, nursery classes, playgroups and day nurseries. All four types of provision are seen as happy, busy, caring environments, but they vary greatly in terms of staffing levels, training and material provision.

The authors look at the 'play' of three- to five-year-old children and the activities of the adults who care for them. They examine in detail children's choices of materials and their use of them, with special attention given to the way language is used by both children and adults during play. They also describe adults' expectations of the various provisions and the values of the activities pursued in them. Of special interest is the emphasis placed by adults upon fantasy play, and the often large discrepancy between expectation and practice. Also covered are the difference in the play activities of part-time and full-time nursery school children, and the transition from pre-school to first school.

The book will be of particular interest to pre-school practitioners, to developmental psychologists and to educational administrators.

**The Authors**
S. John Hutt is Professor in the Department of Psychology, University of Keele. Until 1973 he was Research Fellow in Biological Sciences at St Catherine's College, Oxford, and Co-Director of the Human Development Research Unit, Oxford.
Stephen Tyler is Educational Psychologist, Stockport Metropolitan Borough Council. He was previously Research Fellow in the Department of Psychology, University of Keele.
The late Corinne Hutt was Reader in the same Keele department; she was previously Research Fellow at Lady Margaret Hall, Oxford, while working in the Human Development Research Unit.
Helen Christopherson is Editorial Secretary of the *Observer* magazine. Formerly she was a Research Assistant at Keele University.

**Routledge Education Books**

Advisory editor: John Eggleston
*Professor of Education*
*University of Warwick*

# Play, Exploration and Learning: a Natural History of the Pre-School

S. John Hutt, Stephen Tyler, Corinne Hutt and
Helen Christopherson

*University of Keele*

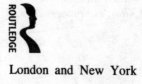

London and New York

First published 1989 by
Routledge
11 New Fetter Lane, London EC4P 4EE

Simultaneously published in the USA and Canada
by Routledge
a division of Routledge, Chapman and Hall, Inc.
29 West 35th Street, New York, NY 10001

New in paperback 1990

Filmset by Mayhew Typesetting,
26 St Thomas Street, Bristol BS1 6JZ
Printed and bound in Great Britain by
Mackays of Chatham PLC, Chatham, Kent

British Library Cataloguing in Publication Data

Play, exploration and learning : a natural
    history of the pre-school. – (Routledge
    education books).
    1. Great Britain. Pre-school children.
    Education
    I. Hutt, S. John
    372'.21'0941
    0-415-05265-3 (pbk)

Library of Congress Cataloging in Publication Data

Play, exploration, and learning : a natural history of the
    pre-school / S.J. Hutt . . . [et al.].
        p.   cm. – (Routledge education books)
    Bibliography: p.
    Includes index.
    1. Education, Preschool – Great Britain – Case studies.
2. Play – Great Britain – Case studies. 3. Child development
– Great Britain – Case Studies.
I. Hutt, S.J. (Sidney John) II. Series.
LB1140.35.P55P56  1989
372.21'0941 – dc 19

ISBN 0-415-05265-3 (pbk)

*To Benjamin, Chloë, Matthew and Simon*

# Contents

## Contents

# Contents

# Figures

*Figures*

# Tables

# Tables

# Preface

This monograph is the report of a study of 'Play, Exploration and Learning in Pre-school Children' commissioned by the Department of Education and Science in the late 1970s. It incorporates the results of a number of studies which were associated with the main study, but which were completed at later dates.

The report has been long in the writing, for reasons which will be only too well known to our colleagues and friends. The report was to have been written by Dr Corinne Hutt. Her untimely death in 1979 was a blow from which her collaborators have never fully recovered. Not only would Corinne have drafted the final report but her files contained much of the unprocessed data upon which it would have been based, and it has been a slow and painful process to piece together the raw data contained in them and to interpret the notes which accompanied the data. Our task has been the more frustrating because our analyses and writing have had to be thrust into the interstices of other full-time jobs. Had Corinne lived, the report would have been prepared sooner; it would also have been immeasurably better. Even had Corinne lived, we would not have been prepared for the two-year period during which our manuscript lay fallow on an official desk awaiting comment, thus further delaying publication.

In preparing this report, we have been helped by many friends, especially Corinne's former graduate students: Mr John Arumainayagam, Mrs Margaret Dash, Mrs Patricia David (formerly Ward), Mrs Norma Anderson, Ms Gay Wilson and Dr Miranda Hughes. We are grateful to all of them for so unselfishly allowing us to quote from their unpublished work.

During the early stages of the study we enjoyed the loyal and able support of our two research assistants, Mrs Barbara Forrest and Mrs Jennifer Wilson.

Our studies would not have been possible without the support of Miss Gwendoline Stubbs, Nursery School Adviser, Mr G. Dibden and Mr A. Riley, former Chief Education Officers, and Miss Joan Wordley, DHSS Day Nursery Adviser, all of Stoke-on-Trent; and Miss Jean Pringle, Nursery and Primary Adviser for Cheshire.

We received a warm welcome from innumerable nursery schools, nursery classes, playgroups and day nurseries. We shall be permanently grateful to the caring adults in charge of these institutions for their courtesy and kindness. At the risk of making invidious comparisons, we would like to acknowledge with especial appreciation the help given us at crucial stages by Mrs Chris Tranter, Miss P. W. Bartholomew, Mrs Barbara Marsden, Mrs Olwyn Shackleton and Miss Mary Kemp.

Throughout our studies, we have been supported and sustained by the members of Liaison Committee A (Nursery Education Research) of the Department of Education and Science. We are grateful to the committee and especially to their Chairman, Miss Mary Puddephat, for their guidance and for their understanding of our difficult predicament following Dr Corinne Hutt's death. The secretariat of the committee has been magnificent throughout, but we should perhaps mention especially the help of HM Inspector Leonard Kay, who gave us wise counsel at a particularly sensitive phase of our studies.

The secretarial staff of the Department of Psychology, Keele University, especially Mrs Dorothy Masters and Mrs Margaret Woodward, have lavished more care and attention upon the innumerable drafts of the manuscript than we deserved or reasonably could have expected; we are deeply grateful to them. They, in turn, received invaluable help during the early stages of drafting this report in mastering the intricacies of the university's word-processing system from Dr Alan Branthwaite, Dr John Sloboda and especially Mr Mark Trueman.

It is doubtful whether the present study would have seen the light of day had it not been for the support of three very dear friends, Ms Josephine Rowley, Professor Olive Stevenson and Mrs Anne Tyler. They alone will be aware of their contribution.

It is hoped that the present report will be of interest to pre-school practitioners, to developmental psychologists and to educational administrators. One of the problems we have had to face is how best to balance the demands of our professional colleagues in psychology for proper representation of statistical analysis, against the need for stylistic 'flow' perhaps more congenial to non-specialists. After some heart-searching we have decided to resolve the issue in the simplest possible way: we have omitted all statistical tests. We therefore must crave the indulgence of our psychologist colleagues: you simply will have to trust us. If we say a finding is (statistically) significant, please accept that the appropriate tests have been applied; if you require the details of such tests, we will provide them.

# The Pre-School Context

# Chapter 1

# Pre-school experience: assumptions and research

## Plowden and the 1972 White Paper

In 1972, the then Secretary of State for Education in England and Wales, Mrs Margaret Thatcher, presented to the British Parliament her controversial White Paper 'Education: a Framework for Expansion'. The White Paper projected an increase in public expenditure upon nursery, primary and secondary schools during the decade ending 1981–2 and projected a contraction in the rate of growth in higher education. The main beneficiary of this shift in government expenditure would be the provision for the under-fives. Prior to 1972, 35 per cent of four-year-olds were receiving state-maintained education. Of these children, approximately two-thirds were in infant schools, the remaining one-third being in nursery classses attached to primary schools or in separate nursery schools. The proportion of three-year-olds receiving nursery education was 5 per cent. The White Paper aimed to increase the provision to that recommended in the report made by the Central Advisory Council for Education (1967):[1] at least part-time places for 90 per cent of four-year-olds and 50 per cent of three-year-olds. This expansion in the nursery provision (Department of Education and Science, 1972) was justified on three grounds – educational, remedial and compensatory. The educational case was presented thus:

> . . . given sympathetic and skilled supervision, children may make great educational progress before the age of five. They are capable of developing further in the use of language, in thought and in practical skills than was previously supposed.

[1] This important and influential report on primary schools, by the Central Advisory Council for Education, is usually referred to by the name of its chairperson, (Lady) Plowden.

Progress of this kind gives any child a sound basis for his subsequent education (p. 5),

together with the remedial case:

The extension of nursery education will also provide an opportunity for the earlier identification of children with special difficulties which, if neglected, may inhibit their educational progress . . . It will be important to ensure that such children's parents are made aware of the facilities available; remedial measures are much more likely to be effective if applied early (p. 5),

and finally the compensatory case:

All children can gain from nursery education but it is particularly valuable for children whose home and life are restricted (p. 7).

In this same section, two further themes may be noted. First, there should be co-operation with other types of provision, such as playgroups, with joint planning between education authorities and other local authority departments concerned with services for the under-fives. Second, special consideration should be placed upon the role of parents, both in supporting and in complementing at home the educational objectives being pursued in the nursery school:

Local education authorities will also wish to adapt and apply to nursery education lessons which can be learnt from the experience of playgroups. The most successful of these have derived much strength from the support of parents, which the playgroups can generate by providing a focus of interests in education in a community (p. 7),

. . . provision for the under-fives should build on, not supplant, parents' own efforts (p. 5).

Throughout the section on provisions for the under-fives (significantly, the longest in the White Paper) can be heard the voice of the Plowden Committee (Central Advisory Council for Education, 1967). Twenty years on it may be helpful to remind ourselves of some of this committee's own deliberations.

One of the most striking features of Plowden's description of the then current nursery scene – the mid-1960s – is its almost total lack of reference to educational objectives. Is this because the educational value of nursery experience is so self-evident as not to warrant discussion, or is this a tacit admission that the need for nursery expansion is not solely, or even primarily, an educational one?

4

Most, but not all, maintained nursery places are given to children who suffer some kind of social handicap. Some children are admitted because they lack companionship, others because their homes are too crowded or poor in other ways. . . . Some are admitted on medical grounds or to help mothers nearing the end of their tether. Some mothers are working, although our enquiries show that this is not the reason for most admissions. Teachers' children get priority because this is a condition for the expansion of nursery education under Addendum No. 2 to Circular 8/60. Since a nursery should not be simply a refuge for children in trouble [sic], some children without handicaps get places, with the unavoidable result that other children in need have to go without (Central Advisory Council for Education, 1967, p. 117).

The case for the *educational* benefits of nursery experience is made in the contribution to the Plowden Committee by the Nursery Schools Association (later renamed the British Association for Early Childhood Education):

The Nursery Schools Association told us they wanted more nursery places because most children can benefit from the physical care, the enriched opportunities for play both indoors and out, the companionship of other children and the presence of understanding adults which nursery education provides. Children need opportunities to get to know people outside their own family circle and to form some relationships which are less close and emotionally charged. The earlier maturity of children increases their need for companionship and stimulus before the age of attendance at school (Central Advisory Council for Education, 1967, p. 118).

To the extent that these 'benefits' are educational in nature, they are acknowledged as being complementary to the events experienced by the child in his own home:

Long before a child is five he is already using words and is often familiar with books, toys and music. The issue is not whether he should be 'educated' before he reaches school age because that is happening anyway. What has to be decided is whether his education is to take place in increasing association with other children and under the supervision of skilled people, as well as of parents, in the right conditions and with the right equipment (p. 118).

However, it is the child from the supposedly 'deprived' or 'inadequate' home background who is seen as the chief beneficiary of nursery education:

> even amongst children below compulsory school age, the growth of measured intelligence is associated with socio-economic features. . . . poverty of language is a major cause of poor achievement and attempts to offset poverty of language are best made as early as possible. . . . thought is dependent on language and some working class children have insufficient encouragement, example and stimulus in the situations of their daily life to build up a language which is rich and wide ranging in vocabulary, is a tool for categorisation and general-isation, and which, being complex in structure, develops concepts of time, space and contingency. The argument thus leads to the conclusion that since development in communic-ation begins in the earliest years, one way in which the consequences of social deprivation can be overcome is to provide richer experience as soon as children are ready for nursery education (p. 119).

Underlying the Plowden Report, the White Paper, and indeed much writing on provision for the under-fives, are a number of basic assumptions: (i) The pre-school years are of special significance in laying down the foundations of later learning; (ii) it is through the child's primary activity during these years – play – that such founda-tions are laid; (iii) children from supposedly 'disadvantaged' backgrounds particularly will benefit from nursery education.

Whilst these assumptions may be self-evident to the nursery prac-titioner, they can be, and have been, challenged by workers in educational research. Clarke and Clarke (1976) have questioned whether the earliest years of life justifiably can be regarded as more 'critical' for the cognitive, social and emotional development of the child than any other period. Hutt (1979a) has argued that 'play' is a jumbo category which encompasses a multiplicity of activities, some of which are conducive to learning, but many of which are not. Ginsberg (1972) and many others have seriously questioned the ideological assumptions underlying the concept of 'disadvantage' in children from economically deprived backgrounds, and whether it is reasonable to look to the educational system to compensate for supposed disadvantage.

It is not necessary to enter into a detailed discussion of these matters, but it is perhaps appropriate to indicate our own stance with regard to the three assumptions above regarding pre-school, before outlining the problems to which we shall address ourselves in this report.

## The significance of the pre-school years

In his review of the psychological aspects of the Plowden Report, Foss (1969) pointed out its strongly biological bias with respect to child development. Not only is the quality of stimulation to which children are exposed important, but so is the stage of development of the recipient's nervous system, a notion reminiscent of the 'readiness' concept of educational theory in the 1930s. The Plowden Report invokes work on 'imprinting' in animals and some supposed analogues in human beings to indicate the importance of 'critical periods' in development at which the nervous system may be especially sensitive to certain environment–organism interactions, with telling effect upon later psychological processes. Whilst nowadays, animal studies are treated with a good deal more caution than was the case in the 1960s, such studies can provide pointers to underlying mechanisms which are difficult to study in human beings. The general proposition raised by them – that the mammalian brain and nervous system may be more susceptible to environmental variations early in life than at later ages – certainly bears some examination.

In purely anatomical terms, the development of the human brain during the first two decades of life is extremely interesting. Tanner (1960), a member of the Plowden Committee, has provided an informative picture, comparing the growth of the brain with general somatic growth and with development of the sexual organs. Taking level of growth attained at age twenty as his norm, Tanner illustrates that, as might have been expected, the fastest development of the sexual organs occurs in the second decade of life. The growth of internal organs and of the skeleton and musculature proceeds more or less linearly from birth to age twenty. The brain, however, achieves most of its mass in the first few years: 60 per cent by age three; 80 per cent by age five and 95 per cent by age seven. A later study by Dobbing and Sands (1973) paints a similar picture. These anatomical findings are paralleled by various indices of psychological maturity. For example, the progression to its adult form of the electroencephalogram – the tiny brain waves which can be recorded from the scalp – is much more rapid during the first five years of life than during the next fifteen (Petersen *et al.*, 1975). Looking at the response patterns of the brain to visual or auditory stimuli – so-called evoked potentials – we obtain a similar story (Rose and Ellingson, 1968). Thus, whilst allowing that neural connections continue to develop throughout life (Yakovlev and Lecours, 1967), there appears to be good reason for treating development during the first five years of life as special from a neurological point of view.

In comparison with later ages, by far the greatest amount of neural organization takes place by the age of five. In short, the *rate* at which brain organization is taking place is faster during the pre-school years than at any later age (Rabinowicz, 1979). If we accept as a general proposition that a biological system is most sensitive to change during stages when it is manifesting its fastest rate of change, there is a sense in which the pre-school years are of special significance. Without wishing to deny the importance of later experiences in determining neurological and behavioural organization, we nevertheless expect the child's brain to be at its most sensitive to change – for good or ill – during these pre-school years.

A study of cognitive development which is of particular interest in relation to the neurological findings is that of Bloom (1964); despite its date it has a refreshingly modern ring. Bloom suggests that changes in cognitive development parallel those in neurological development. Moreover, he argues that the effects of environmental variations upon cognitive development may differ in magnitude according to age. The data upon which Bloom's study are based are derived from several longitudinal studies by earlier authors, the advantage of such studies being that the performances of the same individuals are measured at different periods in their life history. If a plot relative to age is made of the test–re-test correlations between pairs of IQ scores in the same individual, a curve is obtained whose general shape is very similar to that relating brain development and age. Correlations, or the degree of association between two measures at two different ages in the same individual, can be interpreted as a measure of the amount of growth or development which has already taken place. Bloom claims that taking as a 'ceiling' a person's level of intellectual development measured at seventeen years, 20 per cent will have been attained by the age of one year, 50 per cent by the age of four, 80 per cent by eight, and 92 per cent by thirteen. Or, to put it another way, from birth to the age of four years an individual develops approximately 50 per cent of his adult intelligence; from the age of four to eight he develops another 30 per cent and thereafter only 20 per cent.

If, as we have suggested, variations in the environment have their greatest impact upon a biological system at its period of most rapid change, the pre-school period becomes of vital importance. In educational terms, we might expect that interventions during this period will have greater effect than comparable procedures later on. Bloom has estimated, for instance, that extreme environments ('good' or 'bad') in each of the first four years could affect the development of intelligence by 2.5 IQ points per year, whereas similarly extreme environments from eight to seventeen years may have an average effect of only 0.4 IQ points per year.

In the 1960s a considerable number of studies were carried out in the USA of the effects of pre-school programmes upon cognitive development under the auspices of 'Headstart', but very few provided empirical support for Bloom's proposition that an educational programme applied at an early age has greater impact than a similar programme applied later (Cicirelli, 1969). However, as Beller (1973) pointed out, many of the Headstart programmes were methodically flawed, showing little awareness of the vast number of variables affecting cognitive development, the processes involved, or the difficulties of interpreting and comparing studies employing different measuring instruments. Included in Beller's review is a study of his own which stands in marked contrast to many of its contemporaries for its excellent design, execution and analysis. Beller studied groups of children who had entered school at three different stages: nursery school (aged three and a half to four and a half), kindergarten (roughly equivalent to the English infants' class in primary school, aged five) and first grade (primary school, aged six). The children entering school at kindergarten stage were selected so as to be comparable in IQ and sex with the children from nursery classes. A similar selection procedure was adopted when selecting for the first grade class. Thus, during the first grade there were within the same class and with the same teacher approximately equal numbers of children: who were new to school; who had had kindergarten experience; and who had had both kindergarten and nursery class experience. The 'programme' to which only the nursery school children had been exposed had run for four hours on four mornings a week and was described as 'traditional'; it appears closely to have resembled the kind of regime which would be found in any good British nursery school.

On initial exposure to each of the three types of school experience, children were tested on the Stanford-Binet, the Peabody Picture–Vocabulary and Draw-a-Man tests. They were then re-tested at yearly intervals until entry to the fourth grade, that is, at age nine. It was thus possible to compare both the effects of age of entry into the activity programme and the longevity of any such effects. The initial IQs of the three groups were very comparable. After one year the group who had had nursery school experience showed a 7-point increase in (Stanford–Binet) IQ which was maintained throughout the next five years. A smaller increase was observed in the group whose initial schooling was at the kindergarten stage. The IQ of the group whose initial school exposure was at age six remained static throughout the first three grades of primary school. It was also found that marks on a whole range of scholastic tests – arithmetic, reading, spelling – were affected by age of school entry, especially amongst girls. Children who had entered school at the nursery stage were consistently ahead of their age peers from the first to the fourth grades. However, the gap decreased and it is a matter for conjecture for just how long the advantage of nursery school experience may be maintained against a background of social and economic adversity.

Considering together the above findings from neurology and cognitive development respectively, the view prevalent in Plowden and reiterated in almost every text on pre-school education – that the pre-school years are of great importance in laying the foundations of cognitive development – seemed to us a defensible one. Nevertheless, the use of the term 'critical period' (Central Advisory Council for Education, 1967, p. 11) to describe the pre-school years is, in our opinion, unjustified. The term implies a specificity of onset and offset, and an immutability of outcome which cannot be defended even when referring to animal studies (Riege, 1971). The fact that the immature nervous system may be more susceptible to specific experiences than the mature nervous system does not mean that an initially adverse response cannot be mitigated, or an initially beneficial response eradicated. Such long-term effects presuppose a continuation of circumstances which approximate those of the initial experience, be it malign or benign. This point has been eloquently argued by Clarke and Clarke (1976).

## The importance of 'play' in early development

A second underlying assumption of nursery education is that the cognitive, as well as the emotional and social, development of pre-school children depends crucially upon 'play'. Since virtually all the behaviour of children except for eating, sleeping and elimination has in one context or another been called 'play', the view that such behaviour is in some way beneficial is almost irrefutable. As Sylva *et al.* (1980) have commented:

> If the child stands against the garden fence for ten minutes staring absently around him, they [teachers] claim he is 'learning by observing'. If he repetitively puts dough into balls they say that 'the new baby at home is causing him to regress and he needs this simple act' (p. 48).

In a review by Hutt (1979a) of children's activities, some fourteen distinct categories of behaviour were identified, all of which, in one or another context, have been labelled as 'play'. Between them they cover virtually all aspects of children's behaviour. Is there then nothing to choose between them as aids to development? Or do the different types of play subserve different functions? Are some types of play more conducive to learning than others? And what implications does the answer to this question have for the expansion of nursery 'education'? If all types of play are equally valid as learning experiences, is there any need to institutionalize such experiences? Quite clearly advocates of nursery education do not give equal weight to each of the fourteen categories of 'play' identified by Hutt. Nursery schools and classes could hardly continue to exist – except as places for the care of the socially disadvantaged child – were they not to believe that they are specially qualified to provide some basic ingredient for the infrastructure of later education which is not provided by either the home environment or other (cheaper) pre-school provisions.

That what we call 'play' may consist of at least two distinct categories of behaviour which differ from each other in form, causation and function, was indicated by our own early work on how three- to five-year-old children respond to a novel toy (Hutt, 1966). In the course of this and subsequent studies, 128 such children were observed and the pattern of specific exploration was found to be fairly similar in all of them (Hutt, 1970). The children were exposed to the toy (in a room with which they were already familiar) for ten minutes a day for six successive days. On initial exposure, the child would approach and inspect the toy. This visual inspection was followed by a fairly prolonged period of active investigation and manipulation, during which all the children's action patterns were comparatively stereotyped and their posture and expression were interpreted as showing signs of concentration. This 'exploratory' activity decreased exponentially over the six days of the study. By about the third or fourth day a new set of behaviour patterns began to emerge. The child now exhibited a posture and facial expression which we interpreted as 'relaxed' and proceeded to manipulate the novel toy by means of action patterns which were more idiosyncratic and varied in form than on the previous days. It appeared that the child, having acquired information concerning the properties of the novel toy through 'exploration', now utilized that knowledge in 'play'; play activity increased to a peak on the fifth day before also declining (Hutt, 1967; 1970). Implicit in the behaviours we termed 'exploration' was the query: What does this *object* do? whilst implicit in the behaviours we termed 'play' was the query: What can *I* do with this object?

The most interesting inference to be drawn from these studies is that play does not always enhance learning. Where the child's exploration of the novel toy was perfunctory, she did not always acquire further information during subsequent play with the toy. Where information was obtained during play it appeared to be largely accidental. We concluded that play, as opposed to exploration, far from promoting learning may, in some instances, preclude it. In subsequent work, we have shown that the two categories of behaviour originally labelled as 'exploration' and 'play' are distinguishable in other ways. In a mathematical analysis of the 'stochastic' properties of the two (Hughes, 1979), it was found that behaviours labelled as 'exploration' comprised sequences or elements which were much more predictable than was the case with sequences of 'play' elements. Thus, the kinds of behaviour labelled 'play' (Hutt, 1966; 1970) conveyed a much greater element of 'surprisingness': it was much more difficult, given one, two or even three elements of behaviour in a particular sequence, to predict what the child would do next than would be the case during exploratory activities. Further evidence that exploration and play as originally defined were functionally distinct is provided by a later study of their physiological concomitants (Hughes and Hutt, 1980). Measurements were made of heart-rate variability during free play with familiar toys, during a problem-solving task and during 'daydreaming'. Heart rate (i.e. pulse) varies from slow to fast over a considerable range during 'play', whereas it remains fairly steady during 'exploration'. It has been shown (Rolfe, 1973) that steadiness of heart rate is indicative of a high level of concentration (e.g. in landing an aeroplane) whereas variability of heart rate is indicative of relaxation. This suggests that during exploration a child's nervous system is in a quite different state from that during play – in one case, highly attentive, in the other case much more relaxed. The state of the nervous system – as indicated by heart-rate variability – is not substantially different from that observed during daydreaming (Hughes and Hutt, 1980).

Although our distinction between exploration and play was echoed by other psychologists (e.g. Weisner and McCall, 1976), it seemed to cause concern amongst nursery teachers, who felt that exploratory behaviour had as much claim to the title 'play' as behaviours having a more antic quality. In an endeavour to reconcile our views with those of our colleagues in nursery education, we therefore decided (Hutt, 1970) to replace the terms *exploration* and *play* with two rather more descriptive terms, originally employed by Berlyne (1960): respectively, *epistemic* behaviours and *ludic* behaviours. The important distinction, with regard to both the form and the motivation of children's behaviour, originally represented by exploration/play was carried over into the new terminology. The primary function of epistemic behaviour was acquiring information; the primary function of ludic behaviour was self-amusement. We further decided to acquiesce with the views of teachers that both could be encompassed by the term 'play'. It was later argued that nearly all the 'play' activities of the under-fives could be subsumed under one or other of the two main categories, epistemic or ludic behaviours. A taxonomy was thus derived, having motivational as well as functional properties (Hutt, 1979a; 1979b). That is, those behaviours we categorized as epistemic behaviour were associated with relative physiological relaxation. A presentation of the complete taxonomy will be deferred until Chapter 16, where it will be employed to systematize some of the observations to follow.

From the point of view of the present research, we were led to the conclusion that one of the most valuable contributions to the evaluation of nursery practice would be a detailed 'natural history' of the activities of children and caring adults in the various provisions. That is, a description of what children do in different nursery environments; what is the role of adults in the determination of children's activities; how children and adults interact in the various pre-school provisions; what are the effects of such interactions; and how they may relate to the adjustment of nursery children in the primary school. In each case, we were concerned to find how children's epistemic or ludic behaviours might be related to their motivational state. Before discussing these studies, however, we need to consider one further issue.

## The 'compensatory' role of pre-school experience

The third major assumption of the Plowden Report and of the 1972 White Paper was that 'children whose home and life are restricted . . . can gain from nursery education' (Department of Education and Science, 1972, p. 7). A similar view predicated the Headstart programmes referred to earlier. Unfortunately as Cicirelli (1969), Beller (1973) and many other authors have pointed out, the short-term gains in cognitive and social abilities which frequently are found following intervention programmes are usually short-lived, even in well-executed studies such has those of Schweinhart and Weikart (1983). However, as Sylva (1983) has noted, in a recent review of this so-called wash-out effect of early educational programmes for 'disadvantaged' children, the long-term effects may not be altogether gloomy. The Consortium for Longitudinal Studies (1983) has brought together the results of the eleven most rigorously controlled Headstart studies with samples of children in excess of one hundred. The consortium claimed that despite wash-out of the initial cognitive advantages, attendance at pre-school does have long-term effects upon a child and her family, there being, between the initial exposure to pre-school and the long-term outcomes, a 'sleeper effect' (Kagan and Moss, 1962). Thus, pre-school, especially amongst economically disadvantaged or ethnic minority groups, may serve as an 'inoculation against failure' (Woodhead, 1985). However, taking the consortium findings as a whole, the long-term outcomes of the so-called sleeper effect are curious. As Clarke and Clarke (1981; 1982) have noted, whilst the initial pre-school programmes (especially Weikart's Ypsilanti pre-school curriculum, whose theoretical base was Piagetian) were intended to enhance cognitive development, their long-term outcomes were judged in terms of socio-economic criteria, such as savings on special educational needs, release of mothers from the home for economically productive activities, the ability of the children, now teenagers, to support themselves financially, lower crime rates and having fewer children! The psychological processes, however, whereby these outcomes have their effects may have less to do with the original pre-school programmes *per se* than changes in parental aspirations and attitudinal changes in the child and his family towards positive achievements and greater control of their own lives. Weikart nevertheless is enthusiastic about the consortium's findings, portraying pre-school education for disadvantaged children as a wise financial investment and proselytizing the need for greater federal resources. So clear are the long-term *financial* benefits of such investment, he claims, that 'The long-term effect of pre-school is simply not an issue any more in the United States' (Makins, 1985). *Pre-school education for disadvantaged children is a wise financial investment* (paraphrase by Sylva, 1983). Sylva's (1983) own more measured conclusions regarding the consortium's findings are that they 'justify cautious optimism about cognitively-structured early education'.

Inherent in this discussion is the idea that economic deprivation may entail certain shortcomings of experience in children's early life which ultimately will be manifested in poor educational performance. It was for this reason that we also proposed to undertake a study of the everyday experiences of four-year-old children in their own homes. How different are the homes of working-class and middle-class children in providing opportunities for learning, social interaction and conversation? How do such factors as the child's sex, age and position in a sibship relate to such opportunities? If nursery education is supposedly complementing the home experiences of children, is it not essential to find out what these experiences are? If the view advocated by the White Paper – that nursery education should be complementary to the everyday learning experiences of the home – is to be anything but a pious hope, then teachers need to know what experiences they supposedly are complementing. Or, if we are to regard nursery education as providing a counterbalance to some supposed insufficiencies in the home learning experiences of children from a deprived background, is it not essential to establish what these insufficiencies are – or indeed, whether they exist? It was therefore decided to initiate a study of children's experiences in the home. This study is presented in a report separate from, but complementary to, the present one (Davie *et al.*, 1984).

## Outline of this report

The present report is divided into three parts. The first part (Chapters 1 to 3) is largely introductory. In Chapter 2, we set the context in which the subsequent studies took place. In Chapter 3, before going on to describe the activities of the pre-school, we examine the aims and objectives of pre-school provision as seen through the eyes of both parents and staff in the various provisions. We also examine nursery school staffs' perceptions of their pupils.

The second and largest part of the study (Chapters 4 to 11) is descriptive and is concerned with the question of what actually goes on in various pre-school provisions – hence the subtitle of this report. Chapters 4 and 5 explore the interrelation of adults' and of children's activities in the pre-school. Chapter 6 looks at the expectations of parents and pre-school staff with regard to the purposes of materials and at the way in which materials are actually used. Because adults, especially teachers, accord a special importance to the role of fantasy play in pre-school children, Chapter 7 is devoted to a detailed examination of such play and to the views of teachers regarding its importance. In Chapter 8, we examine the time dimensions of children's play: how long they attend to particular activities and the determinants of their approach to and departure from activities. The use of language in the pre-school forms the basis of Chapter 9: how conversations are initiated in the pre-school, how adults respond to children's approaches and how they extend conversations. Chapter 10 is concerned with the adjustment of new children to nursery school. The advent of a child to pre-school is a fraught experience both for the child itself and its parents. How well will the child settle into this new world? It may be remembered that Plowden sought the admission of the majority of pre-school children initially on a part-time basis. In Chapter 11 we examine the differences between full-time nursery school children and part-timers in terms of their cognitive and social development.

The third part of the study (Chapters 12 to 14) is concerned with some of the possible effects of pre-school participation upon cognitive and social processes. In Chapter 12, we examine two studies of the short-term effects of fantasy play upon IQ: and in Chapter 13 four studies of the effects of fantasy play upon more specific intellectual functions – memory, problem-solving, conservation and creativity. In Chapter 14, we ask what differences may be discerned in primary school between children who have, and those who have not, had the benefit of pre-school experience in terms of their responses to social constraints. Finally, in Chapter 15 we bring together the main themes of our findings and in Chapter 16 discuss their implications in relation to provision for the under-fives.

# Chapter 2

# The context of the study

The history of provision for the care and education of young children spans nearly four hundred years, from the beginning of the seventeenth century to the present day. The nature of the provision has taken many varied forms, to a large extent reflecting changing social attitudes towards children and childhood. Currently, provision for the under-fives in England and Wales may be divided into two groups on administrative grounds: the first group is the responsibility of the Department of Education and Science (DES) while the second comes under the auspices of the Department of Health and Social Security (DHSS). Within these two groups several forms of provision may be identified. These forms are distinguished by both functional and organizational criteria, and may be divided into four major types: (i) the nursery school; (ii) the nursery class; (iii) the day nursery; (iv) the playgroup. These four types of pre-school establishment form the basic contexts for the work described in this book.

## Nursery schools and classes

The Department of Education and Science is responsible for nursery schools and nursery classes, whose purpose is to provide educational experience for children below school age. The provision is made by Local Education Authorities (LEAs) and is usually available to all families within a given catchment area.

Nursery schools are autonomous, specially equipped schools catering for the educational needs of children between the ages of three and five years. Exceptionally, two-year-old children may be admitted or five-year-olds retained where the school or family has a special need. Nursery schools operate a normal school day from

17

approximately 9.00 a.m. to 3.30 p.m. In the main, children attend for either the morning or the afternoon sessions but for some children attendance is full-time.

Nursery schools are under the direction of a head teacher, and the qualified teaching staff are usually assisted by trained nursery nurses and assistants. Nationally the ratio of qualified *teaching staff* to pupils is approximately 1:23 (Tizard *et al.*, 1976c) and the overall staff: child ratio is, therefore, superior to this. The DES suggests that a ratio of 1:13 is acceptable and most local authorities attempt to maintain such a ratio. Places in nursery schools are free to parents except for a charge for meals where the child is provided with a dinner.

Nursery classes are similar to nursery schools in most functional and organizational aspects, but are differentiated by their incorporation into a primary or infant school, although often the classes form separate units within the school grounds with their own outdoor play areas. As with nursery schools, the majority of children attend on a part-time basis, for five sessions each week. However, admission into nursery classes tends to be at a rather later age and as a consequence the average age of the children within them is usually slightly higher than in nursery schools. Staffing of nursery classes varies but generally includes both teachers and nursery nurses.

## Day nurseries and playgroups

Day nurseries and playgroups are the responsibility of the Department of Health and Social Security. The principal purpose of the local authority is to provide care for children as a substitute for that of the home, where they or their parents are considered to be in special need of such help. The categories of children eligible for admission are given in Ministry of Health circular 37/68, which states that 'priority will normally need be given to children with only one parent, who has no option but to go out to work'. Handicapped children, children with sick or handicapped parents and children of socially impoverished or strained home environments are also given priority status and families are often referred by health or welfare services. Day nurseries cater for children between the ages of six weeks and five years (although in some cases very young children may be excluded) and operate an 'extended' day (usually 8.30 a.m. to 5.30 or 6.00 p.m.). Most children attend full-time for five sessions a week. The day nursery is open all the year and is staffed by qualified nursery nurses under the direction of a senior nursery officer (formerly designated 'matron'). Qualified teachers are not

18

normally members of day nursery staff, although some local authorities now employ peripatetic teachers who work in co-operation with several nurseries. A staff:child ratio of 1:5 is recommended but the proportion of staff may be increased if there is a large percentage of children below two years. A charge for the provision is made to parents according to means.

The playgroup movement started in 1962 as a result of dissatisfaction with the shortage of places for pre-school children provided by local authorities. Since its inception the movement has grown steadily and in 1987 the Pre-school Playgroups Association (PPA) had a membership of approximately 14,000 individual groups. Since 1970 responsibility for the care of pre-school children in playgroups has rested with the local authority social services department and ultimately with the DHSS. Playgroups, although usually run privately or by a voluntary body, are covered by the Nurseries and Child Minders Regulation Act (1948) as amended by Section 60 of the Health Services and Public Health Act (1968). The guidance of the standards for the day care of young children contained in Ministry of Health circular 37/68 also applies to this form of provision which has to be registered with the local social services department. Playgroups exist, primarily, to provide children with opportunities for play and the chance to mix with other children, and to offer support for mothers. Most playgroups meet in a village or community hall, which they often share with other forms of activity. Admission is usually open to anyone who can afford to pay the fee charged and normally children between the ages of two and five years are catered for. Playgroups vary widely in the numbers of children they take, the figures ranging from below ten to over thirty; the average number attending a session is twenty (Pre-school Playgroups Association, 1987). Attendance is on a part-time basis and many more children may be on a register than attend a single session. Playgroups tend to meet regularly for half-day sessions, and many only open two or three times a week. Management of the playgroup is usually by an elected committee, but day-to-day running is in the hands of a supervisor who is frequently assisted by mothers participating on a rota. Indeed, it may be stated that active parental involvement in the organization and running of the playgroup forms an important part of the explicit ethos of the playgroup movement. Playgroups are financed largely through the fees which the parents pay but approximately a quarter receive some assistance from the local authority.

Other forms of provision for the under-fives – e.g. child-minders, private nurseries, one o'clock clubs, nursery centres, mother–toddler clubs – also exist and provide useful services but are not described here. (For descriptions of some of these, see Van der Eyken, 1974; Pringle and Naidoo, 1975; Ferri *et al.*, 1981.)

## Areas of study

In the course of the project, nurseries in two contrasting areas were studied. The first area, hereinafter designated Area A, is formed by the northern part of the county of Staffordshire in the North Midlands. It includes an industrial city (Stoke-on-Trent) and the neighbouring semi-rural borough of Newcastle-under-Lyme. Both parts of this area of study have a comparatively long tradition of support for nursery education commencing with the opening of the first nursery class in 1918, followed by the founding of a local branch of the Nursery Schools Association in 1929. The current provision of nursery schools and nursery classes in this area is generally good by national standards, a state that may be attributed to at least two factors: first, a demand for female labour in a profitable post-war export industry created a need for some nursery provision; second, a local authority with an interest in the education of the young ensured that the need was met. The area also contains numerous playgroups and six day nurseries providing alternative and contrasting forms of pre-school provision.

During the course of the project the nurseries of a second area, hereafter termed Area B, consisting of parts of neighbouring Cheshire were included in the study. Although this area as a whole differs in many ways from the main area of study, the three particular towns in which the nurseries were situated – Crewe, Winsford and Macclesfield – share many features with Area A.

Until comparatively recently Cheshire has had a fairly limited nursery provision. Over the past fifteen years a programme of building nursery units attached to infant schools has markedly changed the picture so that provision of places in the county is now generally good. In addition, whereas many of the schools and classes in Area A were designed and built more than twenty years ago, those in Area B have benefited from the most modern ideas in design and use of materials. However, other differences, apart from the length of the nursery tradition and modernity of the buildings, separate nurseries in the two areas. Whereas nursery schools have been a prominent feature of the provision in Area A, the LEA provision in Area B has focused on the nursery unit or class which is part of an infant school. Moreover, whereas in the first area the emphasis in the nursery schools and classes is on the provision of full-time places, that in the second area is on part-time education for the under-fives. These differences in the provision in the two areas make comparisons between them interesting.

## Aspects of current provision

The descriptions of the different types of nursery given at the beginning of this chapter apply generally but variations in provision do exist and more detailed information about the nurseries in the two areas of study was collected at the start of the project.

In order to establish certain background information about the nurseries to be used in the studies, a structured interview was conducted with head teachers, playgroup supervisors and senior nursery officers. Initially interviews were carried out in nurseries in Area A, the sample including twenty-one nursery schools, six day nurseries, eleven nursery classes and eleven playgroups. Whereas all the nursery schools and day nurseries in the area were visited, a random selection of approximately one-quarter of the available playgroups and nursery classes was made.

A similar set of structured interviews was conducted in seven nursery classes and one nursery school in Area B. It should be noted at this point that in Area A nursery classes are distinguished from nursery schools not only by their attachment to a primary school but also by the practice in Stoke-on-Trent of staffing nursery classes with nursery nurses alone, the head teacher of the school being in charge of the class. The results of the interviews are presented below.

## Full-time or part-time provision

In general, in recent years, it has been felt to be desirable that children should attend nurseries for sessions whose duration is less than that of the normal school day, although in some circumstances full-time attendance may be necessary (Department of Education and Science, 1972, para. 25). In some instances, therefore, a child may attend a nursery on a full-time basis, spending a period of time at the nursery which is equivalent to or even greater than that of the normal school day. Whether part-time as opposed to full-time nursery provision has any particular consequences for the *education* of the under-fives remains to be established (see Chapter 11). Much variation exists in the length of nursery day available in the different contexts. Day nurseries and playgroups present the most striking contrast here: day nurseries provide full extended day care throughout the week; playgroups tend to operate from two to seven sessions per week with individual children attending from one to three times per week. At the time of the interviews, in Area A nursery schools and classes both tended to provide more full-time than part-time places, although there was much variability between schools. The ratio of boys to girls was approximately the same in each kind of nursery, and corresponded to census data. In Area B (seven nursery classes and one nursery school) only 7 per cent of the 562 children attending the eight units received full-time education. Thus, whereas the emphasis in Area A had been on the provision of full-time places in schools, that in Area B was fixed on part-time nursery education.

## Age range of the children

The range of the children's ages was greatest in the day nurseries which admitted children six weeks after their birth and in some cases retained them until they were of compulsory school age. Playgroups, too, tended to have a wider range of children than nursery schools or classes, in many cases admitting children from two years of age and again permitting attendance until five. Although the majority of nursery schools and classes admitted children upon their third birthday, the average age for admission was approximately three years six months for nursery schools and three years ten months for nursery classes.

In part the delay in admitting children to the educational establishments resulted from an excess of demand for places in the schools. Waiting lists were common but varied in length greatly from nursery to nursery and depended partly upon the criteria used in their creation. When the interviews were conducted, the length of the waiting lists was on average greatest in the nursery schools and least in playgroups. Since collection of these data, however, pressure for places would appear to have diminished somewhat, although this again varies greatly from nursery to nursery. The majority of nursery schools allowed a child's name to be placed on the waiting list on or after the child's second birthday. Thus, on average, the child would have to wait a further one and a half years before gaining a place in the school. The waiting period was approximately the same in the day nurseries and nursery classes but rather less (on average ten months) in the playgroups. However, children for whom attendance at a nursery was considered to be a high priority tended to be accommodated much more rapidly.

The age range of the children in Area B was approximately the same as for nursery schools in Area A, but the average age of admission was slightly lower and waiting lists were correspondingly shorter.

## Backgrounds of the children

In the course of the interview nursery staff were asked whether the fathers of the children in the nursery were predominantly manual or non-manual workers, or whether there was a balance between the two. Although accurate information on the social background of the children in the nurseries proved to be difficult to obtain in the structured interview, the view furnished by the interviewees was that in the majority of nurseries in the study most fathers were more correctly classified as manual workers rather than non-manual workers under the Registrar General's classification.

Other aspects of the children and their background were touched upon in the course of discussion during the interview. In general, responses revealed the anticipated pattern whereby day nurseries appear to have the most children suffering from a variety of difficulties while playgroups have least.

The interviewers also attempted to establish the proportion of mothers employed outside the home in Area A. In the day nursery the information obtained was that 93 per cent of the mothers worked, whereas in the nursery classes and schools the average were 50 and 45 per cent respectively. In the playgroups a mean of 18 per cent of mothers working was obtained. These figures do not, however, distinguish between full- and part-time work and quite often mothers were said to be working evening shifts.

The fathers of the children in the nurseries in Area B again appeared to be engaged predominantly in manual work and in three of the eight nurseries it was stated that a large proportion of the mothers worked, although mostly in part-time employment.

## The nursery environment

At an early stage in the project we set out to find out the characteristics of the different pre-school environments in which the children found themselves. The importance of play in facilitating each child's development is part of the holy writ of the nursery education movement, the role of the caring adult being to provide a 'rich, exciting, secure and challenging environment' in which 'the adult is ready to

23

furnish ideas and information whilst dominating [sic] the child's play' (Cass, 1975a). This role is to be achieved by the provision of materials and opportunities for different forms of play. Simple though this must seem, there are innumerable differences between different pre-school environments with regard to their ideology, how they are organized and the resources available (both in material and human terms). The next part of this chapter presents a study whose aim was to describe the organization and resources of the different forms of nursery establishment listed above.

In order to investigate the availability and use of materials and activities in various forms of pre-school provision, observations were made in eight randomly chosen nursery schools, eight nursery classes, eight playgroups and six day nurseries. Whereas a random selection of nurseries in Area A from the first three categories was made, all the day nurseries in this area were used.

Each establishment was observed on two separate mornings, observations being recorded on a checklist (see Appendix A). Records were made at intervals of 20 minutes using a scan method of sampling (Altmann, 1974). In the 30 seconds preceding the scan, the observer recorded the types of activities available to the children in the playroom or playground according to a set of predetermined categories. During the scan, the numbers of children and adults at each type of activity were recorded. Where children or adults were engaged in activities not specifically catered for by the checklist, a written description of the activity and the number of individuals engaged in it was added to the observation record. A minimum of four scans per session was made, the average being six.

## Organization of the session

Previous studies have emphasized the role of 'free-play' in the routine of the nursery (Clarke *et al.*, 1969; Tizard *et al.*, 1976a). In the present study 'free-play' periods, in which the child was able to choose his activity from several available with minimal constraint, were contrasted with periods of organized activity led by an adult, where the children were constrained to attend. Activities which may have been planned or structured from the *adult's* point of view were classified as 'free-play' if there were no constraints upon the children to participate with the adult. The study revealed comparatively little organized activity in any of the four types of nursery, the emphasis being overwhelmingly on 'free-play' in each. The amount of organized activity in the alternative types of nursery differed, but so too did the variability with which it occurred. Least variability was found in playgroups, which on average had fewest organized activity periods, and most in nursery schools, which together with nursery classes had the greatest degree of organization of the child's time. Nearly all the organized activities and those which were seen at some time in all establishments could be classified into three homogeneous categories according to their content. The first category, of organized story or singing sessions, occurred often in all forms of nursery, forming the preponderance of organized sessions in nursery schools and playgroups. The second category involved the playing of musical instruments or participation in assembly, and was prominent in nursery classes and day nurseries. The third category consisted of activities using an audiovisual aid such as a record player, radio or television. Use of such aids comprised an important part of the organized time in the nursery classes but was seldom observed in other forms of nursery. These three categories accounted for the vast majority of organized sessions observed.

## *Range of activities*

Although organized periods undoubtedly play an important part in the nursery routine, the overall emphasis in most nurseries would seem to be on the provision of a range of activities from which the child can select during 'free-play'. In each type of nursery certain groups of materials were omnipresent (Table 2.1), though they might appear in other nursery contexts as well. Almost every nursery provides a 'home' or 'house' corner for imaginative games (although, interestingly, other provision for fantasy play is usually more limited), a book corner and some miniature adult objects (representational objects), e.g. toy cars. Brush painting was observed to be freely available in nursery classes (NC) and nursery schools (NS) but was rather less common in playgroups (PG) and day nurseries (DN), whilst other forms of painting were also noted. Most nurseries provided a range of table-top activities involving drawing, games or puzzles, while construction toys of various forms and sizes were frequently seen. Often, as well, construction of pictures or models with paper materials or card was encouraged by the setting up of a collage or modelling table, while a form of malleable material such as clay or dough was common.

Most of the occupations available indoors involved the children in play with comparatively little gross physical activity. In three of the four types of context large items of physical apparatus such as climbing frames, slides and tricycles tended to be reserved for use outside

25

TABLE 2.1: *Materials and activities commonly available indoors*

| NS | NC | PG | DN |
|---|---|---|---|
| Plasticene/dough | Brush paint | Collage/Cut | Fine constr. |
| Brush paint | Puzzles | Puzzles | |
| Large constr. | Drawing | Books | Books |
| Fine constr. | *Rep. objects | Physical | Home corner |
| Books | Home corner | Vehicle ride | *Rep. objects |
| *Rep. objects | | *Rep. objects | |
| Home corner | | Home corner | |

*Representational objects: play, with objects of various kinds, e.g. cars, garages, farms, animals, zoos, each object being a representation of a feature of the real world.

when the weather and the nursery routine permitted, but it was notable that in playgroups this reservation was less common and opportunities for physical play were present throughout the session. Interestingly, some activities were observed but rarely. For example, although some of the nurseries visited had record players, tape recorders or television, little use was made of these media and in some instances staff reported antipathy towards their use. Pets of some kind were observed in several nursery schools and classes (where children were sometimes asked to assist in their care) but seldom in playgroups or day nurseries. In the case of playgroups it may be seen that the keeping of animals in a building which has to serve other purposes as well may present organizational problems, but such problems are less obvious in day nurseries. Several nurseries had woodwork benches but sometimes equipment associated with these were either lacking or only occasionally available. Although some staff encouraged this kind of activity, involving sawing and hammering, many others expressed reservations on the grounds of noise and more particularly safety. In general, safety, noise and the possible mess that an activity could create were key factors in determining its availability. Obviously some activities require more staff attention for these reasons alone, and given limited staff resources only a few activities requiring constant staff supervision can be permitted at any one time.

Analysis showed that the number of different types of activity simultaneously available during free-play tended to be greatest in playgroups and least in day nurseries. Table 2.2 shows the mean number of activities available at any one time in the different forms of nursery. It should be noted that the figures reflect the number of

TABLE 2.2: *Mean number of activities available at any one time*

|      | NS   | NC    | DN   | PG    |
|------|------|-------|------|-------|
| Mean | 7.75 | 10.84 | 7.07 | 11.36 |
| SD   | 1.76 | 2.13  | 2.73 | 2.06  |

different activities actually seen to be available and excludes those which were only potentially available. Nursery schools and classes may not differ from playgroups in the number of potentially available activities but their availability is usually determined by some systematic procedure, whereas the playgroups in our survey tended to bring out most of their equipment and apparatus at the start of the session and leave it out for the whole period. The playgroups observed in this study were usually situated in large indoor areas such as church halls, space therefore permitting the setting out of large numbers of different kinds of activities. A similar picture obtained in several of the nursery classes, where the rooms were again quite large. The situation in nursery schools and day nurseries was more variable. In particular where day nurseries were family-grouped rather than age-ordered, very few activities tended to be available for the child at any one time.

## Discussion

The main area of study for this project, Area A, has had a long tradition of pre-school provision in general and nursery education in particular. Until recently, this provision has centred on the nursery school and the day nursery, but recently nursery classes and playgroups have figured prominently. The history of the development of pre-school provision in Area A would appear to resemble in form the development nationally (Blackstone, 1971), although in terms of magnitude of provision the area would appear to have always maintained a somewhat better than average position. The second area used in the project represents an interesting comparison in terms of both the development of provision and of the form that the provision now takes. Whereas nursery schools have been a prominent feature of the provision in Area A, the LEA provision in Area B has centred on the nursery class attached to the infant school. Moreover, whereas in Area A the emphasis in the nursery schools and classes is on the provision of full-time places, that in Area B is on part-time education for the under-fives. Staff are able to adduce cogent arguments for the relative merits of full-time and part-time placement. Teachers who argue for whole-day attendance at the nursery suggest that the children benefit from the closer relationships that consequently develop, both between children and their peers and between children and staff. Staff who advocate part-time nursery places suggest that this form of provision is more appropriate for the majority of three-to-five-year-olds, and stress the importance of not forcing the child at too early an age. In general, however, there is agreement that the type of place offered should reflect the child's or in some cases the family's needs, an example of an ethos that is found repeatedly in the nursery world. The argument about the type of place that is provided is related in part to the question of the age of admission of the child. As stated, although nursery schools and classes in both areas do admit children from their third birthday onwards, or in exceptional cases slightly earlier, the average age for entry is somewhat later. The position does not appear to be an uncommon one (see, for example, Watt, 1977). However, from their comments during the interview some staff clearly felt that early entry into the nursery was not necessarily desirable, suggesting either that the children were not always ready to take full benefit of the experiences offered by the nursery or that a prolonged stay in the nursery would lead to boredom for the child in the months prior to entry into the infant school. In this, the nursery staff who put forward this view would appear to be mirroring the opinions of some parents (Watt, 1977; Shinman, 1981). In most cases, however, the actual age of the child upon entry to the nursery would appear to depend largely on force of circumstances. Although provision in Area A is good, it still does not seem to meet demand in particular localities, as evidenced by the long waiting lists of some nurseries, containing some children of eligible age. Several studies have examined parental attitudes to pre-school provision (Parry and Archer, 1974; Abbott, 1978; Ward, 1982) and their reasons for wanting or not wanting a place for their child. In Area A, where nursery education is long established, parents seem to be well aware of the availability of nursery provision, often because they themselves attended some form of nursery (Ward, 1982). However, previous studies have suggested that there is a differential utilization of nursery provision according to the social class of the parents. In Fife, Watt (1977) states that, contrary to earlier findings, the proportion of nursery places occupied by children of working-class families was commensurate with their numbers in the community as a whole, although the situation tended to vary from one neighbourhood to another and 'problem' families were under-represented amongst those taking up places. Similarly, in both Areas A and B of the present project all forms of pre-school provision tended to have many more working-class than middle-class families among their clients. Working-class representation tended to be proportionally greatest in the day nurseries and least in the playgroups. In addition, playgroups tended to have the smallest proportion of working mothers. In some cases the hours worked by the mother coincided with the school day. Alternatively, some mothers worked evening shifts. However, there is some suggestion of demand for an extended day greater than that met by the day nurseries alone.

Children with specific problems or handicaps appear to be distributed unevenly among the different forms of nursery, the day nursery, not surprisingly, catering for the greatest number of children with difficulties. The number of handicapped children was least in playgroups, although the figure obtained for Area A appears to be quite typical of the picture in playgroups nationally (Pre-school Playgroups Association, 1987). Few nurseries of any type rejected outright the notion of accommodating children with handicaps, but most staff had reservations about their ability to cope with severe handicap or a significant proportion of mildly handicapped children.

In the areas of organizational background and the families catered for we can perceive differences between the types of pre-school provision. However, in terms of the material provision made for the children within these establishments the similarities are great. It is apparent that there is general agreement in the pre-school world concerning the range of activities which are appropriate for children between the age of three and five years. In some instances these activities may supplement those that the nursery workers know to be available to the child in her own home. In other instances, however, the nursery adopts a different position from the home. For example, whereas the child may spend a significant proportion of time in her own home watching television, the use of this medium in the nursery is rare and strictly limited.

The agreement about what is suitable for the under-fives in nursery provision has been reached over a long period of time. Recent innovations in nursery provision, such as the playgroup, have consciously used as their model the established practice of the nursery school or class, and the close interconnections of the pre-school world are reflected in the training of nursery nurses. This agreement, as we have termed it, occurs not only at the material level, dictating the forms of materials and toys to be made available, but also at the theoretical level, where it appears as a belief in the value of play in the development of the child. It is to this belief and the ideological framework in which it is placed that we turn in the next chapter.

# Chapter 3

# The aims and objectives of pre-school provision

The previous chapter has outlined the physical setting of the nursery and the material provision made within it. Important though this provision is, it represents only one component of the total nursery environment. As important in the determination of the value of the nursery experience to the young child is the theoretical framework which underpins the provision that is made for her play. As we have seen, there is general agreement between members of staff in the different forms of pre-school provision concerning the kinds of activities which are appropriate for the development of the three- and four-year-old. The existence of this agreement suggests a common underlying model about the nature of childhood and the role of the nursery within a larger social context. In the studies of the present chapter we examine the views of both staff and parents on the purposes of the nursery, and the benefits that they believe accrue to children as a consequence of their nursery experience.

As Watt (1977) points out, nursery education (as represented by nursery schools and classes) may be seen as the meeting point of two systems: the vertical system of 'education through schooling' in which nursery education forms the first rung of an ascending ladder which the child will continue to climb until late adolescence; and the horizontal system of 'provision for the under-fives' to which nursery education contributes substantially. Nursery education is able to identify with both systems since it has strong professional and administrative links with the former and shares a mutual interest in terms of its clientele with the latter. However, it is likely that the aims and objectives of the staff in nursery education will be different from those of their counterparts in other sections of the two systems, if only because of the existence of this dual set of relationships. Thus, although a certain amount of attention has been dedicated to the investigation of teachers' attitudes and role perceptions in general, those of teachers in nursery education in particular are worthy of further study. Rather less consideration has been given to the attitudes and self-perceptions of nursery nurses in nursery education and to those of staff in other forms of pre-school provision and a study of these is worthwhile in its own right. However, of particular interest would be a study enabling comparisons of the attitudes and role perceptions of all caring adults in all forms of pre-school institutions. Therefore, as an initial part of the project it was decided to investigate these aspects with the staff in the different forms of nursery in Areas A and B.

From our pilot work, we felt it highly probable that the historical traditions of the pre-school world would exert a powerful influence on contemporary aims and attitudes in the nursery. Indeed, Roberts (1975) suggests that in the formulation of aims for nursery schools and classes, in particular, due account should be taken of past changes of emphasis in the field of nursery education. Roberts doubts the value of specifying particular goals for the school, arguing that the child should be looked upon as a unique individual with particular abilities and disabilities, and that planning should proceed at an individual level. In defining her own series of aims for nursery staff she stresses that the staff should attempt to look at the children as a number of separate persons while ensuring that provision is made for fun and enjoyment. Roberts goes on to state that the area of greatest importance is that of social education, which she argues must be based on an understanding of emotional growth. These sentiments are also reflected in the findings of the study of Parry and Archer (1974) in which they surveyed schools with a tradition of 'good' nursery education, and in a national survey of teachers in nursery schools and classes (Taylor *et al.*, 1972). In the major study by Professor Philip Taylor's team, nursery teachers were found to give greatest priority to social development. This emphasis on the social purpose of nursery education was independent of other variables such as the social class of the children in the nursery and the number of children to be taught.

## Pre-school staff: their characteristics and views of pre-school experience

Since these views were published, however, nursery and playgroup provision has greatly expanded and a large number of differing influences may have affected staff attitudes and the formulation of aims. Moreover, while the views of nursery teachers are of primary importance, those of other groups of nursery staff require careful

31

consideration in the attempt to describe the ideological framework of the nursery. In the light of this we initially decided to probe the views of staff in pre-school provision in Areas A and B by means of a short questionnaire, based upon, and therefore similar to, that used by Taylor *et al.* (1972). The main difference lies in the brevity of the questionnaire used here and the exclusive use of closed rather than open questions. The questionnaire was distributed amongst staff in each form of nursery and a comparatively high response rate was obtained in all cases. Respondents were allocated to one of five groups: Nursery School Teacher (NST), Nursery School Nursery Assistant (NSA), Nursery Class Teacher/Assistant (NC), Playgroup Staff (PG) and Day Nursery Staff (DN).

The first section of the questionnaire elicited biographical details from respondents. There were significant differences in age between the groups of staff. Nursery nurses in day nurseries tended to be younger than staff in the other groups, with 43.2 per cent of the respondents in this category aged less than 21 years. The overall difference in ages between the groups of nursery staff was highly significant. The relative youth of the day nursery nurses was also reflected in their comparative inexperience and the small number having children of their own (Table 3.1). In contrast, the nursery assistants in educational establishments were highly experienced, while almost all the staff working in playgroups (97.9 per cent) were themselves mothers.

All the teachers who responded to the questionnaire possessed teaching certificates but only two were graduates. All the nursery assistants had NNEB (Nursing Nurses Examination Board) certificates. Of the forty-four playgroup staff who replied, most had some form of brief training in child care, while four (9 per cent) were qualified teachers and ten (23 per cent) were trained nursery nurses. Comparatively few of the respondents belonged to external organizations concerned with the care and education of the young

TABLE 3.1: *Percentage of staff in each form of nursery having children of their own*

| Category of staff | % |
| --- | --- |
| NST | 60.6 |
| NSA | 51.3 |
| NC | 59.4 |
| DN | 18.2 |
| PG | 97.9 |

TABLE 3.2: *Percentage of staff responses emphasizing particular motives for working in nurseries for different forms of nursery in Area A*

| | Salary | Security | Good hours & holidays | No alternative | Family pressure | Opportunity of going to college | Interesting work | Worthwhile work | Best work | Work with children | Helping disadvantaged children | Other |
|---|---|---|---|---|---|---|---|---|---|---|---|---|
| NST | 0 | 5.3 | 1.8 | 1.8 | 3.5 | 0 | 17.5 | 12.3 | 12.3 | 36.8 | 5.3 | 3.5 |
| NSA | 0 | 1.3 | 0 | 1.3 | 0 | 2.6 | 27.6 | 19.7 | 7.9 | 35.5 | 3.9 | 0 |
| NC | 0 | 0 | 0 | 0 | 0 | 0 | 35.5 | 12.9 | 8.1 | 43.5 | 0 | 0 |
| DN | 0 | 2.5 | 0 | 0 | 0 | 1.3 | 18.8 | 30.0 | 1.3 | 20.0 | 26.3 | 0 |
| PG | 0 | 0 | 5.7 | 0 | 1.1 | 1.1 | 31.0 | 18.4 | 5.7 | 33.3 | 2.3 | 1.1 |
| Overall | 0 | 1.7 | 1.7 | 0.6 | 0.9 | 1.1 | 26.2 | 19.3 | 6.6 | 33.1 | 8.0 | 0.6 |

child, e.g. the British Association for Early Childhood Education (BAECE) or the Organisation Mondiale pour l'Éducation Prescolaire (OMEP). Approximately 20 per cent of the staff who replied to this question belonged to such an organization, a much lower proportion than that cited in the study by Taylor *et al.* (1972). However, many more teachers than nursery assistants belonged, a majority of teachers in the survey (54.8 per cent) being members of BAECE.

Finally in this section, staff were questioned about their primary motives for working in a nursery. Staff were asked to indicate the two items from a list which best expressed their reasons for wanting to work in a nursery. This question contained a degree of ambiguity in that respondents frequently reported that their motives for entering nursery work differed from their reasons for continuing in the field. In spite of this caveat, the responses show some interesting differences between the contexts. Table 3.2 shows the proportion of staff responding on each item for each type of nursery. As with the study of Taylor *et al.* (1972), the primary area of motivation may be described as vocational, the most frequently cited motives being 'work with children', 'interesting work' and 'worthwhile work'. Day nursery nurses tended to emphasize 'helping disadvantaged children' more than the other groups, while the only group to mention the hours of work as an important factor were the staff in the playgroups. None of the respondents indicated that salary played an important part in their choice of work.

The second section of the questionnaire dealt with the benefits of pre-school provision. Staff in nurseries were invited to indicate

TABLE 3.3: *Percentage of staff responses emphasizing particular benefits derived by the children from particular forms of nursery*

| | Training | Good physical care | Correct attitude to school | Foundation for school work | Enjoyment | Emotional security | Self-confidence | Enhanced ability to mix | Stimulation of interests | Wider experience | Realized potential | Enhanced intellect | Enhanced language |
|---|---|---|---|---|---|---|---|---|---|---|---|---|---|
| NST | 0.0 | 0.0 | 3.2 | 11.1 | 1.6 | 1.6 | 12.7 | 4.8 | 7.9 | 15.9 | 11.1 | 1.6 | 28.6 |
| NSA | 0.0 | 0.0 | 1.3 | 12.8 | 0.0 | 0.0 | 5.1 | 11.5 | 16.7 | 7.7 | 17.9 | 2.6 | 24.4 |
| NC | 0.0 | 0.0 | 4.8 | 9.5 | 0.0 | 4.8 | 6.3 | 23.8 | 12.7 | 7.9 | 14.3 | 0.0 | 15.9 |
| DN | 0.0 | 3.9 | 1.3 | 1.3 | 2.6 | 15.8 | 6.6 | 14.5 | 9.2 | 11.8 | 17.1 | 6.6 | 9.2 |
| PG | 0.0 | 0.0 | 2.3 | 8.0 | 10.2 | 0.0 | 13.6 | 31.8 | 10.2 | 8.0 | 11.4 | 0.0 | 4.5 |
| Overall | 0.0 | 0.8 | 2.4 | 8.4 | 3.3 | 4.3 | 9.0 | 17.9 | 11.4 | 10.1 | 14.4 | 2.2 | 15.8 |

which of a series of possible benefits they felt children were deriving from their nursery. In addition, they were asked to select the two areas in which they felt children were gaining most from their time in the nursery. It was clear that many members of staff included in the study felt that the benefits of nursery provision for the children were widespread, several respondents opting to indicate all the possible benefits listed. For the purposes of analysis use was made of only those questionnaires where the respondent had chosen and indicated the principal areas of benefit. Frequencies of response on a particular item were calculated, and subsequently the percentage of responses to a particular item compared to the total number of responses was obtained. Table 3.3 presents these data.

Overall, the benefits considered to be most important were:

1 the ability to mix with others;
2 enhanced language development;
3 the opportunity to discover and use potential.

Staff in the nursery schools and classes tended to emphasize language development more than those working in the other two contexts. Staff in day nurseries gave emotional security greater precedence than did the others, while playgroups in particular emphasized the role of the nursery in getting children to mix well together and the development of self-confidence.

The various items in this section of the questionnaire may be divided into three categories:

TABLE 3.4: *Percentage of staff responses emphasizing general areas of benefit derived by the children from particular forms of nursery*

|       | Training and care | Socio-emotional | Intellectual |
|-------|:-----------------:|:---------------:|:------------:|
|       |                   | development     | development  |
|       | %                 | %               | %            |
| NST   | 14.3              | 20.6            | 65.1         |
| NSA   | 14.1              | 16.7            | 69.2         |
| NC    | 14.3              | 34.9            | 50.8         |
| DN    | 6.6               | 39.5            | 53.9         |
| PG    | 10.2              | 55.7            | 34.1         |

1 training and care;
2 socio-emotional development;
3 intellectual development.

Table 3.4 shows an analysis of the data using these categories and reveals marked differences between the responses obtained from staff in different forms of nursery (it should be remembered that the responses listed are of those areas in which the staff consider the children are deriving *most* benefit). The emphasis on socio-emotional development in the playgroup is most marked, while the emphasis on intellectual development is greatest in the schools. The view of the nursery as a foundation for later schooling is found most often in the educational establishments.

In the next question, staff were asked to consider six different programmes which could be implemented in a nursery and to rank the programmes in their own order of priority. Details of the programmes are given in Table 3.5(a). Although the programmes are certainly not mutually exclusive, the order in which staff placed them yields insights into the emphasis staff place on particular aspects of the running of the nursery (see Table 3.5(b)). Overall, it may be stated that there was a great deal of similarity between the groups. All groups of nursery staff placed programme (e) – emphasizing the need to allow the child to develop his potential at his own rate within a caring and supportive environment – as the first priority, while 'effectively occupying the child's time' or 'actively involving the parents' received comparatively little support in any form of nursery.

All respondents, with the exception of two playgroup supervisors, stated that the children's activities in the nurseries were planned to

TABLE 3.5(a): *Item in questionnaire dealing with pre-school programmes*

Below there are six statements about programmes which might be implemented in the running of a nursery. Some of the programmes are obviously compatible with each other, but we would like your views on their relative merits. Will you please read the statements carefully and when you have read them, indicate the order of priority you would give them by putting a 6 against the programme you would approve most, other things being equal, and number them all down to 1 for the programme you would stress least.

A nursery should have a programme:

(a) which develops within an overall plan those skills that children should acquire before they commence school ☐

(b) of varied activities which effectively occupy the child's time ☐

(c) which allows the child the opportunity for free expression and play with a little guidance from adults ☐

(d) which concentrates on the social and emotional aspects of the child's development ☐

(e) which allows the child to develop his potential at his own rate within a caring and supportive environment ☐

(f) which actively involves parents in the development of the child's skills ☐

TABLE 3.5(b): *Order of priority given to alternative programmes by staff in different types of nursery*

|  | First prog. | Rank | Second prog. | Rank | Third prog. | Rank | Fourth prog. | Rank | Fifth prog. | Rank | Last prog. | Rank |
|---|---|---|---|---|---|---|---|---|---|---|---|---|
| NST | e | 5.7 | c | 4.1 | a | 4.0 | d | 3.5 | f | 2.4 | b | 1.4 |
| NSA | e | 5.4 | c | 4.4 | a | 3.8 | d | 3.4 | b | 2.5 | f | 1.5 |
| NC | e | 5.4 | c | 4.4 | a | 3.9 | d | 3.7 | b | 1.9 | f | 1.6 |
| DN | e | 5.4 | c | 4.3 | d | 4.0 | a | 2.7 | f | 2.5 | b | 2.3 |
| PG | e | 5.1 | c | 4.7 | a | 3.4 | d | 2.8 | b | 2.6 | f | 2.5 |

**TABLE 3.6(a):** *Item in questionnaire dealing with the primary role of the adult in the nursery*

Probably all of us would agree that the primary role of the adult in a nursery is to create a safe, happy and stimulating environment.
However, we may have differing views about other aspects of the role. Please tick the statement below which agrees most closely with your own attitude:

(a) The adult should assist the child to develop his potential by guiding, encouraging and instructing the child in the performance of desirable activities.

(b) By guiding and encouraging the child in those activities that the child wishes to do.

(c) By providing an environment with a wide range of materials and activities in which the child can play and explore in his own way.

**TABLE 3.6(b):** *Number and percentage of staff endorsements of differing forms of role for staff in the pre-school*

|  | Role (a) | | Role (b) | | Role (c) | | Total |
|---|---|---|---|---|---|---|---|
|  | no. | % | no. | % | no. | % | no. |
| NST | 16 | 50 | 6 | 19 | 10 | 31 | 32 |
| NSA | 17 | 45 | 4 | 11 | 17 | 45 | 38 |
| NC | 9 | 29 | 5 | 16 | 17 | 55 | 31 |
| DN | 4 | 9 | 1 | 2 | 38 | 88 | 43 |
| PG | 7 | 16 | 9 | 20 | 29 | 64 | 45 |
| Total | 53 | 28 | 25 | 13.2 | 111 | 58.7 | 189 |

some extent. However, when asked about their attitude to the role of adults in the nursery, the staff in the various contexts tended to give different replies (Table 3.6). The need for some guidance and instruction tended to receive greater emphasis in the nursery schools and classes than in the day nurseries and playgroups where the view that staff should allow the child to play and explore in his own way predominated. Overall, the differences between the groups on this question were statistically significant.

A comparison of the responses of nursery nurses working in

different forms of pre-school establishment proved rewarding. As previously noted, nursery nurses employed in day nurseries tended to be younger than those working in the educational establishments. They also tended to be less experienced and less likely to have children of their own. Motives for entering the work were generally similar but day nursery nurses were more likely to emphasize the 'compensatory' aspects of their work, a finding which is reflected in their according 'emotional security' a more prominent place among the benefits derived by the children. Day nursery nurses tended to rely more on day-to-day planning than the nursery assistants in the other two forms of nursery and similarly placed greater emphasis on allowing the child to play and explore in his own way. Thus, although the nursery nurses in different establishments have in most cases received similar training, some of their subsequent attitudes to their work may be seen to differ from one type of establishment to another.

The questionnaire study was repeated using the staff of nursery schools and classes in Area B. Because of the historical differences in the state provision between the two areas it was felt that a comparison of responses obtained in each area would be of interest.

In terms of biographical details the staff in Areas A and B tended to be similar with the exception that nursery assistants in Area B tended to be younger and less experienced than those in Area A. Teachers in Area A also tended to be older and more experienced than their counterparts in Area B, but the differences between the groups were not significant. The benefits of nursery education emphasized by the staff were similar in both areas, although staff in Area B placed slightly less emphasis on the enhancement of language abilities, and slightly more on the development of the ability to mix. The rating of alternative nursery programmes was similar in both areas, although nursery nurses in Area B tended to give slightly greater priority to programmes (d) and (f), emphasizing both the social and emotional aspects of the child's development and the need to involve parents. More teachers in Area B admitted to planning activities on a daily rather than a longer-term basis but no significant differences in staff attitudes to adult roles in the nursery could be found. Thus, generally, the two areas appeared to be remarkably similar in the responses of the nursery staff to the questionnaire. As a consequence, in the following inter-item analysis the two sets of staff from nursery schools and classes were combined.

More experienced teachers tended to consider that their role should include a degree of guidance for the child and a similar trend with experience was seen in nursery assistants. No effects of the social class of the children upon the nursery staffs' view of the nursery programme could be discerned. However, respondents who viewed their children as coming from a predominantly working-class background tended to emphasize the view that the nursery was providing a wider range of experiences than the home. Teachers tended to stress the need for adult guidance of play more in nurseries with a middle-class representation while the opposite was true of the playgroup supervisors.

Analysis of the responses of teachers and nursery assistants in the educational establishments showed that, generally, whatever their views about the programmes to be run, they saw enhanced language development as the principal benefit of nursery education. However, the group of teachers and assistants who saw the nursery as furnishing a good foundation for later schooling tended to emphasize programme (a) which specifically sets out to develop skills necessary for later schooling within an overall plan. Perhaps not surprisingly, this group also emphasized the need for the adult to guide the child in his activities.

Within the different forms of pre-school provision there appear to be interesting similarities and differences between the staff. In the main, staff in nursery education tend to be experienced in terms of both their training and the length of time they have been working with the under-fives. There is also a strong probability that staff in nursery schools and classes will have children of their own. This last factor also pertains to playgroup staff, but the training of playgroup supervisors is usually more limited than that of their counterparts in nursery education. Staff in day nurseries prove to be an exception to the general rule of experience in caring for young children. The reason for this may lie in the working hours involved in employment in a day nursery and the difficulties these impose upon the combination of work and the raising of a young family. However, differences in response to other questions also serve to differentiate day nursery staff from others in pre-school provision. Analysis of the data reveals an emphasis upon the compensatory role of the day nursery by its staff, an acknowledgement that is highly appropriate in the light of the differences between the children in day nurseries and those in other forms of provision. Nursery nurses in day nurseries stress this as a particular motive for working in that form of pre-school provision, but with this exception the motives underlying the nursery staffs' wish to work with young children are very similar. In each case the motives for undertaking this work would seem to be vocational rather than social or economic. Interestingly, the only group to mention good hours and holidays as playing an important part in determining their choice of occupation were the playgroup supervisors. Approximately 30 per cent of the supervisors responding in the questionnaire study possessed either a teaching qualification of a NNEB certificate. (Nationally, in 32 per cent of playgroups at least one member of staff has an NNEB certificate (Pre-school Playgroups Association, 1987).) In the case of approximately one-third of the supervisors, they will have had contact with, or been trained for work in, nurseries within the educational system. Since the vast majority of supervisors themselves were mothers, it seems likely that in some instances the playgroup provides an opportunity for continuing to work with young children while raising a family with a reduced conflict of demands. In other cases there would seem to be some evidence of mothers becoming interested in nursery work as a consequence of having children of their own. The pattern of entry into playgroup work may therefore be rather different from that found in other nurseries, although the underlying motives are obviously similar.

Several statements concerning the aims of the pre-school may be found in the literature on early childhood education. Often these aims are couched in very general and vague terms (Dearden, 1969). However, there would appear to be a great deal of agreement between the staff in different nursery establishments concerning the benefits derived by the children from the nursery, although the emphases vary between one form and another. In part these differences in emphasis reflect the varied histories of pre-school provision. Day nursery staff, for example, see good physical care and the provision of emotional security as important benefits of their type of nursery. Playgroup staff differed from the other staff in their greater emphasis on the rewards of enjoyment, self-confidence and an enhanced ability to mix. Turner and Green (1977) report a similar emphasis upon socio-emotional development in playgroup supervisors. Staff in nursery schools and classes placed somewhat greater weight on the intellectual and linguistic gains made through nursery education. However, staff in all four forms of provision saw the socialization of the child as being of great concern. Despite some differences in emphasis there appears to be a consensus about the form of programme a nursery should run. The greatest surprise here, perhaps, lies in the comparatively low ranking accorded to the programme describing the active involvement of the parent in the development of the child's abilities. As various authors have stated, parental involvement can take different forms and be broken down into different levels (Gordon, 1968; Watt, 1977). The form of involvement proposed by the questionnaire item concerned the integration of the parents in the process of tuition rather than the allocation of the parent to an auxiliary role in the nursery. Playgroups in particular frequently emphasize the role parents have to play in the running of the nursery (Pre-school Playgroups Association, 1987; Watt, 1977). However, the present study shows that, in comparison with other types of programme, even with this group of nursery staff the involvement of parents is given a fairly low priority. Interestingly, the groups according parental involvement the lowest priority were the nursery nurses in the two forms of educational establishment. Watt (1977) also found some nursery nurses unwilling to concede a role for parents in the nursery, and suggested that some nurses might see such a role to be pre-emptive of their own. Such reasoning may underlie some of the responses from nursery nurses to this question in the present study, although it should be pointed out that a degree of variability in the responses existed.

Almost without exception nursery staff indicated that they tended to plan the child's day to a certain extent, whether on a day-to-day basis (as indicated by day nursery and playgroup staff) or on a longer-term basis (as favoured by staff in nursery schools and classes). The length and degree of planning is obviously an important part of the structure of the nursery and is related to other aspects of the role of the adult. As Laing (1973) states, skilled teachers of pre-school children structure the nursery environment either deliberately or intuitively. He goes on to opine that debate should not centre upon the merits of child-centred as opposed to structured approaches but upon the *degree* of structure. Parry and Archer (1974) concur that there is a need for some degree of structure in good educational practice. However, they state that a too scientific and structured approach can actually interfere with the atmosphere in which a young child learns best. The views of the nursery staff in the present study would appear to be congruent with this last statement, as witnessed by the pattern of responses to the final question concerning the role of the nursery staff.

Closer inspection of attitudes towards the role of staff in the nursery is permitted by analysis of the answers to the final part of the questionnaire. Taylor *et al.* (1972) provided the nursery teachers in their survey with four alternative views of their own role in the nursery: two child-centred and two teacher-centred; two child-directed and two teacher-directed. In their study the majority of teachers preferred the teacher-centred/child-directed role. The findings of Abbott (1978) were generally similar. In the present study nursery staff were given three alternative attitudes to the role of the adult in the nursery (see Appendix B). Although differing slightly from those of Taylor *et al.* (1972), the roles could be construed as:

1 teacher-centred/teacher-directed;
2 child-centred/teacher-directed;
3 child-centred/child-directed.

The most popular option in the previous studies was deliberately excluded in order to make a clearer distinction between teacher-centred and child-centred roles. In contrast to the previous studies, results show a distinct emphasis on child-centred approaches. This is particularly true of day nurseries and playgroups, but the emphasis is rather less clear amongst the staff in schools, teachers in nursery schools being evenly divided between teacher-centred and child-centred approaches.

## Parental and staff views of the purposes of pre-school provision

In a follow-up to the study cited above a colleague, Patricia Ward, presented a new questionnaire to groups of staff in playgroups and nursery schools and to the parents of children attending these two forms of pre-school provision (Ward, 1982). From the responses to the questions in the initial part of the questionnaire, which contrasted nursery schools with playgroups, it was clear that both sets of parents were satisfied with the provision in which their child was currently involved. Teachers emphasized the value of the structure inherent in nursery school sessions and the qualities of their own professional training while playgroup supervisors emerged as a group strongly committed to the publicized playgroup ethos of community involvement and parent participation.

In the next question Ward asked respondents to select two main purposes of pre-school provision from a given range of twelve, which are shown in Table 3.7. It is clear from analysis of this table that both parents and staff in nursery schools and playgroups see the primary purpose of pre-school provision as being of benefit to the child rather than to the mother or the family as a whole. All staff groups and the playgroup parents made 'giving children wider experience with people, equipment and space' the main choice of purpose. Nursery school staff also frequently selected the development of the child's intellect in general and of his language in particular. Playgroup staff tended to emphasize the social purposes of pre-school provision. Thus a different set of questions elicited responses which are broadly congruent with those given to the first questionnaire.

It is interesting to note that nursery school parents indicated that they considered a major purpose of pre-school provision to be preparation for later schooling. Other studies have also shown that working-class parents see nursery provision in this way (Newson and Newson, 1968; Tizard, 1978). Discussion with parents in the present study revealed that they saw pre-school as a means of preparing the

TABLE 3.7: *The supposed purposes of pre-school provision**

| Question no. | Purpose | Respondents | | | | |
|---|---|---|---|---|---|---|
| | | Nursery teachers | Nursery assistants | Playgroup supervisors | Nursery school parents | Playgroup parents |
| 1 | It frees mothers to go out to work | — | — | — | 5 | — |
| 2 | It gives mothers time to themselves | 5 | — | 5 | — | 5 |
| 3 | It replaces old-style large families | 5 | — | 5 | — | — |
| 4 | It gets children ready for school | 20 | 27 | 10 | 70 | 25 |
| 5 | It breaks the child away from the mother | 5 | 10 | 20 | 5 | — |
| 6 | It gives children wider experience with people, equipment and space | 75 | 69 | 80 | 40 | 85 |
| 7 | Children get bored at home | — | — | — | 5 | — |
| 8 | A child needs the company of other children | 10 | 16 | 35 | 40 | 50 |
| 9 | It helps mothers to make friends | — | — | 10 | — | — |
| 10 | It fosters a child's intellectual development at her own rate | 35 | 43 | 20 | 30 | 15 |
| 11 | It fosters a child's independence | 15 | 16 | 15 | — | 20 |
| 12 | It fosters a child's language development | 35 | 21 | 5 | 5 | — |

*Percentage of group choosing each purpose as one of their *two* selections (therefore total responses per group = 200 per cent).

child for the *routine* and *discipline* of school rather than an intellectual training. Many of these parents had children who had attended playgroups before entering nursery school. It is possible, therefore, that they see the nursery school day as conforming more to the ethos of the primary school than would the playgroup situation. As a result they may believe that the nursery school prepares the child for the world of school more adequately than continued playgroup experience would do. Playgroup supervisors and parents were in closer accord in generally emphasizing the social aspects of group life. This finding could be due to the fact that playgroup parents are more actively involved in the playgroup and so become imbued with the playgroup philosophy. Playgroup staff were less likely to indicate the encouragement of intellectual or linguistic development as a major purpose of their form of provision. This result is interesting in the light of research carried out by Turner and Green (1977), who found that playgroup supervisors denied any cognitive aim in their work, yet in practice their interactions with the children did in fact contain styles destined to foster cognitive development.

The two questionnaire studies reported above reveal interesting similarities and differences between staff in different kinds of pre-school provision. Both studies reveal the child-centred orientation of the adults working with the under-fives. Yet, neither necessarily leads to a conclusion that nursery staff place a low priority on intellectual development as has sometimes been alleged. As Curtis (1986) points out, different aims may assume priority depending on the particular needs of the children and the circumstances pertaining at any given time. What is interesting about the studies reported here is the *relative* emphasis given by staff in different forms of pre-school provision when they are asked to make statements about priorities. It may also be recognized that there have perhaps been shifts in opinion amongst nursery staff during the course of the research project described here. Thus, for example, when Curtis and Blatchford (1980) administered a questionnaire to nursery teachers working with socially handicapped children they found that the majority of respondents marked intellectual development either first or joint first with social development, teachers' comments indicating the need for sensitivity to the child's individual requirements. This suggestion that staff should be aware of the particular needs of the children in their care requires further elaboration. Accordingly, in the next study to be described we concentrate upon the nursery staffs' perceptions of children in order to discover in greater detail which characteristics they feel it is most important to recognize in fostering development.

## Nursery staff's perceptions of pupils

A questionnaire consisting of closed questions places constraints upon the form of response that can be made. In order to enable staff to explain more clearly their approach to individual children we conducted a further study based upon interviews using a technique that has become known as the *repertory grid technique*. Because interviews were conducted on an individual basis and lasted for approximately one hour this study was limited to staff in nursery education. The subjects of the study were twenty teachers and twenty nursery nurses drawn from the twelve nursery schools and classes. Interviewees were told that the purpose of the exercise was to 'see the children through their eyes'. By means of a systematic procedure, staff were requested to describe and contrast the characteristics of six boys and six girls chosen at random from the register.

The procedure had three principle phases:

1 Elicitation of constructs: staff were presented with the names of children in groups of three (triads). They were then asked to say in what way two of the children were alike and differed from the third. What staff said about the pair of children was recorded as a 'construct', e.g. 'aggressive'. They were then asked to describe the single child, and a second 'construct' was noted, e.g. 'timid'. In this way, through repeated presentation of names of children in different combinations, a series of 'construct pairs' was obtained for each member of staff.

2 Elicitation of construct polarities: each staff member was requested to discuss the construct pairs supplied in the light of the objectives of the nursery: then they were asked to say which aspect of the pair (if either) they would seek to encourage, e.g. would they wish to encourage 'cooperation' (say) as opposed to 'a refusal to join in'? Thereafter, staff were asked to look at the construct pairs they had given and determine, as far as possible, which of the characteristics it was most important that staff should be aware of. Construct pairs were accordingly ranked in order of importance by the subject.

3 Location of elements on construct dimensions: as a final part of the procedure each staff member was asked to rate the twelve children on each construct pair using a seven-point scale. Thus, if the construct pair was 'plays cooperatively' versus 'plays alone' these terms were placed at each end of a scale with five intermediate points. Each child was then placed on this scale and a note made of her position.

45

At the end of the procedure staff were asked if there were any other characteristics of the children that staff should be aware of. Throughout the interview the terms employed by the subject were recorded verbatim, although requests for clarification of meaning were made where there was possible ambiguity.

In total 374 construct pairs were elicited from the 40 members of staff. Teachers tended to supply rather more constructs than nursery nurses but the difference between the groups was not significant.

Since overlap or equivalence between construct pairs was suspected, constructs believed to be concerned with essentially the same areas were assigned to categories, with the rider that, because of the way in which constructs were elicited, no two constructs supplied by the same subject could be assigned to the same category. The constructs were placed in sixteen major categories and thirty-seven subcategories. The areas thus differentiated are indicated in Table 3.8 and definitions and examples of each category are supplied in Appendix B. As Smith (1970) points out, constructs elicited still require understanding on the part of the experimenter and categorization of similar constructs may lead to a loss of meaning. In order to guard against this to a certain extent, reliability of categorization was ascertained by resort to comparison with independent assessors.

The frequencies with which constructs of a particular superordinate category were elicited are given for teachers and nursery nurses separately in Table 3.9. Generally, the two groups of subjects are very similar on this measure, the only significant difference occurring with constructs pertaining to the child's home background. Significantly more constructs were supplied by teachers than by nursery nurses in this area. The most frequently elicited constructs for both groups referred to the child's personality.

Table 3.10 shows the most frequently elicited constructs by subcategory for teachers and nursery nurses. Both groups frequently mentioned the child's overall level of intelligence and the ability to mix, the latter assuming particular importance for nursery nurses.

Analysis of the constructs elicited according to the experience of the subjects revealed few differences. Experienced teachers tended to produce more constructs than less experienced teachers but the reverse trend was observed in the responses of nursery nurses.

Analysis of polar preferences on constructs showed that staff felt it highly desirable that children should mix well, that they should be confident and emotionally well adjusted, and that they should converse freely with adults in the nursery. Emphasis was also given to the importance of the development of linguistic facility. It was clear that staff attributed little importance to the co-operativeness of

TABLE 3.8: *Categorization of constructs elicited by the Repertory Grid Technique*

| Category | Subcategory |
|---|---|
| 1 Child's relationships with children | (i) Ability to mix |
| | (ii) Aggression |
| | (iii) Leader–follower |
| 2 Child's personality | (i) Confidence |
| | (ii) Loquacity |
| | (iii) Boisterousness |
| | (iv) Disposition |
| | (v) Emotional adjustment |
| 3 Child's relationship with staff | (i) Independence |
| | (ii) Conversation |
| 4 Attitude to staff | (i) Eagerness |
| | (ii) Co-operativeness |
| 5 Play | (i) Play ability |
| | (ii) Play preference |
| | (iii) Play value |
| | (iv) Play type |
| 6 Concentration | |
| 7 Ability | (i) Intelligence |
| | (ii) Awareness and comprehension |
| 8 Language | (i) Speech |
| | (ii) Use |
| 9 Creativity | |
| 10 Self-help | |
| 11 Physical development | |
| 12 Age | (i) Chronological age |
| | (ii) Maturity |
| | (iii) Rate of development |
| 13 Sex | |
| 14 Home background | (i) Stability and security |
| | (ii) Physical care |
| | (iii) Care and interest |
| | (iv) Expectations |
| | (v) Status |
| | (vi) Family |
| | (vii) Parting and separation |
| 15 Settling in | |
| 16 Miscellaneous | |

TABLE 3.9: *Rank order of superordinate construct categories by frequency of elicitation*

| Rank | | Construct | Total | | Teacher | | Nursery Nurse | |
|---|---|---|---|---|---|---|---|---|
| | | | no. | % | no. | % | no. | % |
| 1 | 2 | Child's personality | 70 | 18.72 | 37 | 18.23 | 33 | 19.30 |
| 2 | 1 | Child's relationship with children | 48 | 12.83 | 22 | 10.84 | 26 | 15.20 |
| 3 | 14 | Home background | 37 | 9.89 | 26 | 12.81 | 11 | 6.43 |
| 4 | 12 | Age | 31 | 8.29 | 17 | 8.37 | 14 | 8.19 |
| 5.5 | 7 | Ability | 29 | 7.75 | 15 | 7.39 | 14 | 8.19 |
| 5.5 | 5 | Play | 29 | 7.75 | 13 | 6.40 | 16 | 9.36 |
| 7 | 8 | Language | 25 | 6.68 | 15 | 7.39 | 10 | 5.85 |
| 8.5 | 4 | Attitude to staff | 24 | 6.42 | 12 | 5.91 | 12 | 7.02 |
| 8.5 | 3 | Child's relationship with staff | 24 | 6.42 | 11 | 5.42 | 13 | 7.60 |
| 10 | 16 | Miscellaneous | 12 | 3.21 | 7 | 3.45 | 5 | 2.92 |
| 11 | 6 | Concentration | 11 | 2.94 | 7 | 3.45 | 4 | 2.34 |
| 12 | 9 | Creativity | 10 | 2.67 | 4 | 1.97 | 6 | 3.51 |
| 13 | 13 | Sex | 8 | 2.14 | 5 | 4.13 | 3 | 1.75 |
| 14.5 | 11 | Physical development | 7 | 1.87 | 6 | 2.96 | 1 | 0.58 |
| 14.5 | 15 | Settling in | 7 | 1.87 | 4 | 1.97 | ·1 | 1.75 |
| 16 | 10 | Self-help | 2 | 0.71 | 2 | 0.99 | 0 | 0.00 |

TABLE 3.10: *Frequency and proportion of the most frequent categories of constructs by type of staff*

| Rank | Nursery teachers | | | no. | % |
|---|---|---|---|---|---|
| 1.5 | 2(i) | | Confidence | 11 | 55 |
| 1.5 | 7(i) | | Intelligence | 11 | 55 |
| 3.5 | 1(i) | | Ability to mix | 10 | 50 |
| 3.5 | 12(i) | | Chronological age | 10 | 55 |
| 5 | 2(iv) | | Disposition | 9 | 45 |

| Rank | Nursery nurses | | | no. | % |
|---|---|---|---|---|---|
| 1 | 1(i) | | Ability to mix | 14 | 70 |
| 2 | 7(i) | | Intelligence | 12 | 60 |
| 3.5 | 2(iii) | | Boisterousness | 11 | 55 |
| 3.5 | 5(ii) | | Play preference | 11 | 55 |
| 5 | 1(ii) | | Aggression | 9 | 45 |

TABLE 3.11: *Rank ordering by importance of elicited constructs by teachers and nursery nurses*

| Teachers | | | Nursery nurses | | |
|---|---|---|---|---|---|
| Rank | | Category | Rank | | Category |
| 1 | 14 | Home background | 1 | 8 | Language |
| 2 | 12 | Age | 2 | 14 | Home background |
| 3.5 | 7 | Ability | 3 | 12 | Age |
| 3.5 | 8 | Language | 4 | 3 | Child's relationship with staff |
| 5 | 3 | Child's relationship with staff | 5 | 2 | Child's personality |
| 6 | 2 | Child's personality | 6 | 7 | Ability |
| 7 | 11 | Physical development | 7 | 1 | Child's relationships with children |
| 8 | 1 | Child's relationships with children | 8 | 9 | Creativity |
| 9 | 6 | Concentration | 9 | 5 | Play |
| 10.5 | 9 | Creativity | 10 | 4 | Attitude to staff |
| 10.5 | 5 | Play | 11 | 6 | Concentration |
| 12 | 15 | Settling in | 12 | 13 | Sex |
| 13 | 4 | Attitude to staff | | | |
| 14 | 13 | Sex | | | |

*Note* A category must have been elicited more than once to be included in analysis.

the child (although some nursery nurses considered that it was important) or the child's play preferences.

Analysis of the staff rankings of their own constructs in order of importance produced some interesting findings (Table 3.11), suggesting that the frequency with which a construct is elicited is not always a good index of the importance that may be attributed to it. For instance, whereas constructs relating to the child's relationships with other children were the second most frequent category elicited, they were ranked eighth and seventh in order of importance by teachers and nursery nurses respectively. Where constructs referring to the child's home background had been elicited these were accorded considerable importance by both teachers and nursery nurses. The child's home background can thus be seen as an important factor in the explanation of the child's behaviour by nursery staff. Overall, the rank ordering for the two professions was very similar.

As a final part of the analysis each completed repertory grid was subjected to a principal component analysis. In each case the first pair of components accounted for more than 70 per cent of the variance. Generally, the first component could be interpreted as a measure of social maturity but interpretations of the second component were more difficult and more varied.

In general, the findings of this study are congruent with those obtained from the questionnaire study. The principle area of concern for staff working with the young child is his social development. The constructs that related to this area showed a fine degree of discrimination between different facets of this development. By contrast, where constructs pertaining to other areas of development – intellectual, physical or linguistic – were elicted they tended to be more global and less precisely defined. It was also noteworthy that whereas staff were willing to attribute negative values to a child's social behaviour, they were less willing to do so for other aspects of behaviour where the positive pole was stressed. For example, although staff were content to state that a particular child was bright, they would label other children as 'less bright'. Staff denied that they preferred to work with the brighter children, stating that they saw it as a duty to share their time evenly between children; where a discrimination between children was made it was on the grounds that less bright children required greater assistance.

The child's ability level was seen as being something that staff should be aware of, but particular aspects of intellectual ability considered especially important remained undisclosed. As in the questionnaire study, language development was separated from other cognitive areas and given prominence. This finding is supported by the work of Clift *et al.* (1980), who report: 'Aspects of language development were seen as distinct from and almost independent of areas related to cognitive or intellectual development, and of social aims' (p. 44).

However, whereas Clift *et al.* found teachers making statements of aims concerning language development more frequently than nursery nurses, both groups in the present study attributed importance to this area. Indeed, the nursery nurses from whom a construct concerning language development was elicited, as a group accorded this area greatest importance. Teachers ranked it behind home background, age and general ability.

Both groups emphasized that it is important that nursery staff should be aware of the child's home background. It will be remembered that in the questionnaire study the programme which suggested a need for the active involvement of parents in the nursery routine was given a low priority, yet from the present study it is obvious that staff recognize the powerful influence of the home upon the child's performance. It may be argued that knowledge of the home background is used to explain the child's behaviour in the school, although most staff stressed that they were reluctant to 'judge' any of the parents of their children. The use of 'home background' as an explanatory concept is well documented (e.g. Goodacre, 1968; King, 1978).

## Discussion

The studies presented in this chapter reveal a general similarity in the approach of nursery staff, with minor differences reflecting the kind of training they have received and differences in the groups of children with which they work. In the main, the emphasis in nursery work remains centred on the child and the need to provide an environment in which he can develop in his own way and at his own pace. This ethos is of great importance in determining the nature of the experiences available to the child in the nursery. Only amongst the teachers in the nursery schools is it possible to detect a clear division in attitude between those who believe in a relatively unstructured nursery environment which has its own unique educational identity and those who view the nursery and the education available within it as a precursor of the infant school. Whereas the former emphasize the benefits of free play with limited adult intervention, the latter group tend to emphasize the development of skills required in the infant school with adult guidance according to a given plan. This dichotomy might in some respects be analogous to that described by King (1978) in his observations on the infant school, in which he sees a division between the majority who accept the infant school ethos wholeheartedly and those whose attitudes reflect an ethos more typical of the junior school. In this case the division would be between people sharing a common nursery ethos and those whose views embrace the attitudes and practices of higher levels of the school system.

Three previous studies have employed repertory grid techniques in order to elicit the perceptions of primary school teachers (Nash, 1973; Taylor, 1976; Aitkenhead, 1978). Nash (1973) in his study of primary school children and their teachers reported that the two most common constructs used by teachers were 'well-behaved – poorly-behaved' and 'high-ability – low-ability'. Taylor's (1976) study also suggested that academic criteria predominate in the teachers' perceptions of their pupils. Aitkenhead's (1978) work examined the views of reception class teachers. The results of his study suggest that there are differences among reception class teachers as to the ways in which they perceive their pupils; some teachers stress social adjustment while others attend mainly to ability and achievement from an early age. In general, more academic criteria are more commonly found later in the school year. Combining the findings of these studies with those of the present, one may hypothesize that there is a continuum in the perceptions of teachers at different stages of the educational process. At the nursery stage the emphasis is placed firmly upon social adjustment. In the reception class this emphasis shifts through the course of the year towards more academic criteria. This trend continues with the increasing age of the child until in later primary school these aspects of academic ability and social control of the child predominate.

King (1978), through observation of infant teachers' actions, suggested that these were related to the ideas they held about the nature of young children and the nature of the learning process. These ideas formed coherent sets or ideologies. For the most part these ideologies were unconsidered by the teachers because they were taken for granted, but occasionally they were made more explicit, as in the writing of letters and guidance notes for parents. The prevailing ideology of the infant school finds official expression in the Plowden Report (Central Advisory Council for Education, 1967), and is essentially one of child-centredness. Within this there are important elements of 'developmentalism', 'individualism', play as learning and childhood innocence (King, 1978). It is possible to make similar inferences for staff in all forms of nursery. How these ideologies are reflected in practice is the concern of the next part of this book.

# What happens in different pre-school provisions?

# Chapter 4

# Adults' activities in pre-school

In recent years there has been much interest in the analysis of the teacher's role in the nursery school in terms of both theory and practice (e.g. Bereiter and Engelmann, 1966; Blank, 1973; Woodhead, 1976). These studies suggest that where some children appear not to benefit from nursery education the remedy lies in a modification of the adult's role. However, few studies have closely examined the role of the teacher prior to the operation of a programme of intervention and fewer still have considered the role of other adults involved in the care and education of the pre-school child, such as nursery nurses and playgroup supervisors.

One of the earliest studies of the adult's contribution to children's nursery experience is that of Thomas (1973). The aim of the study was to investigate the value of nursery education through an examination of the language elicited in the nursery situation. Recording therefore focused on verbal interaction between the child and the staff of the nursery. The results revealed a lack of awareness on the part of the children of the adult's role as a source of information, as witnessed by the paucity of the children's questions. In addition, the responses of the adults failed to indicate awareness of a child's particular need for communication, for stimulating his curiosity or for presenting sufficient speech patterns for imitation. For Thomas the linguistic evidence revealed a confusion of roles between the teacher and the nursery nurse, only the dinner lady seeming confident of hers. The use of language in the nursery will be considered in more detail later (Chapter 9). Of more relevance here is Thomas's strident criticism of the nursery routine she observed, and the limited adult–child interaction within it.

55

The experiences presented during the day were invariable, the pattern of activities were repetitive and the equipment emphasized gross motor activity . . . The value of their self-chosen activities was doubtful. Awarded no adult support, either as an individual or as a group, they selected their activity at random. It was rarely matched to their experiential or ability level (Thomas, 1973, p. 215).

Having studied nursery staff at work within a traditional nursery routine, Thomas is clearly arguing for a change in the role of the staff. A rather more supportive view of the behaviour of nursery staff is provided by a study reported by Tizard *et al.* (1976b) in which a time-sampling method was employed to examine aspects of staff behaviour in six pre-school centres. The centres differed in their educational orientation and the subjects involved in the study included both trained and untrained staff. Staff behaviour was categorized according to content. As complete a record as possible was made of what staff said and did. Reassuringly, in view of some of Thomas's criticisms, in none of the centres could staff be described simply as 'care-taking'. However, certain teacher-specific behaviours, such as Socratic questioning, demonstrating, or giving children extensive information or explanation, occurred rarely. Half of the centres selected contained predominantly working-class children, half predominantly middle-class. The 'cognitive content' of staff behaviour, defined as the proportion of time in which the staff were observed helping the child to learn non-disciplinary matters, and the total amount of talk to children were observed more frequently in the centres catering for middle-class children. Dealing with play equipment and minimal supervision, i.e. merely watching the children without interacting in any way with them, occurred more often in the working-class centres. Comparison between trained and untrained nursery assistants revealed no consistent trends, although there was a marked tendency for the cognitive content of staff behaviour to be highest among the nursery nurses working in schools. Tizard *et al.* (1976b) argue from this evidence that the strength with which staff believe they should influence children's cognitive development is more important than their training.

In a study of ten playgroups situated in areas of social need in Belfast, Turner and Green (1977) elicited information about the aims of the playgroup leaders by means of a questionnaire and a semi-structured interview, prior to observation of adult–child interactions in the playroom. The observational data were examined to determine the time devoted to the promotion of each of the five aims obtained from the questionnaire and the interview. When the time spent by the different leaders on the promotion of the aims was averaged the following order emerged: cognitive, socio-emotional, aesthetic development, preparing for school, and physical development. The time actually devoted by staff to cognitive aspects was nearly eight times that spent encouraging socio-emotional development. Interestingly, this order differed markedly from the professed order of aims of the leaders. Turner and Green suggest therefore that further observations of day-to-day nursery practice are desirable.

Cashdan and Philps (1975) report data obtained from pilot observations of teachers in the nursery classroom. Analysis showed that wide variation was evident in both verbal and non-verbal spheres. Incidence of higher-level non-verbal activities (i.e. demonstrating, helping, investigating or examining and showing) was uniformly low. Although most of the teachers in the pilot study were already quite spontaneously comparing children's abilities, competencies and social success – as evidenced by their responses on a repertory grid procedure – observation showed that they rarely acted in a way suggesting that they might try to modify these perceived differentials.

Two of the studies outlined above (Thomas, 1973; Turner and Green, 1977) tended to concentrate on the content of interactions between staff member and child, while the more general overviews of the other two (Cashdan and Philps, 1975; Tizard *et al.*, (1976a)) do not provide information on the sequences of staff behaviour.

In the previous chapter we looked at the differential involvement of adults in the various activities of the nursery. In this chapter we investigate the role of the adult in more detail by means of two direct observational studies. The first study was concerned with how adults, within the different forms of pre-school provision, allocate their time amongst different roles. The second study examined the deployment of adults' attention in relation to the varying demands made upon them.

## How adults spend their time

The study was carried out in seven nursery schools, five playgroups, five day nurseries and five infant schools having nursery classes attached to them. The subjects were eleven teachers (NST) and eleven nursery assistants (NSA) in nursery schools, eleven playgroup supervisors or assistant supervisors (PG), eleven day nursery nurses (DN), and ten nursery assistants and one teacher in nursery classes (NC). Staff were observed in the nursery during periods of free-play, each subject being observed for a period of 30 minutes on each of two separate days.

Within the observation session a time-sampling procedure was adopted employing a predominant activity-sampling convention and a time interval of 15 seconds (Hutt and Hutt, 1970; Tyler, 1979). Prior permission for the study had been obtained from the establishments involved, but since the study was alternated with others where children acted as the focal point, staff were unaware that they were being observed at any particular session. The behaviour of the staff member was noted on a checklist using a series of behavioural categories defined in Appendix C. For the most part observations were of staff behaviour in the playroom but some outdoor observations were also included.

Inter-observer reliability tests were performed on three separate occasions. It proved difficult to obtain satisfactory levels of reliability on some of the categories. Consequently only the more global categories, whose reliability was deemed to be adequate, were used in the analysis. The reliability coefficients obtained for these categories are quoted in Appendix C.

The proportion of time spent by nursery staff in the different forms of activity is represented for each context in Figure 4.1. Associative activity, where the adult was an active participant in the child's play, predominated in both types of educational establishment whereas non-associative or independent activities were most common in playgroups and day nurseries. The proportion of monitorial activity was similar in all situations, tending to be more common outdoors than indoors. Differences in the behaviour of the staff at this level can be accounted for by reference to specific features of each nursery environment. Day nursery staff tended to have to deal with younger children as well as with the three-to-five-year-olds found in the other forms of nursery. The duties of the nursery nurses therefore included a greater degree of 'care-taking', necessitating more time being spent in routine activities that did not involve children.

Differences in staff behaviour became even more apparent when consideration is given to the length of time an adult spent in a given type of behaviour before switching to another. The mean activity spans for each form of activity are shown in Table 4.1. Significant differences exist between groups on spans of associative activity, nursery teachers having the longest spans and playgroup supervisors the shortest. However, it must be noted that in each type of provision, the activity spans are dismally short.

FIGURE 4.1: Percentage of time spent by adults in different activities

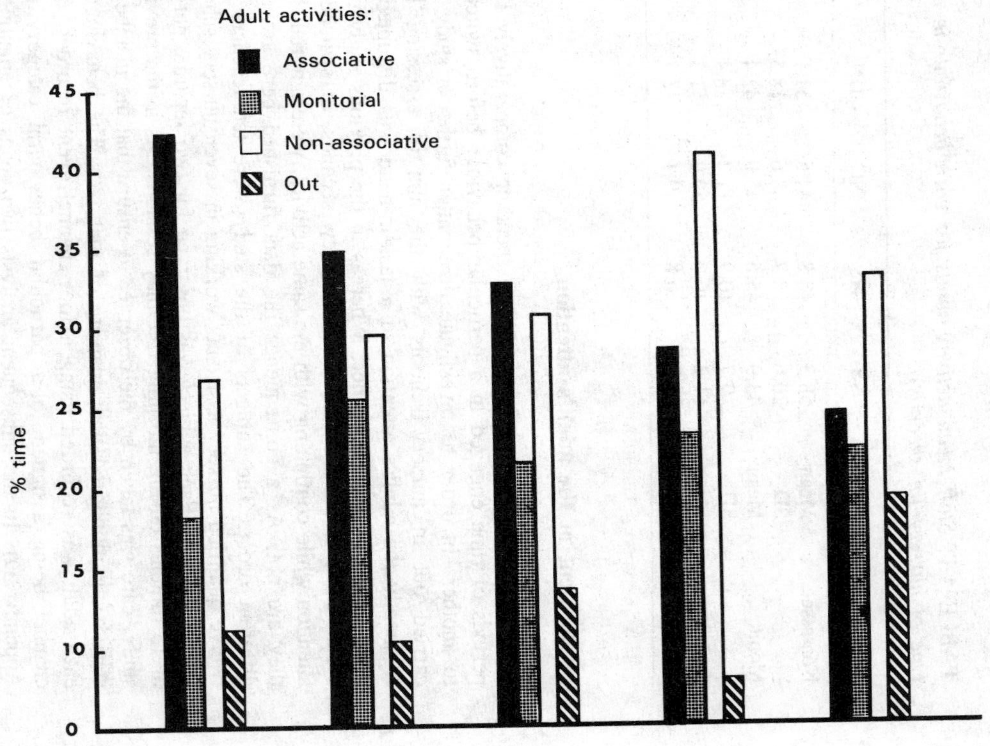

TABLE 4.1: *Staff mean activity spans for each behaviour in each type of nursery (in seconds)*

|            |      | NS   | NS   | NC   | DN   | PG   |
|------------|------|------|------|------|------|------|
| Non-assoc. | Mean | 58.3 | 48.8 | 44.5 | 51.1 | 52.7 |
|            | SD   | 20.6 | 8.7  | 8.6  | 18.5 | 13.8 |
| Monit.     | Mean | 43.9 | 45.6 | 45.9 | 42.4 | 46.9 |
|            | SD   | 9.7  | 10.9 | 11.2 | 8.4  | 19.1 |
| Assoc.     | Mean | 61.2 | 49.0 | 50.0 | 51.5 | 43.4 |
|            | SD   | 14.0 | 6.8  | 9.1  | 13.7 | 10.0 |

## Deployment of the adult's attention

A picture emerges, therefore, of staff spending comparatively short periods of time engaged in a particular behaviour before switching to another. In order to investigate this matter further a study was carried out in nursery schools with the aim of assessing how frequently the adult's attention to a task-in-hand was disrupted by other demands made upon her. Whereas in the previous study brief breaks in an activity of the order of a few seconds, or switches in attention while continuing with the same activity, were ignored, here they are not. As a consequence the data furnished here are of a different order. The subjects of the study were ten teachers and twelve qualified nursery assistants working in seven nursery schools within Area A. Each subject was observed for two separate periods of 15 minutes during morning free-play sessions. As in the previous study, care was taken by the observer to ensure that the member of staff being monitored was unaware of that fact. The behaviour of each adult was recorded using a four-channel event recorder, each channel being assigned to a particular behavioural category (see Appendix D). In the subsequent analysis two spans of attention to children were distinguished. The first (designated Child 1) denoted a span of attention given to a particular child. The second (termed Child 2) was a measure of the attention span on a task involving children, wherein attention could be switched from one child to another, yet maintained on the task. Mean attention spans for the different categories of behaviour for each form of training are given in Table 4.2.

The spans of attention to child-oriented tasks (Child 2) approximate to the spans of associative activity found in the previous study as would be anticipated from the definitions of each. However, as expected, in general the attention spans obtained are considerably

TABLE 4.2: *Mean attention spans for teachers and assistants in nursery schools for each category of behaviour (in seconds)*

|      | Adult | Child 1 | Child 2 | Look/watch | Overall |
| ---- | ----- | ------- | ------- | ---------- | ------- |
| NST  | 47.5  | 21.8    | 60.7    | 12.4       | 27.4    |
| SD   | 24.3  | 9.8     | 45.0    | 7.3        | 8.9     |
| NSA  | 40.3  | 19.0    | 36.2    | 10.1       | 22.0    |
| SD   | 22.0  | 6.9     | 12.5    | 6.9        | 8.2     |

Notes Child 1: span of attention for individual child.
      Child 2: span of attention for child-oriented task irrespective of attention to particular child.

shorter than the activity spans. The differences between mean spans for teachers and for nursery assistants are not significant, but as in the preceding study there is a tendency for the teachers to have longer spans. However, the standard deviations also reveal that the teachers tend to be more variable on these measures than the nursery assistants. When adults were engaged in activities which did not involve children (tidying-up, marking the register, etc.) their attention spans were longer than when they were working with children. This was largely due to the fact that the adult's attention was frequently distracted from a particular child or task by the behaviour or requests of other children. If we consider the duration of child-centred bouts irrespective of the children involved, we see that these are considerably longer and approximate to the duration of the adult-only activities.

From the studies reported here a picture emerges of a general similarity in the organisation of different forms of pre-school provision. In each nursery context the emphasis rests squarely on the provision of free-play sessions with limited periods of organized activity. The content of both free-play and organized periods in the different forms of provision tends to be broadly similar in terms of the materials provided, the activities encouraged and the extent of adult participation. Where differences do emerge they appear to derive from practical aspects of the running of the nursery rather than from a clear divergence in ideology or aim. Indeed, the similar aims of the nursery staff described in Chapter 3 appear to be clearly reflected in the observed practice of this chapter.

As we saw in Chapter 3, the nurseries observed tended to be reasonably well provided with materials and equipment appropriate to the age level of the children catered for. Nurseries tended to provide the children with a choice of several different activities at any one time, some of which were likely to have high levels of adult participation, e.g. collage, and some low levels of adult involvement, e.g. sand and water play.

## Discussion

As was found in the study of Tizard *et al.* (1976a) it would seem that the context of the nursery has a greater influence than the effect of training on the behaviour of the nursery staff. Tizard and her colleagues found that the cognitive content of the behaviour of assistants was not greater in those who had received a NNEB training, but was greater in those working in schools rather than in nurseries. In the present study, associative activity, including behaviour with a high cognitive content, was most frequently observed in nursery assistants working in conjunction with teachers in nursery schools and observed least frequently in the staff working in day nurseries.

In general the distribution of staff time in different activities may be seen to be in accord with the tenet currently widely held that learning in the nursery should be self-paced and self-directed. Involvement of adults in children's activities is not only limited, however, it also tends to be quite brief when it occurs. In general this could be seen to be desirable in terms of the structuring of staff time and optimally effective in terms of the contribution to the child's processes of learning. Children's attention spans tend to be short at this age and matching the adult participation spans to them seems likely to be a useful strategy. However, other studies to be described later suggest that the length of involvement with a single child is only partially determined at a conscious level by the adult. The major factor would seem to be the relative fluidity of the free-play situation. Interruptions, which can be shown to be largely adventitious, whether from other children or from other members of staff, often serve to terminate involvement with a particular child. That most adult activity spans are of less than a minute may be of some concern because it implies that periods of concentrated work with a child who may require this form of attention are often precluded. In all forms of nursery, but perhaps in the educational establishments in particular, the difficulties of sustaining attention to instruction, demonstration or investigation must be frustrating to both adults and children. It could be argued that to promote more effective learning for some children both a spatial and a temporal rearrangement of duties is desirable so that two or three adults working with a class or group of children take on clearly different but complementary roles for certain periods of the day. Such a revision would entail a degree of structuring of the nursery environment which is not generally seen at present.

This chapter and the preceding one have attempted to describe the nursery environment in which the pre-school child is expected to learn and develop. The following chapters describe the ways in which the child avails himself of the opportunities which this environment provides.

# Chapter 5

# Children's activities in pre-school

In the previous chapters we have attempted to provide an outline of typical nursery provisions. Thus far we have been primarily concerned with the attitudes and roles of nursery staff and the material resources of the nursery environment. Now we turn to the children who are the *raison d'être* of the nursery establishments. The present and subsequent chapters are devoted to the description of the behaviour of children attending different forms of pre-school provision, with the aim of affording a detailed analysis of the ways in which children avail themselves of the resources and opportunities for play presented by the nursery environment. At which activities do children in nurseries spend most time? Are there sex differences in the choice of activities? How long do children remain at an activity before they leave and choose another? What factors influence the initial choice of activity? The studies described in this and the succeeding chapters represent our attempts to answer at least some of these questions. However, before turning to the studies themselves, a brief comment is necessary on some of the methods we have employed in the course of the project.

**Play and observation**

A major facet of the project was the use of observational techniques of various kinds. The use of direct observation in the study of behaviour has a long history in the discipline of psychology (Hutt and Hutt, 1970). Its use in the study of practice in education is of more recent origin, but in the past decade it has been extensive. Whereas the majority of large-scale studies reported in the literature

have tended to concentrate on a particular technique of direct observation (e.g. time-sampling) the present project has made use of
various techniques in comparatively small-scale studies, methods
being adopted as appropriate to the purposes of the study and the
subjects being observed. For example, where an outline of the
pattern of the nursery day was required a system of observation
employing a scan technique and a simple checklist was adopted (see
Chapter 2). Alternatively, where greater detail about intervals was
required, techniques involving the use of mechanical event recorders
or radio microphones were employed. In each case an attempt was
made to focus on particular aspects of the nursery. This approach is
in marked contrast to those employed by other researchers
investigating nursery practice who have tended to adopt a single
comprehensive instrument in order to measure behaviour (e.g.
Tizard *et al*. 1976b; Sylva *et al*., 1980). Both approaches have their
particular strengths and weaknesses. It is reassuring, however, to
find that although different methods of observation have been
employed and although researchers have given somewhat different
emphasis to particular aspects of the nursery environment, in
general, there is a high degree of concordance in terms both of the
results obtained and of the conclusions that researchers have drawn
from them. In the present project, although the sample sizes of
particular studies may be small, there is marked agreement between
studies.

The above points have been made because we have encountered
a healthy initial scepticism towards the use of observational techniques in the nursery from the staff in whose nurseries we have
worked. Rightly, staff have suggested, prior to the commencement
of a study, that the presence of an observer in the room might have
an effect upon the behaviour of some children, and that the effect
would not always be predictable.

Certainly, carrying out observations in the context of the nursery
may present problems, but these are not necessarily insurmountable.
Connolly and Smith (1972) report a study which was designed to
assess the reactions of pre-school children to a strange observer. In
particular, note was taken of the number of approaches towards the
observer made by children during the course of ten periods of observation. It was found that in both the day nursery and the nursery
school the incidence of approaches to the observer declined rapidly
over a series of eight visits, suggesting that children tend to habituate
quite rapidly to the presence of the observer. In a second study,
Connolly and Smith (1972) categorized the form of children's
approaches to the observer, who adopted different patterns of
response in different nurseries. The observer's response ranged from

65

total passivity to interaction with the approaching child including both smiling and talking. Almost all kinds of approaches occurred with increased frequency at those nurseries where the observer interacted with the children. Evidence was also obtained of a *decline* in approach frequencies both through individual one-hour sessions and through successive weekly visits where the observer was essentially passive. Connolly and Smith conclude that for the majority of children, at least, responses to a passive observer in the nursery fall to a low level within a few sessions. A similar conclusion may be drawn from a study by Davie *et al.* (1984), whose purpose was to assess the possibility of observing young children in the home when the observer was present in the same room as the child. As in the previous studies in the nursery, it was found that approaches to a passive observer declined rapidly through a series of observation sessions.

As a result of these studies it was decided that in the present project, where observation was to take place in the playroom of a nursery, the observer would adopt an essentially passive role. This point was explained to nursery staff who were also requested to minimize their approaches to the observer. In addition, several visits to the nursery were made by the observer prior to the commencement of data collection for a particular study in order that the children might become accustomed to her presence during periods of play. Our own impressions as observers were in accordance with the findings of the studies cited above, approaches to us by children being fairly low in frequency. However, the fact that approaches to the observer are infrequent does not preclude the possibility that the presence of the observer affects other behaviour patterns which are not directed towards her. For example, some children may avoid the activities which require greatest proximity to the observer; alternatively, they may be attracted to these same pursuits. Such evidence as we have upon which to base a judgment as to the effect of the presence of the observer upon children's behaviour is highly impressionistic. Frequent discussions with staff upon this point revealed no evidence of a *systematic* effect of our presence. Indeed, staff usually volunteered the opinion that after the first few sessions of observation our presence in the nursery had no noticeable effect upon the children. In addition, staff themselves often appeared to forget that we were there and were sometimes startled by our approach at the completion of a period of observation.

Previous studies of children's play have tended to adopt a variety of different methods of observation and systems of categorization of behaviour. In some instances researchers have chosen to adopt relatively simple pencil and paper methods of recording data, whereas in others recourse to sophisticated electronic recording devices has been made. Similarly, whereas in some studies the child's behaviour patterns have been divided into *molecular* units on the grounds of morphology, in other studies researchers have preferred to categorize the behaviour into *molar* functional units. It may be argued that no one method of observation or form of categorization is inherently superior to another. Rather, each may be more suited to a particular purpose. In the studies described in these pages several different systems have been adopted as appropriate to the particular aims of each study. Details of the systems employed may be found in the relevant appendices.

## Activities in the pre-school

In Chapter 2 we described the basic provisions made by each form of nursery. In a second part to her questionnaire study, Patricia Ward invited nursery staff and parents to select the five activities which they considered most important from a list of seventeen common activities (Ward, 1982). Figure 5.1 shows the results.

Overall, highest ratings are given to books and stories, painting and pre-reading activities, group music and singing, collage and the use of apparatus for physical activity. Those activities attracting lowest overall ratings were dry sand, jigsaws, large blocks, woodwork and representational objects. A notable feature of the results is the high value placed upon the provision of books and materials, especially by teachers, every teacher in the sample population selecting this activity. Nursery assistants, in general, conformed to the overall pattern, but as a group chose pre-reading and pre-maths activities most frequently.

Playgroup supervisors produced a rather different picture, however, emphasizing water play and large climbing equipment and trucks. As we have seen, this emphasis is often reflected in practice by the comparative importance given to these activities in the actual provision. Ward suggests that in part the value accorded to these activities may be a result of the difficulty the group may have encountered in either raising the funds for, or acquiring permission to use, the apparatus. Also, of course, since the equipment is expensive it may be felt that children do not have such facilities at home. By contrast, playgroup supervisors accord lower value to pre-number and pre-reading activities, again preferring overall to emphasize activities which encourage social development.

The parents of nursery school children, in an interesting corollary to their responses to the question concerning the purpose of

FIGURE 5.1: *Choice of activities*

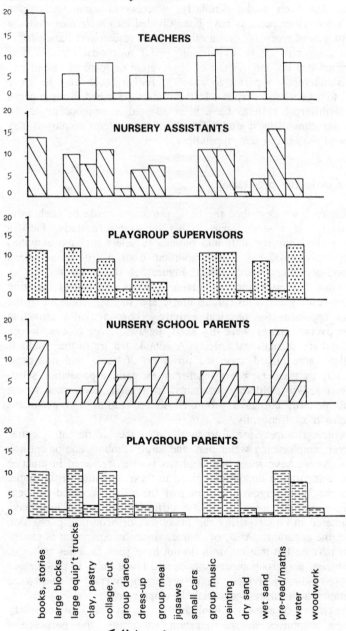

FIGURE 5.2: *Percentage of scans during which children's different activities are in use in each of four pre-school provisions*

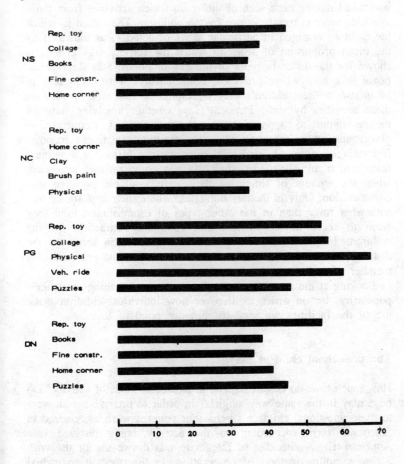

pre-school provision, chose to emphasize 'academic' activities. Playgroup parents' responses, however, were more closely related to those of playgroup supervisors.

Ward's study reveals the views of adults about the value of particular activities within the pre-school curriculum. We shall now turn to the views of the children as witnessed by their behaviour.

## Children's use of activities

In the course of the observational study described in Chapter 2 it was noted during each scan of the room which activities from those available were currently in use by the children. The extent to which the children engaged in particular kinds of activity, as indicated by the mean proportion of scans in which the activity was in use, is shown for the different types of nursery in Figure 5.2. Representational toys and, where provided, home corners were often seen to be in use in the children's play – despite the low value placed on these activities by staff. Physical play, whether involving static or mobile items of apparatus, was observed most frequently in playgroups where these activities are commonly available indoors. Interestingly, although sand and water troughs formed a prominent feature of many playrooms, their use was comparatively infrequent when the amount of time that they were available is taken into consideration. Only in the day nurseries, where their appearance was somewhat rarer than in the other types of establishment, did they seem to serve as a principal and continuing attraction for the children. In part, this finding can be explained in terms of the distribution of a major resource of the nursery – the presence of a member of staff.

Looking at the activities themselves tells us something about their popularity, but in order to discover how individual children make use of the facilities we need to shift our point of focus.

## The pre-school child at play

How much time do children spend at particular kinds of activity? Do boys play in the same way as girls? In order to provide the answers to these questions, children's behaviour patterns were categorized in functional terms according to the activity being pursued (see Appendix E). A checklist of categories was drawn up for use with a time-sampling method of observation. In this method individual children were selected and observed for two separate periods of thirty minutes, making a total of one hour of observation per child. The behaviour of the child was recorded upon the checklist according to the predetermined categories at intervals of fifteen seconds as timed on a stop-watch. Two conventions were employed, depending upon the type of behaviour to be recorded. Most categories were sampled by a convention of predominant activity sampling (Tyler, 1979). However, those categories of the child's behaviour relating to interaction with peers and adults, or affect, were one–zero sampled

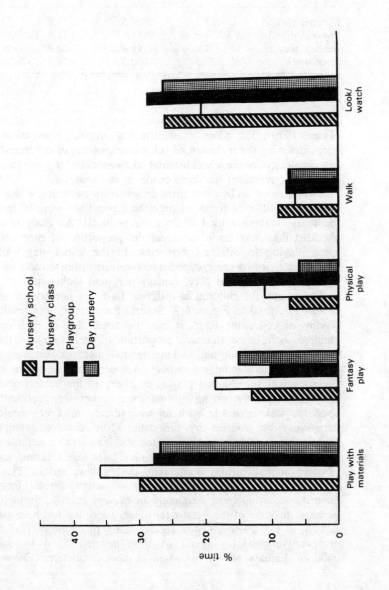

FIGURE 5.3: *Percentage of time spent in each of five main types of activity in the four provisions*

TABLE 5.1: *Percentage of time spent in different forms of activity by children in different nursery contexts*

| Play activity | Context | | | |
|---|---|---|---|---|
| | NS | NC | PG | DN |
| Material play | 27.3 | 36.5 | 28.8 | 26.4 |
| Physical play | 7.3 | 11.6 | 17.6 | 7.3 |
| Fantasy play | 9.7 | 15.8 | 10.9 | 12.4 |
| Look/watch | 27.3 | 20.3 | 27.9 | 26.1 |

(Tyler, 1979). The adoption of different sampling conventions was necessitated by the inclusion of behaviour patterns of different levels of complexity in the checklist and allowance for the use of these different conventions has been made in the analysis.

Twelve boys and twelve girls drawn from nurseries within each of the four different forms of pre-school provision were included in the study, making a total of 96 subjects in all. An analysis of the checklist data was made to reveal the proportion of time children spent playing in different activities. In the initial stages of the analysis activities were grouped into the superordinate categories of: material play, physical play, fantasy play and look/watch.

The results for children in different forms of nursery are shown in Table 5.1 and in Figure 5.3. Several features of these results are worthy of comment. First, it may be noted that in each context children spend a considerable proportion of their time not actively engaged in a pursuit but looking around them or watching other children or adults indulging in play. A superficial assessment of this finding might suggest that play is desultory in the nursery with the children frequently gazing around them rather than concentrating upon the task in hand. Such an assessment, however, would not necessarily be justified by the data. More detailed examination reveals that children spend more time watching (with a definite focus of attention) than looking, and one may infer that a certain amount of observational learning is occurring during these periods. Play with materials is the most common form of activity in all forms of context, occurring most frequently in nursery classes. Surprisingly, perhaps, in view of the great deal of attention that has been paid to fantasy in the literature over recent years, this type of play has a comparatively small amount of time devoted to it by nursery children. Fantasy play is discussed in more detail later (Chapter 7), but it is worth noting here that other forms of activity appear to predominate in the child's play. Of the four superordinate categories of play, that of physical play is the only one that differentiates significantly between nursery contexts. Physical play was observed most frequently in playgroups and it should be noted that this is the context where provision for this activity was made most frequently indoors. That children in the nursery classes exhibited the greatest amount of fantasy play may, in part, be explained by reference to the age structures of the children within the different forms of nursery. Although all the samples of children from the four types of nursery included in the study had similar average ages (all children observed were between three years nine months and four years six months) the nursery classes tended to contain more four-year-olds and fewer three-year-olds than the other types of nursery and consequently tended to contain overall groups of children with higher average ages. It may be argued that fantasy play is likely to occur most frequently and to be most elaborate where there is least likelihood of interruptions from younger and less mature children.

The differences in the proportions of time spent in different types of play in different forms of provision which have been commented upon thus far fall short of statistical significance since there is much individual variation between the children in each sample group. However, the finding that children engage in most physical play in the playgroups is a significant one and may be seen as a reflection of the differences in the level of provision for this type of play indoors in this form of pre-school setting (see Chapter 2).

Analysis of the children's activities at this level of the superordinate play category is consistent with the findings of the study reported above whose focal point of observation was the group rather than the individual. The consistency of the findings between the two studies would suggest that although differences between contexts for particular types of activity may not be particularly great there may be persistent underlying trends present in the data. A similar point may be made in the discussion of the more detailed analysis of the checklist data which follows.

Details of the proportion of time spent in particular categories of activities for boys and girls in differing forms of pre-school provision are presented in Table 5.2. Inspection of this table yields an impression of the overall similarity of the play observed in the different contexts and of the absence of marked sex differences. The *quality* of the play within the particular activities described is not here in debate. Rather one is struck by the way in which children in different contexts devote similar proportions of their time to the same kinds of activity.

73

**TABLE 5.2**: *Percentage of time spent in different forms of activity by boys and girls in different nursery contexts*

| Activity | NS | | NC | | PG | | DN | |
|---|---|---|---|---|---|---|---|---|
| | Boys Mean | Girls Mean | Boys Mean | Girls Mean | Boys Mean | Girls Mean | Boys Mean | Girls Mean |
| Sand | 5.4 | 5.0 | 8.1 | 4.1 | 3.5 | 5.1 | 0.8 | 0.0 |
| Water | 1.2 | 0.5 | 9.2 | 11.5 | 1.3 | 7.5 | 5.8 | 3.5 |
| Clay | 0.8 | 4.3 | 4.9 | 7.4 | 2.1 | 3.7 | 1.6 | 0.5 |
| Painting | 3.6 | 1.2 | 2.2 | 4.3 | 5.2 | 3.1 | 7.1 | 2.4 |
| Collage/Cut | 2.6 | 6.5 | 1.6 | 3.0 | 7.3 | 1.8 | 1.5 | 5.3 |
| Construction | 8.2 | 2.4 | 8.6 | 3.1 | 5.0 | 6.2 | 11.2 | 7.6 |
| Puzzles/sort | 5.9 | 2.6 | 4.0 | 0.4 | 2.9 | 1.5 | 1.5 | 1.1 |
| Colour/draw | 0.5 | 4.1 | 0.0 | 0.6 | 0.4 | 0.9 | 0.2 | 2.7 |
| Music/noise | 1.6 | 1.2 | 0.2 | 0.9 | 0.3 | 0.4 | 2.0 | 1.0 |
| TV/stories | 5.4 | 3.5 | 0.4 | 0.0 | 0.5 | 2.1 | 2.2 | 4.8 |
| Books | 4.5 | 1.0 | 1.7 | 4.0 | 1.3 | 0.0 | 1.0 | 2.3 |
| Object manip. | 2.6 | 1.0 | 1.5 | 0.6 | 5.0 | 1.9 | 3.1 | 2.6 |
| Object hold | 3.7 | 3.5 | 4.1 | 7.3 | 9.4 | 8.2 | 5.3 | 4.5 |
| Physical | 6.0 | 7.9 | 7.6 | 9.5 | 21.0 | 10.8 | 8.4 | 5.0 |
| Push–pull | 0.5 | 0.3 | 3.2 | 2.8 | 2.6 | 0.9 | 1.0 | 0.3 |
| Walk/run | 8.1 | 6.4 | 5.3 | 7.7 | 5.6 | 8.8 | 7.8 | 9.2 |
| Gesture | 1.5 | 4.7 | 0.9 | 1.2 | 2.1 | 0.8 | 2.7 | 4.9 |
| Dressing up | 2.9 | 0.0 | 9.7 | 6.6 | 8.1 | 9.2 | 7.1 | 0.0 |
| Rep. object | 4.3 | 4.1 | 10.0 | 7.7 | 5.9 | 10.3 | 4.8 | 3.7 |
| Fantasy object | 4.8 | 0.6 | 10.8 | 4.8 | 4.4 | 2.6 | 2.1 | 6.3 |
| Fantasy person | 4.2 | 3.3 | 2.6 | 2.7 | 1.4 | 1.5 | 4.5 | 8.2 |
| Immat. fantasy | 3.4 | 0.7 | 5.6 | 2.9 | 0.8 | 1.5 | 1.2 | 1.9 |
| Look | 10.6 | 8.1 | 7.5 | 7.4 | 10.9 | 12.4 | 11.8 | 10.4 |
| Watch | 15.9 | 19.9 | 10.5 | 15.1 | 16.4 | 16.0 | 12.7 | 17.3 |
| Help/care | 0.5 | 0.4 | 1.3 | 1.5 | 0.4 | 1.8 | 0.8 | 2.4 |
| Tidy/pinafore | 2.4 | 2.7 | 1.4 | 1.7 | 1.3 | 1.3 | 2.6 | 2.2 |

Perhaps surprisingly, in view of the considerable body of work which describes and discusses the differences in the patterns of development in boys and girls, the present study presents little evidence of sex differences in the amount of time children devote to particular forms of nursery activity. For example, one might anticipate from both studies of play in young animals and previous studies of play in humans that boys would tend to engage in more physical play than girls. However, in the present study only in one context, the playgroup, does the time devoted to physical play in boys significantly exceed that in girls. This finding may be related to a tendency to inhibit gross motor activities in the other forms of pre-school context, a tendency which is not shared by the playgroup which permits and encourages this form of activity indoors. In two other types of activity there is an apparent sex difference in three of the four contexts. There is a tendency for girls to devote more time to collage activities than boys while the reverse applies to play with constructional toys. In the case of collage the customary presence of an adult rather than the nature of the activity itself may be the factor which tends to predispose girls rather than boys towards it. Hutt (1972) argues that girls tend to be oriented towards people whereas boys are oriented towards objects. The adults in the nursery are foci for the attention of children, particularly girls, who spend much of their time communicating with members of staff (see also Chapter 9) and the unequal distribution of adult time between activities may influence children's choice of activity. Arguably, this influence will be greatest amongst the girls and may explain their tendency to engage in more collage activities than boys. Constructional toys receive less attention from adults but represent attractive equipment for manipulation and use in playful quasi-antagonistic encounters. As such they may be more powerful stimuli for boys than for girls. Almost any nursery worker will admit that it is exceedingly difficult to prevent boys manufacturing guns.

Other features of Table 5.2 require comment and explanation. One category of behaviour that was of interest to us was that of *object hold*. In a study of the play of nursery aged children in their own home (Davie *et al.*, 1984), it was observed that children between the ages of three and five spend relatively large proportions of their time holding objects as they play. These objects include not only soft toys but also ordinary household items, e.g. spoons, tins. In order that a comparison between the behaviour observed in the nursery and that observed in the home might be made, a category of *object hold* was included on the checklist employed in the present study. Inspection of Table 5.2 reveals that the holding of objects by children in the nursery does not, on average, occupy a considerable proportion of their time.

Analysis of the individual categories of fantasy play shows that all four categories were observed in each form of nursery context but that, overall, representational object play tended to occupy the greatest proportion of time. Immaterial fantasy play tended to be the form least commonly observed.

FIGURE 5.4: *Percentage of time spent in 'joint' activities with adults or with other children in the four provisions*

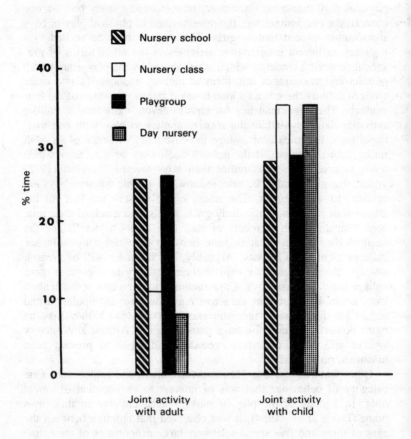

The findings of the observational study reported in Chapter 2 suggest that books are common features of the nursery environment which are readily accessible to the children. However, examination of the data accruing from the present study suggest that children devote comparatively little time to looking at books. Again the presence of the adult may be a major influence here, since it was observed that children seemed to prefer to examine books in the company of an adult or to have a story read to them.

The expressed aims of the pre-school world suggest that encouragement of the child to socialize, especially with peers but also with adults, is of paramount importance. Observations upon social interactions were, in fact, included in the present study. The proportions of time children spent in joint activity with adult and peers respectively for each context is shown in Figure 5.4. The differences in the proportions of time spent in activity with adults between contexts may be related to the differences in the staff:pupil ratios and to how accessible the adults are for interaction. Children spend most time in joint activity with adults in nursery schools and playgroups. In the former context, as we saw (Chapter 4), adults spend a considerable amount of time in activity with children; in the latter context the adult:child ratio is particularly good. Least time in joint activities with adults is spent in day nurseries and nursery classes.

However, the commensurate rises in the amounts of time spent in joint activity with other children in these two contexts are limited in extent and also do not completely compensate in temporal terms alone. For reasons that will be argued elsewhere, this finding may prove to be of particular importance in the discussion on the salient differences amongst varied forms of pre-school provisions.

## Indoor and outdoor activities

The majority of the observations recorded in the study described above occurred within the nursery buildings. From both our own observations and from our discussions with staff we formed the opinion that important quantitative and qualitative differences distinguished play indoors from that occurring outside and that these differences warranted systematic investigation. A further small study comparing the form of play occurring in the two areas was therefore undertaken. The subjects in this study were eighteen children aged between three and a half and four and a half years. The subjects were drawn from several nursery schools and the sample was divided equally between the sexes. Observation of the children at play was conducted during the summer months when the weather permitted extended periods of outdoor activity. Each subject was observed for equal periods of time indoors and outdoors and on average for fifteen minutes in each location. The method of observation adopted was identical to that employed in the preceding study. For the purpose of analysis the activities of the children were grouped into six superordinate categories: material play; physical play; fantasy play; walk/run; look/watch; and 'other' (which included non-playful activities). The amount of time spent in the different forms of activity as defined above was calculated as a

TABLE 5.3: *Mean percentage of total observation time spent by nursery school children at different activities outdoors and indoors*

| Activity | Outdoor play | | | Indoor play | | |
|---|---|---|---|---|---|---|
| | Boys | Girls | Boys + Girls | Boys | Girls | Boys + Girls |
| Material play | 2.6 | 18.7 | 10.6 | 55.6 | 48.3 | 51.9 |
| Physical play | 56.1 | 42.2 | 49.2 | 2.8 | 1.5 | 2.1 |
| Fantasy play | 5.7 | 8.1 | 6.9 | 5.7 | 11.7 | 8.7 |
| Walk/run | 15.0 | 13.7 | 14.4 | 4.6 | 3.1 | 3.9 |
| Look/watch | 17.8 | 13.3 | 15.6 | 27.8 | 28.5 | 28.1 |
| Other | 2.8 | 3.9 | 3.3 | 3.5 | 6.9 | 5.2 |

proportion of the total observation period for both indoor and outdoor play. The results of this analysis are presented in Table 5.3 by sex and location. Inspection of the table shows, perhaps not surprisingly, that physical play predominates outdoors but occupies little of the children's time indoors, whereas the reverse is the case for material play. Fantasy play occupies similar percentages of time indoors and outdoors, the figures increasing slightly in the former condition. Whereas the category *walk/run* occupies a greater proportion of time outdoors the reverse is true for *look/watch*.

Consideration of the findings from studies that have already been described suggests that the amount of time spent at different kinds of activity indoors and outdoors is in large part a reflection of differences in the availability of materials and apparatus in the two situations. Many more opportunities for material play are provided inside the nursery compared with the play area outside. In the latter context there may be a sand pit and/or water trough and occasionally paint, puzzles and other easily movable equipment. However, the predominant resources of the outdoor areas tend to be items of apparatus which encourage physical play. Conversely, provision inside the nursery building tends to centre upon activities yielding behaviour here designated as material play to the virtual exclusion of opportunities for physical play. The results for material and physical play presented in Table 5.3 are consistent with these differences in provision. Interestingly, when the results for girls and boys are compared in these two categories of behaviour, differences emerge. Indoors, the proportions of time spent in material and physical play are similar in each sex, boys tending to devote slightly more time to each category. In the outdoor area girls spend less time at physical play and more at material play than boys.

Comparison of the time spent in fantasy play indoors and outdoors revealed less marked differences. The boys observed in this study spent the same proportion of time in this type of play in each situation. The girls tended to spend rather more time in fantasy play than boys overall, and to spend more time in this behaviour indoors. These differences may be related to the provision made for play in the two environments.

There is a substantial difference between the amount of time spent in look/watch and in walk/run in the two contexts. None of the children spent much time walking and running inside, a finding which may be due to constraints, both spatial and verbal, placed on this behaviour and to the availability of a wide range of activities in close proximity. Outdoors, however, children spent nearly 15 per cent of the time walking and running, which may again be a reflection on the emphasis placed upon physical activity outdoors. The amount of time devoted to looking and watching was about twice as great indoors as it was outdoors. There is a slight difference between the sexes in these categories of behaviour. Boys spent slightly more time engaged in walk/run in both settings.

The present study, therefore, reveals interesting, although perhaps not surprising, differences in children's play indoors and outdoors. An overall picture emerges of most time being spent indoors at activities which involve materials accompanied by much looking and watching, while outside most time is spent in physical play and walking and running. This picture pertains to both sexes but the effect of play area is exaggerated in boys.

## Discussion

Ward's (1982) work quoted in this chapter reveals the views of nursery staff on the relative value of particular forms of activity within the pre-school environment. Whereas teachers in nursery education tend to place emphasis upon activities which are obvious precursors to later schooling (such as looking at books and items concerned with pre-reading and pre-maths skills), playgroup supervisors lay greater stress upon forms of play involving materials (such as sand and water and physical play). The differences between the various forms of provision are interesting and have a number of possible origins. First, in the geographical area of Ward's (1982) study, it is customary for playgroups to be working with children who on average are rather younger than their counterparts in nursery school or class. Play with sand and water, as opposed to play with forms of equipment more specifically oriented towards cognitive skills, may be felt to be more appropriate for children at the lower end of the age range catered for by pre-school provision. Second, some playgroups have stated to us that they have no wish to pre-empt the work in the cognitive domain that occurs in the reception class of the infant school or even the nursery school or class. The supervisors expressing this view felt relatively unqualified to teach in this sphere, although the latest publication of the Pre-School Playgroups Association (1987) would suggest that such a view is not necessarily held by all concerned with playgroups. Third, it is possible that a fundamental distinction between playgroups and nursery education exists, with playgroups drawing on those rather more traditional views of nursery practice which tend to emphasize play with materials. By contrast, nursery education may be influenced by its links with higher levels of the educational system and the need for some form of educational accountability. Whereas both groups are able to justify their practices in general terms, in recent years the onus has been upon professional staff to demonstrate the effectiveness of their provision. Such a demonstration may be provided by reference to the progress made by the children as a consequence of their stay in the nursery. It is difficult to quantify or even describe some of the changes which may take place in the child's socio-emotional state, so emphasis may be given to more cognitively oriented areas where evidence of change is less subjective. The effect of this shift in emphasis may be to lead staff in nursery education to place greater value upon those activities and pieces of equipment which have a tangible impact upon the child's development. It is interesting to note that parents' views tended to reflect those of the staff whose establishment their children were currently attending. Furthermore, parents in the area of study tended to place their children first in a playgroup and then to move them to a nursery school or class as the children approached school age, suggesting that a change occurs in parental view, with the development of the child.

The distinction between the views of playgroup supervisors and of staff in nursery education as to the relative merits of particular forms of activity is, to a certain extent, reflected in practice in the greater encouragement given by playgroups to physical play. The finding that children in playgroups tend to engage in more physical play than their peers in other forms of provision may be a reflection not only of the greater access these children have to equipment that permits this kind of play, but also of the greater value playgroup supervisors place upon it. The fact that physical play occurs much more frequently outdoors in the other contexts suggests that this form of play is often inhibited indoors. There may be a variety of reasons for this. First, in a crowded playroom there is clearly an increased safety risk if children are permitted to engage freely in physical play. Second, by its very nature, physical play is noisier and more distracting for children attempting to concentrate upon more sedentary pursuits. Third, given the orientation of the staff already described, staffs may wish to channel children towards situations in which learning of a cognitive nature more obviously occurs. Although possibilities for cognitively oriented approaches undoubtedly exist outdoors, staff *tend* to see such approaches as being primarily based upon the equipment available indoors and are inclined to use the outdoor play area almost exclusively for the encouragement of physical and social play.

Interestingly, there is less looking and watching outside on the part of the children. This may be a response to the reduced number of different types of stimuli, presenting the child with an easier choice in his selection of activity. There may also be an implicit agreement between staff and children about what one does outdoors as opposed to the indoor situation. Certainly, this argument is supported by the change in the adult role from an essentially participatory form indoors to a predominantly monitorial form outdoors. The children's activities outdoors are concerned with *doing* rather than thinking and children are more positive in their selection of activity. The agreement between adult and child is sometimes challenged indoors where the prohibition upon certain forms of physical play is occasionally made explicit. This prohibition may be the reason for a failure to find sex differences in three of the four contexts. Perhaps boys in nursery schools, nursery classes and day nurseries would engage in more physical play than girls if they were permitted to do so indoors like their peers in the playgroups.

Although, as we have said, playgroups tend to emphasize the child's development in the physical and socio-emotional domains, this does not mean that they eschew entirely the cognitive aspects of the child's development. As Turner and Green (1977) found, playgroups also make use of activities which potentially possess a high cognitive context. The difference is not absolute but one of emphasis.

A finding of particular interest in the study of children's play reported in this chapter is the comparatively small amount of time given by children to play with sand and water. This finding is somewhat surprising given the stress laid on the need to provide these materials found in the literature available to nursery staff. Even in the playgroup, where play with water is seen by staff as being of particular importance, the quality of play at the water trough does not assume especially high levels. In order to examine the underlying reasons for this finding we turn in the next chapter to the question of what the children do with particular materials.

81

# Chapter 6

# Use of materials

## Parental and staff views of the purposes of materials

The studies of the previous chapter revealed how children spend their time in the nursery when allowed to choose their own activity from amongst the range involved. In the next three chapters we examine in greater detail the behaviour of children at a particular activity and some of the ways in which they go about selecting that activity.

We have previously alluded to the questionnaire study of our colleague, Patricia Ward (Ward, 1982). In a third section of her questionnaire, Ward asked nursery staff and parents to select one from amongst six possible purposes for the provision of a particular activity during a play session. Each possible purpose presented to the respondents arose during discussions with a group of staff in interviews conducted prior to the commencement of the questionnaire study. Although activities may have a number of different purposes associated with them, staff were asked to indicate which of these they considered to be most important. The activities selected for comment included four which involve the use of basic materials: dry sand, water, painting and collage.

The question concerning the purpose of providing dry sand in the nursery evoked a great diversity in the response pattern in all groups. Teachers and nursery assistants in nursery schools most frequently opted for the reason that this material enabled children to use their imagination, although 26 per cent of the teachers were also of the opinion that its primary purpose within the nursery is to facilitate the release of emotional stresses. A quarter of the nursery assistants suggested that dry sand assists children in learning to share and co-operate with others. In contrast, both sets of parents and the playgroup supervisors stressed that this material provided opportunities for a great deal of enjoyment during children's play. Several teachers and nursery nurses shared the idea that this is the primary reason underlying the provision of dry sand in the nursery. Interestingly, only three teachers felt that dry sand had a primary role in the learning of mathematical concepts, which was a response open to them; no respondents in any of the other four groups selected this reason.

Water and dry sand have many physical properties in common and frequently similar equipment is made available to the children for play with each medium. Yet, whereas the most popular reasons for the provision of the dry sand trays fell into the affective domain, we see a shift towards the cognitive domain in the responses to the question concerning the reasons for providing water play in the nursery. Whilst no group produced a clear consensus of opinion about the merits of water play, the greatest proportion of teachers and nursery assistants gave a cognitive aim as their most favoured reason for its provision, suggesting that it provides an opportunity for experimentation which may include facets of measurement. Playgroup parents also frequently gave this as a prime reason for water play, but most frequently playgroup supervisors and parents of children in both forms of pre-school provision were of the opinion that water play is principally provided for the enjoyment that it brings.

A substantial minority of nursery assistants and playgroup supervisors were also inclined to believe that this medium is useful for bringing about the release of emotional stress in the children playing with it. Some respondents thought that water play helped children to share and co-operate with others but very few thought that the primary reason underlying its place in the nursery is that mothers may not be prepared to accept the mess that it may create in their own homes.

Turning to brush painting, we find that the majority of nursery staff thought that the primary purpose of painting is that it allows the child to express herself. Some 27 per cent of all parents thought that painting is provided for the children's enjoyment compared with 14 per cent of staff who chose this reason, the playgroup staff providing a higher proportion of this response group than either teachers or nursery nurses. Some parents also believed that painting as an activity serves to stimulate the child's imagination, a primary reason for its provision that was seldom suggested by members of staff. Interestingly, no members of staff responded by saying that painting serves to release emotions or facilitates the learning of colours, although some parents were of the opinion that the latter is a primary purpose for its provision.

The most popular reason given by teachers and nursery nurses for collage and other associated activities requiring cutting being given a place within the nursery curriculum is an educational one. A considerable proportion of the staff in nursery schools felt that these activities were very useful when accompanied by an adult in the facilitation of the children's language department. Playgroup supervisors and parents were either less aware of this or perhaps were more sceptical of making such a claim, most suggesting instead that the primary purpose of collage or a similar activity is to give children experience of different materials and to allow them to experiment.

Overall, the results of this part of Ward's study suggest that as a group teachers prefer to emphasize the effect of the provision of materials upon the cognitive elements of development, in comparison with their colleagues in other areas of the pre-school world. On the whole, Ward concludes, teachers seem to be conscious of the need to provide different activities because they are expected to foster the child's intellect or language, although it must be stated that as a group teachers are often divided as to the primary purpose behind the different activities. This last statement is also true of the other groups who responded to the questionnaire. The nursery assistants vary only slightly from the teachers in the overall pattern of their views, though tending to stress the effects of pre-school provision in meeting children's socio-emotional needs. Playgroup staff tend to lay much more emphasis on the enjoyment that an activity may furnish and the social purposes that it may serve.

It is obviously true that the activities discussed in Ward's study may well have a number of purposes associated with them, the relative importance of which may vary with the perceived individual needs and stages of a particular group of children. That a diversity of opinions concerning the purposes of specific nursery activities would exist, might be anticipated from the literature on children's play. Raw materials such as wood, stone, sand, water, clay and paint frequently have particular merits attributed to them, not least the ability to increase the young child's *aesthetic* appreciation of the natural constituents of his physical environment. An awareness of the different types and forms these materials can take and of the variety of products to which they can give rise will undoubtedly increase the child's store of physical knowledge. But much more is implied by the emphasis which play with these materials frequently receives:

Some play materials do seem to offer children particularly satisfying outlets for their impulses of love and hate, destruction and aggression. A child needs to be able to mess and destroy without feeling wicked and guilty. To learn that feelings can be safely expressed and redirected into creative and constructive activities when so desired; that when things have been destroyed in anger no irreversible harm has necessarily been done (Cass, 1975b, p. 19).

Primitive materials present the child with the problems they provided for primitive man, and what made man intelligent is available for the child. Left to their own devices, children respond readily to this challenge. They find infinite appeal in soil and mud, in sand and water, in making colourful marks on paper; later they enjoy the discipline of wood, of stone and rock, of sound and light. It is the crust of the earth, in all its variations, which most attracts the child. In handling these things the child's powers of concentration are exercised to the full. He is completely absorbed and happy because his deepest needs are satisfied (Yardley, 1973, p. 71).

Both these authors of authoritative texts for members of nursery staff are convinced that children derive considerable and various benefits from play with these materials. The 'needs' of the individual child, however, remain unspecified and the accounts of activities may be picturesque products of an adult mind rather than exact descriptions of the child's reality. In particular, the benefits claimed for these activities remain unsubstantiated. Although, as we have seen, sand and water are almost mandatory equipment for any nursery unit, until very recently there seems to have been little endeavour to describe what the children typically do with the materials, or to verify the particular benefits to be derived. One of our principal tasks in this project, therefore, was to examine exactly what children did with the various materials provided for them.

## What children do with the materials

Children in two forms of pre-school environment, nursery schools and day nurseries, were studied: six of the former and five of the latter. Observations were made on a group of three- and four-year-old children who were selected by age and sex so that the number of boys and girls in each group was the same. An account of the child's behaviour was tape-recorded using a stylized and abbreviated commentary, the child's behaviour being described in terms of discrete motor patterns (e.g. dig, scoop, scrape). The terms used and the definitions applying to each had been agreed upon by the three observers involved in the study after preliminary recordings. One particular activity provided the focus of observation for each session. An individual child would be observed from the moment he commenced play with a particular material until the play episode had clearly finished and the child had moved away. In this manner children were observed at play at seven different material-based activities: dry sand, wet sand, water, brush painting, clay and dough, finger painting, and collage. The recordings made were subsequently transcribed, the durations of each motor pattern or interaction timed, and data concerning the average frequency and duration of pattern obtained. A total of seventy-one children from nursery schools and fifty-nine children from day nurseries were observed at play.

The initial analysis was conducted on the data obtained in nursery schools. The activity patterns associated with each of the different types of material are shown in Figures 6.1 to 6.7. Patterns involved in play itself are shown to the left of the diagram. Most activities had a variety of patterns associated with them and these are shown in decreasing order of frequency from left to right in each figure. On the extreme right of each figure are shown patterns which were not related to the material *per se* but were observed in the course of play with it, e.g. interactions with children or adults.

In nursery schools, *dry sand* was found to be associated with a wide range of patterns, but many of these were not observed in all children, since the average frequency was less than one (Figure 6.1). Instead, two patterns predominated with a very high frequency, namely *scoop* and *pour*. These two patterns also occupied the most time. Thus the overall picture of play with this material is one of restricted stereotypy – the repetition of two actions. A frequently observed piece of equipment provided for play in dry sand or water is a wheel which rotates when the medium is poured over it. Our observations showed that where this wheel is present the stereotypic nature of the play is enhanced with *scooping and pouring* continuing endlessly with little variation. Interestingly, the perseverative form of activity is most evident in the older children, the four-year-olds. It will be seen that the younger children engaged in more of the exploratory patterns like *visual inspection*, *bury hand*, *trickle*. Perhaps for the younger child the experience of playing with this material is still novel; such would not be the case for the older child. Indeed, few older children seemed particularly interested in going to the trough containing dry sand.

Many nurseries provide a second trough containing *wet sand*. A

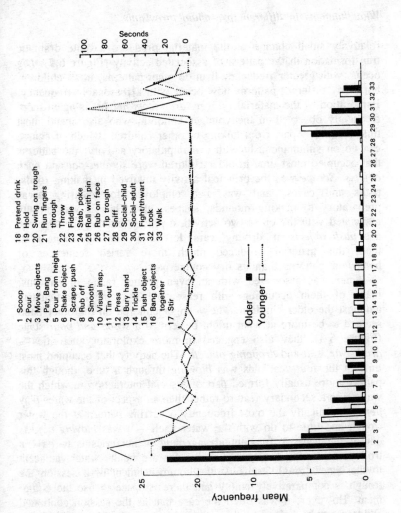

FIGURE 6.1: Frequency of motor patterns shown by older and younger children in play with dry sand

Legend:
- Older (filled)
- Younger (open)

1 Scoop
2 Pour
3 Move objects
4 Pat, Bang
5 Pour from height
6 Shake object
7 Scrape, push
8 Stab, poke
9 Smooth
10 Visual insp.
11 Tin out
12 Press
13 Bury hand
14 Trickle
15 Push object
16 Bang objects together
17 Stir
18 Pretend drink
19 Hold
20 Swing on trough
21 Run fingers through
22 Throw
23 Fiddle
24 Stab, poke
25 Roll with pin
26 Rub on face
27 Tip trough
28 Sniff
29 Social-child
30 Social-adult
31 Fight/thwart
32 Look
33 Walk

relatively small change in the material produces a quite dramatic transformation in the pattern of associated activity (Figure 6.2). *Dig* occurs with greater frequency than do other patterns, in all children, but many different patterns now occur with a reasonable frequency. Exploration of the material (*finger, drop from height*) is again more frequently observed in the younger children, who also spend most time *digging*. Apart from talking to other children, which of course can go on simultaneously with a manipulatory activity, the patterns that occupied most time in older children were *scrape, pat* and *push objects. Scrape* was the principal activity involved in making roads, paths and caves, and was also employed for clearing areas preparatory to making mounds, shapes, etc. Thus it was closely associated with the other two activities: *pat*, in building or shaping, and *push objects* in 'driving' cars, lorries or animals. In general, then, this material produced much more varied sequences of behaviour patterns than its dry counterpart.

*Water* was associated with an even greater range of patterns, many of them occurring with reasonable frequency, particularly amongst the older children. The younger children on the other hand seemed to be more at what might be termed a *scoop and pour* stage (Figure 6.3); they also engaged in more exploratory activities – *drink, stir, spit* and *dropping objects*. The activity that occupied most time in the four-year-olds was *blowing* through a tube, though this pattern more usually formed part of a social interaction in which the water was a secondary feature rather than an aspect of the water play *per se*. Ironically the most frequently occurring pattern at the water trough had little to do with the water itself – it was *moving objects* out of the way. A frequent arrangement in nurseries is to have a trolley, containing the toys available for use in the water, adjacent to the water trough itself. At the commencement of a session the trough is comparatively empty and there is space to use the equipment. However, it was often the case that as the session continued children newly arrived at the water play area would transfer items from the trolley to the trough: movement of objects in the opposite direction was seldom encountered! Thus the trough soon became so cluttered with objects that the children moved them around more often than they did anything else. Moreover, such staff intervention in water play as were observed were frequently connected with this phenomenon, staff removing unwanted toys and replacing them.

Product-oriented activities like *brush painting* (Figure 6.4) and play with *clay and dough* (Figure 6.5) were both characterized by a distribution of patterns which was very different from those already described: many patterns now appear with moderate frequency, none with a very high frequency and few with a very

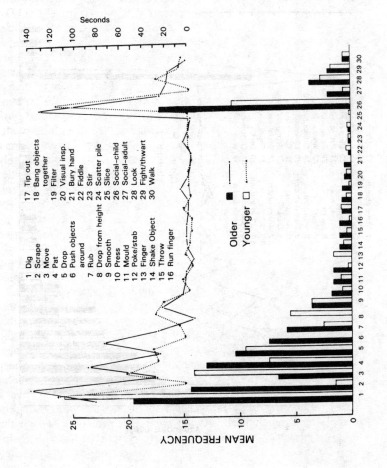

FIGURE 6.2: Frequency of motor patterns shown by older and younger children in play with wet sand

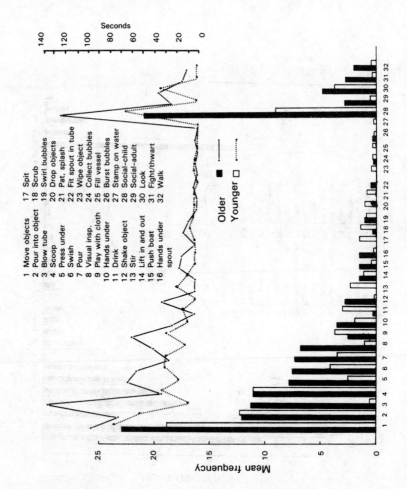

FIGURE 6.3: *Frequency of motor patterns shown by older and younger children in play with water*

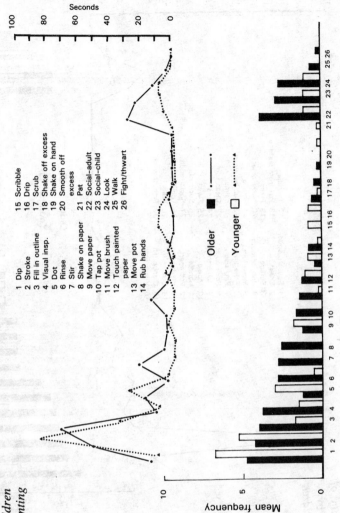

FIGURE 6.4: Frequency of motor patterns shown by older and younger children in play with brush painting

FIGURE 6.5: Frequency of motor patterns shown by older and younger children in play with clay and dough

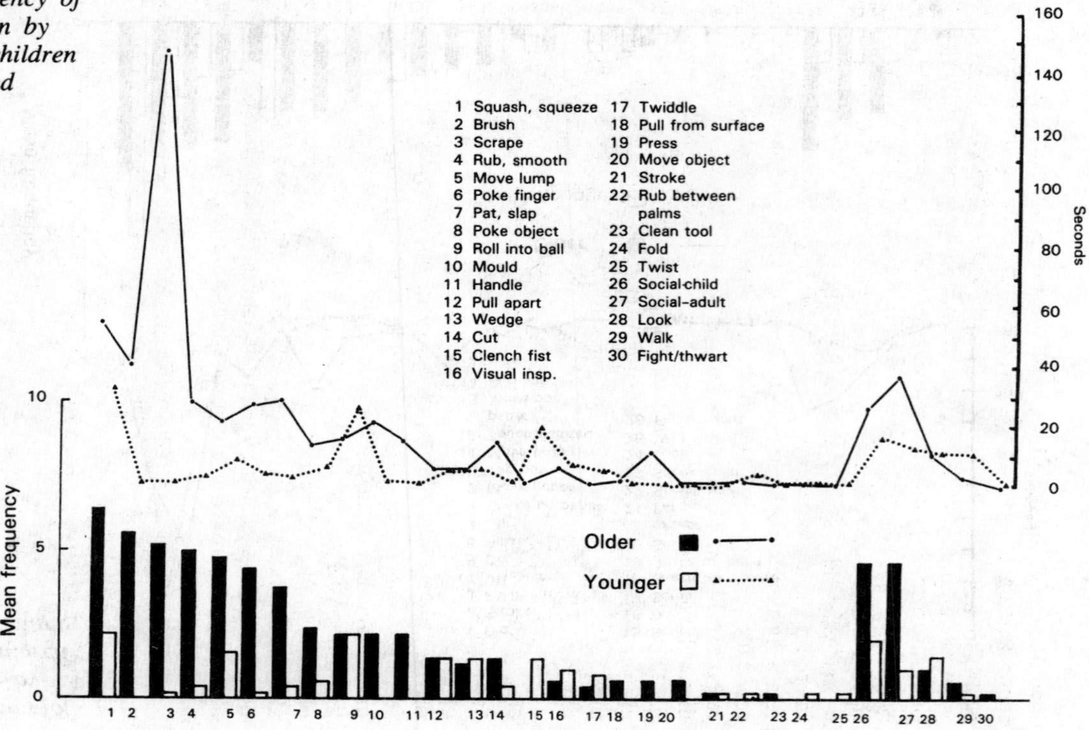

1 Squash, squeeze
2 Brush
3 Scrape
4 Rub, smooth
5 Move lump
6 Poke finger
7 Pat, slap
8 Poke object
9 Roll into ball
10 Mould
11 Handle
12 Pull apart
13 Wedge
14 Cut
15 Clench fist
16 Visual insp.
17 Twiddle
18 Pull from surface
19 Press
20 Move object
21 Stroke
22 Rub between palms
23 Clean tool
24 Fold
25 Twist
26 Social-child
27 Social-adult
28 Look
29 Walk
30 Fight/thwart

Older ■
Younger □

low frequency, so that the overall picture is one of a more even representation of several actions. In brush painting most time was spent doing *strokes*, particularly by the younger children. In fact, the younger children concentrated on the more conventional and directly product-oriented actions, whereas the older children engaged in occasional 'exploratory' activities like shaking paint on paper or tipping the pots of paint. Play with *clay and dough* was very much a four-year-olds' rather than a three-year-olds' activity. What is interesting is that even for the older children these materials were relatively novel; exploratory responses like *squeeze* and *poke* occurred fairly frequently and more often than explicitly functional responses like *mould*. The responses of the younger children were directed even more to the sensory qualities of the material – *clench fist*, for example, was an act performed to feel and to inspect the clay or dough as it oozed out between the fingers. It occupied more time than many other acts and was only observed in the three-year-olds.

*Finger painting*, an activity more rarely available (Figure 6.6), was also an activity which elicited much exploration from both three- and four-year-olds, although the older children showed a wider range of patterns, some of which were rather unusual like *clapping* and *waving* the hands, but again directed to the sensory feedback received. *Rubbing* the fingers in the paint on the surface was the most frequently occurring pattern, and it also occupied most of the time, the younger children spending almost twice as long as the older ones. A good deal of watching (*look*) the efforts of others was also evident in the three-year-olds. The exploratory and observational responses elicited by the material are probably related as much to its comparative novelty as to any intrinsic properties of the material itself.

*Collage* (Figure 6.7), although a product-oriented activity, yielded a similar composition of patterns to that of sand or water, in that one pattern (*sort*) predominated over the others. In this case, however, the act cannot be regarded as merely repetitive since variety was present in the materials being sorted. Moreover, though it occurred very frequently it occupied relatively little time, whereas *gluing* and *cutting* took up a good deal of time.

The social content of these various activities with materials differed markedly. For instance, there was negligible adult participation in play with dry sand and very little in play with wet sand or water. This is perhaps rather surprising in view of the facts that play with these natural materials is emphasized in any text on pre-school activities and that, as we have seen, they provide such an important component of the provision that is made for play. Staff frequently

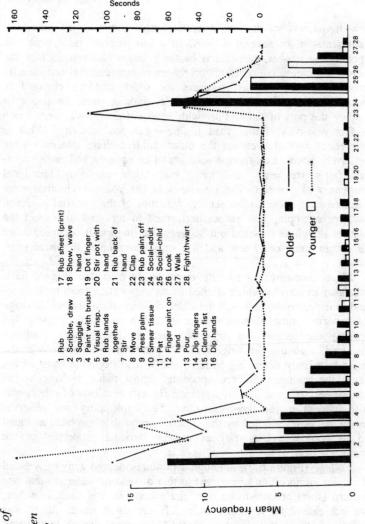

FIGURE 6.6: Frequency of motor patterns shown by older and younger children in play at finger painting

Seconds

| 1 | Rub | 17 | Rub sheet (print) |
| 2 | Scribble, draw | 18 | Show, wave |
| 3 | Squiggle | 19 | hand |
| 4 | Paint with brush | 19 | Dot finger |
| 5 | Visual insp. | 20 | Stir pot with |
| 6 | Rub hands | | hand |
| | together | 21 | Rub back of |
| 7 | Stir | | hand |
| 8 | Move | 22 | Clap |
| 9 | Press palm | 23 | Rub paint off |
| 10 | Smear tissue | 24 | Social-adult |
| 11 | Pat | 25 | Social-child |
| 12 | Finger paint on | 26 | Look |
| | hand | 27 | Walk |
| 13 | Pour | 28 | Fight/thwart |
| 14 | Dip fingers | | |
| 15 | Clench fist | | |
| 16 | Dip hands | | |

Older ■   Younger □

Mean frequency

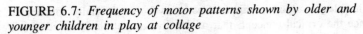

FIGURE 6.7: *Frequency of motor patterns shown by older and younger children in play at collage*

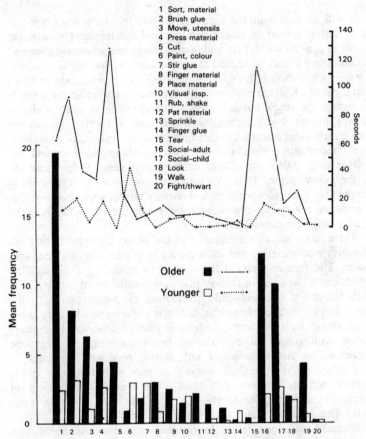

1 Sort, material
2 Brush glue
3 Move, utensils
4 Press material
5 Cut
6 Paint, colour
7 Stir glue
8 Finger material
9 Place material
10 Visual insp.
11 Rub, shake
12 Pat material
13 Sprinkle
14 Finger glue
15 Tear
16 Social–adult
17 Social–child
18 Look
19 Walk
20 Fight/thwart

Older ■ ———

Younger □ ·······

stated that the reason for the provision of these materials was to promote exploration, enjoyment and the release of emotional tensions. Consequently, they may feel that it is less necessary, if not in some instances undesirable, for them to participate in these activities. However, it may justifiably be argued that these materials also have great educational potential in that many basic concepts may be learned and *taught* during children's encounters with them. Yet we observed relatively little use of these materials in a teaching context, except for the demonstration of properties of sinking and floating. Unfortunately, as Kamii and DeVries (1978) point out, principles involved in this case can only be superficially appreciated since the critical concept, that of density, cannot be mastered at this age.

It will be seen from the figures presented that most adult involvement was observed in finger painting and collage, and to a lesser extent in activities with clay and dough. These are, of course, 'messy' activities and it may be argued that close adult monitoring is required, but very often the adult's role is supervisory to the exclusion of being participatory. Collage is an activity that merits particular mention. It is perhaps the single nursery activity during which an adult is almost always present. For the children, this ensures a 'captive' partner for conversation and one does in fact find the most lively discussions and, most importantly, *sustained* discussions, taking place around the collage table. Often the collage activity itself seems to be incidental to the conversation. It is interesting to note that in Ward's study quoted above, nursery teachers and nursery nurses often proposed that a principal reason for providing collage activities is to facilitate the child's language development.

There was some conversation with other children during all activities with materials but most during play with wet sand and with water. The former material lends itself to modelling and moulding which can be utilized in fantasy play, a typically social activity. The high frequency of child–child interaction in conjunction with the water trough resulted from the fact that children would very often 'play about' with the water, usually in pairs. There was little interaction with other children during brush painting, as might be expected, but also surprisingly little during play with dry sand.

To sum up this detailed analysis of play with materials in the nursery school, we see that most materials elicit a variety of responses, always more in the four-year-olds than the three-year-olds. The product-oriented activities like brush painting are more constrained and have fewer exploratory responses associated with them. The less readily available materials like clay, dough and finger paints, elicit a good deal of exploratory activity, even in the older children. Dry sand appears to be a material which is most often played with in a rhythmic stereotyped manner and which does not readily lend itself to innovative uses, despite the variety of other equipment which may be placed in the trough. The incidence of social interaction whether with adults or with children varies considerably over the different activities: most child–child encounters occur during play with water and with wet sand, whereas adult participation is largely restricted to finger painting and collage. This latter activity is a particularly sociable affair.

A similar analysis of play activities in the day nursery yielded much the same picture, often in exaggerated form. For instance, the frequency of *scoop* and *pour* in play with dry sand was even higher than in the school setting; a similar repetitive pattern was also evident in water play. Unlike in the school, water and sand are not available daily in the day nursery (see Chapter 2), so that when they are put out there is a general clamour around the troughs. The younger children played with these materials much more than did the older ones. The abstinence of the four-year-olds seemed to be a matter of necessity rather than of choice. The demand for these materials was often so great that eight or nine children would be crowded around a trough. The play of the younger children, usually being more active and uncontrolled (e.g. splashing), made the scene less attractive for the older ones, who seemed to become more involved in 'productive' activities. During a comparable period of brush painting, for example, the frequency of brush strokes amongst day nursery children was more than twice that found in schools.

The pattern of social interaction associated with these activities in day nurseries mirrored that in the schools, though there was more adult interaction during sand and water play necessitated by the somewhat exuberant activities of the younger children.

## Discussion

Examination of the questionnaire and interview material presented in this chapter reveals the diffuse nature of the claims made for activities, especially for imaginative play. In the main, teachers tend to emphasize the cognitive benefits to be derived, playgroup staff the socio-emotional ones. However, frequent members of both groups cite the enjoyment that is to be gained from an activity. As Ward (1982) states, it might be argued that the reason for the provision will depend upon the child using it and that individual child's needs. However, one would expect that enjoyment would be an intrinsic attribute of *all* activities in the nursery rather than the *main* purpose in the provision of an activity. Where staff have given other reasons underlying the setting up of a particular activity these would at times appear to be at variance with our own observations of the children's behaviour. For example, in the case of dry sand, staff quite frequently suggested that it assisted imaginative play and some suggested that through play with this material children would learn to share and co-operate. Our observations revealed extremely repetitive and stereotyped behaviour in association with this material and little interaction with either children or adults. Why, then, is it so fundamental to nursery practice to provide dry sand for so much of the time? The reason remains obscure.

In the case of water play, staff frequently gave a reason associated with a child's cognitive development for its deployment in the nursery. Yet in our observations, although some *exploratory* behaviour was noted, most of the patterns were essentially *ludic*. In the case of both these materials it is difficult to see how the teacher's claim could be substantiated without greater adult intervention. Undoubtedly, the materials do possess some intrinsic merits, but we feel that these will not be fully realized without an adult posing questions, giving responses and channelling the child's play down new avenues. In Chapter 5 we suggested that both staff and children are in implicit agreement about the kinds of play permissible in the outdoor and indoor areas. Our observations of play with materials suggested to us that a similar set of agreements may obtain in the case of materials. The collage table, for example, is a place where the child will find an adult and where discussion occurs. The tray containing wet sand is a place where a variety of stimuli may be encountered and different games can be played in co-operation with others. The dry sand and water troughs are places to be alone, where play is usually in parallel and where one can shut out some of the hustle and bustle endemic to nurseries. That there is a need for different micro-environments in the nursery is clear. The total environment is not the same for all children since they come to it with different personalities, experiences and needs. For some children contact with other children in comparatively large numbers is something they can take in their stride. Other children require and seek more limited contact and ideally the environment we create in the nursery should be sensitive to their needs. To some extent most nurseries provide niches where the child is able to play in a solitary or parallel fashion if she so desires. Our concern is that these places are too often associated with a particular activity or material.

In addition, children are often thwarted in attempts to make their own associations between materials. Paint is for use on paper on the table or easel, not for mixing in the water tray, and fantasy games cannot be permitted to incorporate particular elements if these are likely to cause mess or disruption, e.g. 'sand cakes' may not be taken into the house corner. Undoubtedly, there are good practical reasons for these policies, as the current set-up of most nurseries stand. But with more imagination and organization the situation could be altered with connections made between activities and events. An overall picture of some stereotypy at the level of both provision and behaviour thus pertains. In our view, staff ingenuity concentrates too much upon particular activities and products rather than upon possible connections between them. This leads to a stereotyped view of the nursery being developed in both staff and children. Thus far we have concentrated in this chapter upon play with materials. However, over recent years another form of play has attracted a great deal of attention and we shall turn to this now.

# Chapter 7

# Fantasy play

## Teachers' views of fantasy play

The Department of Education and Science (1976), *Pre-school Education and Care*, states: 'If we can assume that imaginative play has value in assisting the children's emotional, social and intellectual development, it is important that such play experiences are of high quality and it is necessary for good practice to become much more widespread.' However, the conditional statement follows only if the initial assumption is valid. We would thus question whether it is either logical or in the interests of good teaching practice to embark upon any programme of tutoring or stimulating imaginative play without first examining the evidence for this assumption. There are, in fact, surprisingly few empirical data to indicate what is the role of imaginative play in children's development, intellectually or otherwise. Yet as with play with materials, the claims that have been made for this form of play are far-reaching and most nurseries make some provision for its encouragement. Just as certain kinds of material are almost always present in the nursery, so too are the house corner and the toy railway.

In view of the importance accorded to fantasy play in relation to development in general and to *cognitive* development in particular, it seemed of interest to explore teachers' views on this subject in some detail. Accordingly, one member of our team, Norma Anderson – herself a teacher – interviewed forty of her colleagues, thirty-four of whom taught in nursery schools and six in the reception classes of primary schools typical of Area A (Anderson, 1980). The interviews were tape-recorded except in six cases where teachers either requested the interviewer to take handwritten notes or asked

99

to make written statements. The terms 'imaginative play' (Singer, 1973), 'fantasy play' (Smith, 1977), 'symbolic play' (Sutton-Smith, 1966) and 'socio-dramatic play' (Smilansky, 1968) are frequently used interchangeably. What is common to the definition of each of these terms is the element of *pretence* in the child's play. In a pilot study, it was found that whilst not disputing the synonymous use of the various terms, teachers preferred the term 'imaginative play'; the latter term was therefore employed throughout the interviews. Teachers were asked: how they would define imaginative play and how they would recognize when it was taking place; what benefits the child derives from imaginative play; whether and how teachers should intervene in such play; and what is the role of language.

The attributes of imaginative play which were mentioned by the teachers are shown in Table 7.1 and the benefits of such play in Table 7.2 (the figures do not add up to 100 per cent as a single teacher might mention more than one attribute). Although all teachers were able to give illustrative examples of their own definition of imaginative play, there was no real consensus as to what were its essential attributes. The most frequently reported

TABLE 7.1: *Frequency of attributes of imaginative play*

| Attributes | Frequency | % |
|---|---|---|
| Primary attributes | | |
| 1 Is re-enactment of roles | 12 | 30.0 |
| 2 Is replay of first-hand, observed or fictional experiences | 22 | 55.0 |
| 3 Is based on imitation | 8 | 20.0 |
| 4 Facial expression or speech indicate presence | 7 | 17.5 |
| 5 Language is necessary and indicative of social imaginative play | 12 | 30.0 |
| 6 Is indefinable or difficult to define | 6 | 15.0 |
| Secondary attributes | | |
| 7 Occurs anywhere, at any time, and with any object | 9 | 22.5 |
| 8 Is stimulated by props | 25 | 62.5 |
| 9 Is possible without props | 17 | 42.5 |
| 10 Can be social or solitary, depending on age, child or situation | 20 | 50.0 |
| Nil response | — | — |
| Failure to specify any attribute | 4 | 10.0 |

TABLE 7.2: *Frequency of benefits of imaginative play*

| Benefit | Frequency | % of teachers |
|---|---|---|
| 1 Aids creativity | 4 | 10.0 |
| 2 Gives independence/confidence | 5 | 12.5 |
| 3 Opportunity to adopt superior role | 9 | 22.5 |
| 4 Aids language | 25 | 62.5 |
| 5 Serves emotional needs | 31 | 77.5 |
| 6 Allows enjoyment | 15 | 37.5 |
| 7 Helps consolidate knowledge | 16 | 40.0 |
| 8 Promotes reasoning | 18 | 45.0 |
| 9 Aids socialization | 16 | 40.0 |
| 10 Aids learning of new skills, concepts | 6 | 15.0 |
| 11 Encourages attention | 6 | 15.0 |
| 12 Serves as communication | 9 | 22.5 |
| 13 Supplies a need | 7 | 17.5 |
| 14 Helps observant adult understand child | 6 | 15.0 |
| Nil response | 1 | 2.5 |

attributes were that imaginative play is a replay of first-hand or observed or fictional experiences (55 per cent); that it is a re-enactment of roles (30 per cent); and that it is imitation (20 per cent). The importance of props in promoting imaginative play was mentioned in two-thirds of cases. The unconventional use of props (what Hutt (1966) called 'transformation of function') was particularly highlighted by Anderson; as an example she noted the following incident described by a teacher:

Mark was pushing a pram up and down on the top field. It was unusual for him to be with a pram with dolls and blankets in it, but he wasn't making the noise of the pram, but that of a machine. He was cutting the grass.

Anderson remarks: 'because of a perceived similarity, the child was able to "represent" the mower by a pram, and thus transform its function'.

Only one teacher out of forty was unable to suggest at least one benefit to be had from imaginative play. The range of putative benefits is quite remarkable, covering virtually every facet of cognitive, emotional and social development. Indeed, one is tempted to ask whether there is any aspect of early development which is *not* benefited by imaginative play. The clear favourites are the effects upon emotional needs and upon language development. However, the same incident is capable of being interpreted by different teachers as equally fulfilling an emotional or a cognitive function. For example, a child who repeatedly enacted having a baby beneath a blanket was seen by one teacher as coming to terms with her (the child's) jealousy of a baby brother or sister. The same incident was regarded by another teacher as evidence that the child 'was consolidating her learning and extending her understanding by this process. . ... They fetch out their experiences and re-examine them' (Anderson, 1980, p. 27). The notion that fantasy play may serve a cathartic function in enabling a child to 'act out' some troubling emotional experience has long been acknowledged by developmental psychologists of psychoanalytic persuasion. Moreover, there is no reason to suppose that such acting out cannot simultaneously fulfil other functions, such as the facilitation of language use. However, there is a risk that in ascribing so many functions to imaginative play, one is led away from inquiring further into the *processes* whereby it produces its effects. Imaginative play becomes self-evidently 'a good thing'. As part of the project, therefore, we decided to undertake a series of studies examining fantasy play in detail. The first of these studies is described below.

## Observation of fantasy play in nursery schools

In Table 5.2 of this volume we gave details of the proportions of time children spend in different categories of fantasy play during free-play in different forms of pre-school provision. The aim of the present study was to investigate the thematic content of the play and the interrelationship between the participants, their play and the environment. Thus, whereas the first study examined the behaviour of groups of children observed individually, in the present study it was the *group* of children engaged in imaginative play and their immediate environment which formed the focal point. Through observation a detailed picture of the type and frequency of themes within the children's imaginative play, and of the areas of the classroom where these activities tended to occur, was built up.

Nine nursery schools were used in the course of the study, providing a total of ten complete sessions of free-play. Most of the observations occurred indoors but some outdoor sequences were included amongst the data. Observations continued throughout the period of free-play, but excluded periods of organized activity. During the period of observation the observer scanned the whole classroom and made detailed notes on any readily observable incidents of fantasy play. By scanning all areas of the room sequentially it was ensured that a representative sample from the range of themes occurring was obtained.

The written records were subsequently divided into episodes and events. An *episode* consisted of a period of continuous fantasy play occurring in a single location. An *event* represented a subdivision of an episode and was distinguished from preceding and succeeding events by changes in the theme of the play and/or in the composition of the group of children. For example, an episode might consist of a group of children playing together for a quarter of an hour in the home corner. The episode might be subdivided into several events as follows: (i) a girl playing for the entire period with a doll; (ii) a boy pretending to iron some clothes briefly and then leave the group; (iii) two girls and a boy pretending to eat dinner. Thus, in this instance, the episode of play is divided into three distinct events. However, an episode, although complex, might contain only a single event. For example, a small group of children building a 'fire' from blocks of wood, escaping from the fire, and becoming firemen to quench the blaze would be coded as a single event occurring within an episode, since there is a group and thematic continuity. For the purposes of analysis our central concern was the event. A total of 127 events were distinguished during the ten observational sessions and these were analysed in terms of the following attributes: the *environment* or location in the nursery where the event occurred; the *type* of fantasy play observed (e.g. representational object play or fantasy person play); the *numbers* of children and adults involved; the *duration* of the event; and the *theme*. (For details of these attributes see Appendix F.)

Initial analysis of the data obtained from the study revealed a wide range of thematic material. The frequency of occurrence of different themes is given in detail in Figure 7.1. Themes may be grouped into three major categories: those concerned with *domestic* events; those concerning individuals who might be encountered in the *local* community, e.g. policeman, fireman; and those based upon fictional *media*-based characters, e.g. Batman, Bionic Man. Overall, domestic themes tended to predominate. Interestingly, there appears to be a sex difference in the children's adoption of the different themes in their play, girls tending to spend most time in play involving domestic themes, boys tending to concentrate on local community or media-oriented themes.

Subsequent analysis focused upon the *types* of fantasy play in order to ascertain the factors associated with each. Definitions of fantasy play are given in Appendix F.

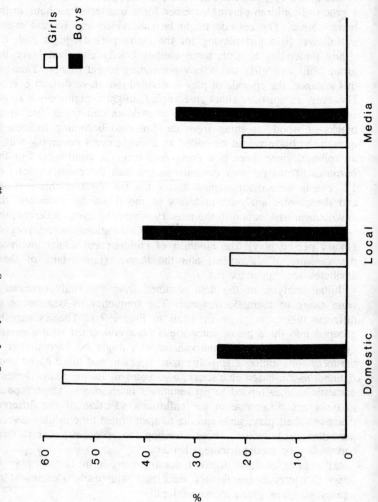

FIGURE 7.1: Percentage of boys and girls seen at different themes

Most nurseries, through the equipment available, make generous provision for representational object (RO) play. Therefore, it is not surprising that this form of play was present in more than half the observed events, nor that it should tend to occur in locations reserved for it. However, a certain amount of RO play occurred in other areas of the nursery also, which may be a reflection of the comparative freedom given to children to move these objects from one part of the nursery building to another. The average group size for this kind of play was 2.3, but children frequently engaged in this kind of play alone. The provision of different representational objects within one area, as in the home corner, appeared to lead to a considerable amount of parallel play. Adults tended not to interact with children engaged in representational object play, and where interaction did occur its duration was brief. The majority of events in which RO play was seen to occur were of medium duration (i.e. of only a few minutes) and nearly half the events involved this form of play exclusively. Nearly all the RO play centred on domestic themes and seldom did more than a single theme occur during an event which included RO play. A picture emerges, then, of RO play as a fairly low-level activity often engaged in in parallel with other children. This finding from the nursery is consistent with that of a study involving the observation of children in their own home (Davie *et al.*, 1984).

One-third of the events included fantasy person play (FP) and these events occurred in four of the five environments, the exception being play with materials. This form of play usually involved groups of children but rarely adults. Adults were only noted twice during events where FP play occurred and on these occasions were not active participants in the game. For example, one boy approached an adult and stated 'I am a Dalek' at which the adult smiled and nodded but did not prolong the interaction further. Fantasy person play tended to occur during events that were either of medium or of extended length. A wide diversity of themes was observed, which included a variety of different roles (Appendix F). Girls tended to select from a smaller range of roles than boys and each sex tended to adopt 'sex appropriate' roles.

Nearly one-fifth of the events included fantasies concerning food which led to the creation of a separate *fantasy food* (FF) category. All except one of these events occurred in, or at least originated in, the home corner, and the theme was almost invariably domestic. An average group size of 2.4 was associated with this kind of play, but as with RO play it was usually conducted solitarily or in parallel. Adult involvement was uncommon and was limited to the 'consumption' of food proffered by the child. Events involving this form of play tended to be of medium or extended length.

More boys than girls tended to be involved in events which included fantasy object play (FO) and although these events occurred in all environments they tended to be concentrated upon the constructional toys. The average group size was 3.4 and children were rarely seen alone during these events. By contrast, adults were rarely involved in the play. This type of play tended to occur during events of medium or extended duration. Themes accompanying this type of play were fairly varied but predominantly 'local'.

Only 23 of the 127 events included immaterial fantasy play (IF). This form of play tended to occur in most areas of the nursery and usually involved groups of children. As with the other forms of play, adults were not closely involved. Immaterial fantasy play tended to occur during episodes of medium length, although the actual incidents were quite brief; this form of play usually occurred in conjunction with other forms of fantasy play. Most often a media theme was involved in events containing IF play.

In a final part of the analysis, a distinction between fantasy play indoors and outdoors was studied. Whereas fantasy play indoors is dominated by RO play with domestic themes, that observed outdoors includes a considerable amount of FO play, FP play and IF play, with themes generally taken from the media. This finding may derive from the relative absence of props and interference by adults whilst the child is outdoors.

## Linguistic correlates of fantasy play

Despite the lack of consensus amongst nursery teachers regarding the definition of imaginative play, if we re-examine Table 7.1 an interesting fact may be noted. Almost all the attributes of imaginative play are ones in which some verbal expression by the child is required before the 'pretend' component of the behaviour becomes evident. Similarly, if we recall the definitions employed in the behavioural study of fantasy play above, it can be seen that at least two of the definitions, fantasy person and immaterial fantasy, are identifiable only by reference to the child's verbal behaviour. Indeed, it may be suggested that the greater incidence of girls' participation in these behaviours relative to boys is due to their supposedly greater verbal fluency in the pre-school period. This suggested to us that a closer examination of the relationship between fantasy play and linguistic ability might be informative.

The present study examined the hypothesis that fantasy play, as measured by time spent in this activity, is related to linguistic ability, as measured by the verbal comprehension and expressive language

TABLE 7.3: *Amounts of fantasy play and Reynell Developmental Language Scores in children rated by teachers as either high or low in imaginativeness*

| | High Imaginativeness | Low Imaginativeness |
|---|---|---|
| Chronological age | 4 years 1 month | 4 years 2 months |
| Mean time spent in fantasy play | 57.42 min | 40.67 min |
| Mean time spent in complex play | 29.92 min | 13.50 min |
| Age level on verbal comprehension scale | 4 years 9 months | 3 years 5 months |
| Standard score on verbal comprehension | + 0.77 | − 1.44 |
| Age level on expressive language scale | 5.0 years | 4.41 years |
| Standard score on expressive language | + 0.85 | + 0.25 |

scales of the Reynell Developmental Language Scales. Thus, children rated by teachers high on imaginativeness should not only manifest high levels of fantasy play – as observed in naturalistic situations – but show high levels of linguistic competence.

The subjects were twelve four-year-old children (six male, six female) from an Area A nursery school. The children were selected by the head teacher as the six who showed the 'most imaginative play' and the six 'who showed least imaginative play'. Each child was observed for a total of 100 minutes during twenty observation periods. A predominant activity scan (Tyler, 1979) was employed with a 30-second observation interval, the child's behaviour being allocated to one of the four categories of fantasy behaviour employed by Davie *et al.* (1984) and listed in Table 7.3, excluding fantasy food. After the observations were completed, each child was assessed on the Reynell Developmental Language Scales.

Table 7.3 shows the mean amount of fantasy play observed in the high imaginativeness (HI) and low imaginativeness (LI) groups respectively. Although HI children did indeed manifest a higher level of fantasy play than LI children, the difference was not statistically significant. The two groups did, however, differ significantly from each other on the second measure, complex fantasy. This consisted of those time intervals in which more than one of the four types of fantasy play occurred. It thus appears that the teachers' judgments of 'imaginativeness' were in very good accord with objective measurements of how children actually behave in the nursery setting.

The teachers' success is perhaps the more impressive since, as we have already seen in the first part of this chapter, they are frequently quite unclear as to what criteria they utilize in recognizing fantasy play. However, we also found that at least two of our definitions of fantasy play rest substantially upon verbal expression. Is it the case, therefore, that in judging one child as being more imaginative than another, teachers are categorizing the former as being more linguistically advanced than the other? This possibility is strongly supported by the data from the Reynell Scales. As can be seen in Table 7.3 the HI group were developmentally in advance of their chronological age on both scales of the Reynell. In contrast, the LI group were performing at a level more appropriate for children of lower chronological age. The difference between the mean standard scores of the two groups was highly significant in each case. The relationship between fantasy and language development is seen even more clearly if Reynell scores are correlated with the observational data irrespective of which 'imaginativeness' group a child belongs to. Highly significant rank order correlations were obtained between the amount of fantasy play and the two Reynell scores; and between the complexity of play and the two Reynell scores. In short, it would appear that the amount of fantasy play in general, and of complex fantasy play in particular, is a good reflection of a child's level of verbal competence – at any rate, to the extent to which this is measurable by a standardized psychological test.

## Fantasy discourse

A further intriguing aspect of the relationship between fantasy play and linguistic competence was observed during our studies of children in day nurseries. Many of the children in the nurseries would be classifiable as 'disadvantaged' on socio-economic criteria. So ingrained is the assertion that children from disadvantaged homes tend to manifest 'poverty of language' (Central Advisory Council for Education, 1967) that the linguistic retardation of the children in day care occasioned little apparent surprise or concern amongst the staff. We ourselves noted that much of the speech of the day nursery four-year-olds was rather infantile, in that there was a high frequency of onomatopoeic terms, like 'choo-choo' or 'puss-puss', and of two- or three-word utterances. It was also observed, however, that these same children, when engaged in imaginative or fantasy play, did use longer and more complex forms of speech. Linguists have made the important and now familiar distinction between linguistic 'competence' and linguistic 'performance': while performance refers to the actual speech one hears, competence refers to knowledge of the rules that apply to the syntactic structure of the language. But more recently, socio-linguists have demonstrated that linguistic forms in any one speaker may differ from one context to another. Bernstein (1973) observes that context exerts control upon syntactic and lexical selection and, moreover, that linguistic codes reflect the social structure.

It was interesting, therefore, to investigate the children's utterances during everyday interactions and during episodes of fantasy play. The speech of fourteen day nursery children (eight boys, six girls) was tape-recorded by an observer, using a radio-microphone, who followed each child at a discreet distance for 30 minutes. Recordings were continued until thirty utterances had been made during non-fantasy activities. The criteria of what was fantasy play again followed the definitions of Davie *et al.* (1984). The ages of the children ranged from three and a half to four and a half years with a mean age of four years two months. Six observers recorded the data, which were obtained from five day nurseries in Area A. The tapes were subsequently transcribed and four measures of linguistic performance, which have been used in other, similar studies, were derived:

1   Mean length of utterance (MLU): the mean number of morphemes per utterance, an utterance being distinguished by intonation, pauses, etc.
2   Type–token ration (TTR): a measure of lexical diversity expressed as a ratio of the number of different word types occurring in a sequence of 200 words (tokens).
3   Number of adverbs (ADV) in the thirty utterances.
4   Number of modal auxiliary verbs (MA): auxiliary verbs which refer to the likelihood, possibility, etc., of the event in the main verb, e.g. *can, must, would, may.*

The following extracts give the flavour of fantasy and non-fantasy discourse respectively.

*Fantasy discourse*

*Episode 1  Setting: making and using a train – three boys.*

Paul:   Let's make a long train 'cos there will be a lot o' people getting on.

Jason:  We haven't got any. . .

Paul:   C'mon, quick – we have t'hurry, guard will blow his whistle – there's lots o' children coming as well.

Mark:    Who's going to be the driver?

Paul:    I am – and you can be the guard and Jason can be the ticket collector. You climb up behind.

Jason:    Blow your whistle, Mark.

*Episode 2 Setting: shopping – two boys and two girls.*

John:    Do you want to buy some sweets?

Jane:    I want some bubble gum.

Rachel:    [Shopkeeper] We only have Polos – do you want them?

Jason:    I'll ask my Dad. Will you come to the shop? I want some Polos.

John:    My little girl wants some Polos and I want some cigarettes and some beer.

Rachel:    What cigarettes do you want?

John:    Those amlets [Hamlets?] that you can smell. What about my beer as well?

Rachel:    We ain't got any.

John:    This is a rotten shop. [To Jane] You can't have any of those Polos till we get home. I've told you before, you're a naughty girl.

*Episode 3 Setting: ? playing witches – three girls.*

Joanne:    I don't know any witches but they live in caves.

Sally:    How do you know?

Joanne:    Because you can't see them, but they go up in people's houses and climb the stairs – like this – when the moon is out. Then they fly to palaces and eat up little boys – gobble them up – like this.

Donna:    I want to be a witch.

Sally:    Let's get some clothes – quickly.

Donna:    I think witches live in houses with pointed roofs and they walk about on tip-toe and chatter to themselves.

Joanne:    We'll make some magic food. I'll get some from the shop on my broomstick.

Sally:    Don't witches have cats? And they sit on the broomstick.

Joanne:    Don't be silly – cats can't ride on broomsticks, they'll fall off.

Donna:    But then the witch can catch them – she can fly through the air.

Joanne:    You are silly – people can't fly.

*Episode 4 Setting: going on holiday – two boys, one girl.*

Susan:    This is our holiday caravan. We're going to the seaside.

Kevin:   You get in there – I'm going to drive. Brm, br. . .
Susan:   No, I will drive.
         [Kevin moves away]
Michael: That's a holiday caravan. Can we go in it?
         [Both Kevin and Michael climb on and 'drive']
Susan:   Only two can fit in – I'll get in here.
         [Rachel approaches]
Susan:   Can she come in?
Kevin:   No. You sit on this seat and be quiet, I'm driving.
Susan:   I'll get inside the caravan. It's nice and dark in there.
Michael: Where are we going?
Kevin:   To Blackpool – by the seaside. Have you packed the
         buckets and spades?
Susan:   Yes – and I've got some food – it's only a little though.
Michael: We can stop at a caf.
Susan:   What do we do if it's raining?
Kevin:   Swim in the sea, of course.
Michael: Drive faster Kevin, someone is trying to overtake us.

(Adults confirm that *none* of these children has been on a seaside
holiday.)


*Non-fantasy discourse*

*Episode 1  Setting: adult preparing to tell a story.*
Mark:    Stephen kicked my leg.
Adult:   Stephen, you're a naughty boy. Get a tissue, Mark.
         [Mark fetches one]
         Have you got a cold?
Mark:    No.
Adult:   Yes you have – go on now – go and play with
         something.

*Episode 2  Setting: Paul is filling the nursery assistant's shoe with
sand while she is drawing some figures.*
Adult:   Paul, what are you doing?
Paul:    ————
Adult:   You are a naughty little boy. Come here – go and get
         the brush and sweep this up.
         [Paul goes – meets Sarah]
Paul:    Where's the brush?
Sarah:   There [pointing].
         [Paul fetches it]

Adult: If you do that again you'll get smacked.
Paul: No.
Adult: Yes you will.

*Episode 3 Setting: four children at water trough.*
Jason: Look, it's coming out of there.
Donna: Pour some more.
Kevin: Pour it really fast.
Peter: More, more, more. . .
Adult: Children, don't make such a mess.
Kevin: I want that bottle.
Jason: You can't have it.
[Kevin and Jason start fighting and Donna takes bottle]
Jason: [To adult] Donna's taken my bottle.
Adult: Donna, give it back to him.
[Donna leaves water]

*Episode 4 Setting: three children watching adult cutting out shapes.*
Joanne: My mummy's got a dress like that.
Adult: Has she?
John: My jumper's that colour.
Adult: No it's not – your jumper is green.
Sarah: That's blue.
John: Go toilet?
Adult: Yes, be quick. Sarah, you stick that on there.
Joanne: Can have one?
Adult: Yes here's a carriage for you – put it on that road there.
Sarah: What's a carriage?
Adult: It's like a cart, drawn by a horse.
John: What?
Sarah: A carriage.
John: What's that?
Adult: I've already told you. Now get on with your sticking.

An interesting picture emerges when we examine the linguistic forms employed by the children during fantasy and non-fantasy play respectively. It can be seen from Figure 7.2 that on all four measures the children scored higher during non-fantasy sessions; three of these differences (MLU, ADV and MA) were statistically significant. In other words, these children were displaying a greater competence in their language usage during fantasy play than could be discerned from their ordinary speech. It was striking that such young children could be almost 'bilingual', having the ability to use

FIGURE 7.2: *Scores on measures of syntax during normal conversation and during fantasy play*

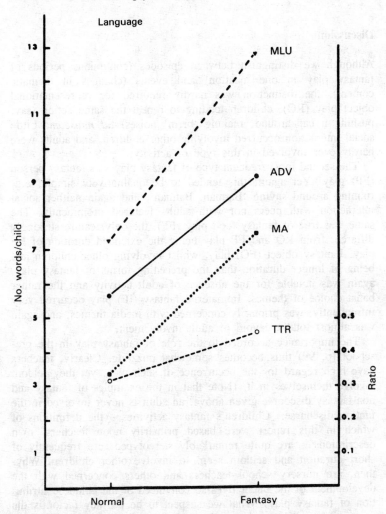

two different speech codes; furthermore, their *performance* in everyday speech gave little clue as to their *competence*, i.e. knowledge of the rules that apply to the syntactic structure of language. As sociolinguists like Bernstein (1973) have frequently pointed out, linguistic codes are realizations of the social structures and dependent upon the context: where children are free from constraint in expressing their

113

thoughts, ideas and experiences, the language used is correspondingly unconstrained.

## Discussion

Although we distinguish between episodes (continuous periods of fantasy play in one location) and events (changes in thematic content), the distinction was hardly required for representational object play (RO), children tending to repeat the same action (say, pushing a car around, making 'brrm' noises) *ad nauseam*. Little social interaction occurred involving other children, and adults were hardly ever involved in this type of activity.

The second most frequent type of fantasy play was fantasy person (FP) play. Yet again, this tended to be qualitatively simple, e.g. running around saying 'Batman, Batman'; and again neither social interaction with peers nor with adults featured prominently. The same was true of fantasy food play (FF), the only feature strikingly different from RO and FP play being the extended duration of FF play. Fantasy object (FO) play, whilst involving other children and being of longer duration than the preceding forms of fantasy play, again was notable for the absence of adult activity and the rather banal choice of themes. Immaterial fantasy (IF) play occurred very infrequently, was primarily concerned with media themes, and again was almost totally devoid of adult involvement.

The importance accorded to the role of fantasy play in the pre-school (p. 99) thus becomes somewhat puzzling. Clearly, teachers have high regard for the occurrence of such play, yet they seldom involve themselves in it. (Note that in the examples of fantasy and non-fantasy discourse given above, an adult is never involved in the fantasy discourse.) Children's fantasy activities – the definitions of which in this report were based primarily upon teachers' own descriptions – are quite remarkably stereotyped, are frequently of short duration and seldom seem to involve other children. Why, then, are nursery school teachers and others concerned with the development of the under-fives so convinced of the unique contribution of fantasy play? What we suspect to be the key factor is the very understandable concern of adults caring for the under-fives with language development; and the correlation of linguistic complexity and certain forms of fantasy play. In fact, it is almost tautologous to state that there is such a correlation, since fantasy person play (FP) and, even more so, immaterial fantasy (IF) are recognizable primarily by the child's language usage. Interestingly, these categories of fantasy play account together for rather less than a third of all such play. Nevertheless, it appears that adults caring for the under-fives – and nursery teachers in particular – attach particular salience to fantasy play involving language. This indeed becomes evident if we examine Table 7.1. Several of the signs by which fantasy play is recognized are ones which involve language: the language provides a commentary upon the child's actions; without such a commentary the child's behaviour appears incomprehensible or bizzare.

Thus, because language is a definitional requirement of certain categories of fantasy play, it is not surprising if adults, and especially teachers, are tempted to see linguistic competence as being *potentiated* by fantasy play rather than a mere accompaniment to it. However, it may be that those children who are linguistically more competent than others express their greater competence during free play. We have defined fantasy as fantasy if it involves *pretence*, irrespective of whether language is also involved. It is likely, however, that the form of pretence which is most salient to teachers is that which involves language – fantasy objects (FO) and fantasy persons (FP) – even though these categories account for only a very small part of all fantasy play. Children who engage in the greatest amount of verbally dependent fantasy play will be picked out as the 'most imaginative' children and vice versa. Thus, our positive correlation between scores on the Reynell Scales and amount of fantasy play is readily comprehensible without resort to a *causal* relationship between fantasy play and verbal ability.

But if fantasy play is not involved in enhancing verbal ability (or perhaps indeed any aspect of cognitive ability) what is its function? We have seen that much 'pretend' play is highly repetitious, and occurs without peer interaction and without adult participation. It tends to occur, in fact, when situational demands are fewest, when the child can pace his own behaviour, can just 'muck about'; in short, when the child is relaxed, or as relaxed as he can be, short of being asleep. Hutt and Hutt (1978) have called this state 'idling' – in the engineering sense, not its moralistic sense. It is a period of recuperation after more demanding periods of information processing (Delius, 1970) and, as we have seen (Chapter 1), it is akin to daydreaming both behaviourly and physiologically.

If then, fantasy play indicates the state of the child's nervous system, a state of relaxation, or 'time-out', this may provide an opportunity for him to manifest skills which may not be apparent when he is more tense – in situations where other, unfamiliar children, or adult authority figures, are present. This may have been the case in our study of day nursery children. In terms of IQ – tested by an 'authority' figure with (for them) an unusual manner of speech – these children were far inferior to their nursery school or playgroup counterparts. Moreover, their apparently 'impoverished' speech caused no apparent surprise amongst the day nursery staff. Yet, as we have seen, the linguistic forms shown by these children in formal situations with adults were totally misleading as a guide to their linguistic competence in general. When engaged in fantasy play, without adult interference, their linguistic forms were rich and sophisticated.

We are thus moving to a position in which we would seriously question the importance placed upon fantasy play as an aid to cognitive development. Rather, we see fantasy play from the child's point of view as possibly serving a recuperative function (Hutt and Hutt, 1978; Hutt 1979a); and, from the adult's point of view, primarily as serving a *diagnostic* function. Thus, fantasy play provides us with a 'looking-glass', whereby we may glimpse the motives, emotions, experience and competence of young children (Hutt, 1979b). We would argue that in many cases where cognitive benefits have been attributed to involvement in fantasy play (e.g. the oft-quoted study by Smilansky, 1968), they could, more parsimoniously, be attributed to the linguistic and social stimulation involved in the tutoring or training process than to fantasy play itself. We shall offer some empirical evidence for this statement in Chapters 12 and 13.

# Chapter 8

# Attention and choice of activity

Of great concern to those involved in the education of the young child is the question of how long, once a stimulus or activity has been selected, attention to it can be maintained. Thus establishment of control of attention, it may be argued, is an important developmental stage. The degree of control established in the pre-school as evidenced by the child's level of activity may serve as a predictor of future social and intellectual performance (Halverson and Waldrop, 1976). This finding is broadly consistent with Kagan's view that children with 'fast tempos' (marked by short attention spans and impulsivity) do not maintain an active involvement in hypothesis verification when confronted with a novel situation (Kagan, 1971). The ability of children to focus upon a particular stimulus or set of stimuli is obviously of concern to nursery practi-tioners whose aim will often be to provide particular activities within a general environment which will enhance the children's level of concentration. A *prima facie* case may be made that the longer a child is able to attend the more efficient his information-processing and hence the better his performance. Such a case is supported by empirical evidence that attentiveness is correlated with task perfor-mance and school achievement through the primary years (Lahaderne, 1968; Cobb, 1972; Samuels and Turnure, 1974). We also have evidence that duration of attention increases with age and maturity (van Alstyne, 1932; Gutteridge, 1935; Crow and Crow, 1963; Mussen *et al.*, 1974; Bruner, 1980). More specifically, it has been argued that the nature of attentiveness shifts from a single-channelled, adult controlled form to a double-channelled, child controlled form during the child's third and fourth years of life – the very years of the child's nursery career (Cooper *et al.*, 1978). In general, then, longer spans of attention to a task or activity may be considered a sign of greater maturity. However, some studies have failed to find such a consecutive relationship (e.g. Clarke *et al.*, 1969; Lunzer, 1958; Tizard *et al.*, 1976b).

The foregoing discussion suggests that the attentiveness of the child is a pertinent factor in any description of the nursery environment. Certainly this view is shared by some nursery practitioners, since degree of concentration was one of the constructs elicited in the repertory grid study previously described (Chapter 3). However, staff did not accord this aspect of the children's behaviour particular prominence, a finding which in itself is perhaps surprising. We therefore decided to examine the attentiveness of pre-school children in order to determine whether certain contexts and types of activity were more conducive to concentration than others. In particular, we wished to evaluate the possible role of the adult as a catalyst in the focusing of children's attention.

## Measuring children's attention

The behaviour of a child in the nursery may be likened to a continuously flowing stream whose successive crests divide it into a sequence of natural units. These units may be categorized with reference to the form of the observed behaviour (e.g. running, jumping, hitting) or the particular objects to which attention is being paid (blocks, toy cars, etc.). If we classify the child's behaviour in the former terms the measures of concentration we obtain may be called 'activity spans': if we choose the latter mode of classification we term the measures obtained 'attention spans' (Hutt and Hutt, 1970). Thus, activity spans are defined in terms of the duration of particular forms of activity and are generally shorter than attention spans.

## The activity spans of pre-school children

The data used for the study of activity spans of children in pre-school were those collected in the course of the checklist study described in Chapter 5. For the purpose of this analysis, the number of consecutive cells of the checklist devoted to a single activity was noted. If during an activity there was a 'break' of more than one time interval (observations were being made in this case at fifteen-second intervals) it was considered that one span had ended before and another had begun after the break. Thus, if a child broke off from an activity and walked around the nursery for half a minute

TABLE 8.1: *Mean activity spans of children in free-play in different forms of pre-school provision*

| Pre-school provision | Without adult (sec) | With adult (sec) | % increase with adult | Overall (sec) |
|---|---|---|---|---|
| NS | 124.4 | 186.0 | 49.5 | 130.8 |
| NC | 126.2 | 161.4 | 27.9 | 126.8 |
| PG | 107.3 | 195.9 | 82.6 | 114.2 |
| DN | 98.3 | 209.9 | 113.5 | 110.7 |

before returning to the same activity or engaging in a new one, two separate spans of activity would be recorded. The presence of an adult at the activity engaged in by the child was also noted. Mean activity spans in time intervals were calculated for each group of children in each nursery context and then converted into seconds. The mean activity spans obtained in the different establishments are shown in Table 8.1. It may be seen from this table that the overall span is greatest in the school and lowest in the day nursery. When, however, account is taken of the presence or absence of an adult, it may be seen that the spans are significantly increased in all four contexts when an adult is present, suggesting that the adult is a potent force in harnessing the child's concentration.

The study previously reported (Chapter 5) contrasting indoor and outdoor play also furnished data on the spans of activity. A notable feature of the activity spans in that study was their brevity. The spans obtained from this second study were of a similar order. Overall, it was found that the mean length is fairly similar for play indoors and outdoors, with a slight tendency in both sexes for spans outdoors to be longer. The differences in spans in relation to sex and type of activity largely reflected the differences in the amount of time spent in these activities, as previously reported. In general, spans tended to be longer for those activities which might be termed 'playful'. The most sustained play in girls occurred at material play inside, while boys tended to exhibit their longest spans in physical play outdoors. Girls and boys had very similar spans for 'looking' and 'watching' and spans for these behaviour patterns tended to be greatest indoors.

A feature of the two studies cited above is the brevity of the measures of activity span obtained. In part, this may be seen as a product of the system of observation and behavioural categorization adopted. It must be remembered, when considering the figures presented, that the definition of a span employed here permitted quite brief changes in behaviour to act as indications of the termination of one span and the commencement of another. However, a consistent picture emerges from both studies of children whose attention to particular activities is frequently interrupted whether they return subsequently to that activity or not.

## Attention spans

In a further study we switched our interest from the individual child's behaviour to the focus of the child's attention, i.e. to what was she paying attention? However in this instance the measurement obtained was of the duration of the child's stay at an activity from the moment of arrival to ultimate departure, without reference to brief interruptions or switches to other activities, i.e. *attention* span. The results obtained from this study are shown in Table 8.2, which gives a breakdown by type of activity and sex. Inspection of this table reveals immediately that attention spans measured in this way are best presented in terms of minutes rather than seconds. At most activities girls stayed longer than boys except at semi-structured activities, where the duration of the spans was approximately similar. The observers noted, however, considerable individual variability.

In some instances, the attention span measured was approximately one minute (i.e. of the order of the *activity* spans presented in the previous studies) extended to over an hour in one or two cases. Most attention spans, however, did not approach this latter figure, as may be witnessed by the averages given in the table.

Consideration of the results accruing from the three studies described above suggests that the concentration of the children in the nursery on a particular activity is typically of the order of a quarter of an hour, this period being punctuated by frequent interruptions or breaks.

TABLE 8.2: *Mean time spent at different types of activity*

|  | Girls | Minutes Boys | G + B |
|---|---|---|---|
| Free-play with materials | 16.2 | 12.2 | 14.1 |
| Product | 14.7 | 10.7 | 12.9 |
| Representational play | 28.3 | 20.2 | 22.4 |
| Semi-structured | 11.6 | 11.8 | 11.7 |
| Overall | 15.3 | 13.0 | 14.2 |

## Factors affecting children's choice of activity

A key factor in determining the duration of a child's stay at a particular activity might be the reason why he became engaged in that activity in the first instance. Was it the presence of an adult or of other children that drew him to the activity or was it some intrinsic feature of the activity itself? Or did he just wander aimlessly into it? Similar factors might affect the reasons for the child's decision to abandon an activity. Was the thing he was making complete? Was another activity suddenly compelling?

One inference that may be drawn from the studies already presented in this volume is that pre-school materials and activities have varying powers of attraction for different children and may present these children with different educational opportunities. All these considerations suggest that the question of what it is that influences the child's choice of activity may be an important one.

Thus far, researchers have paid comparatively little attention to children's behaviour immediately prior to entry into an activity or at departure from that activity. A notable exception to this generalization is to be found in the work of Stodolsky (1974). In observing children's behaviour in pre-schools, Stodolsky found she could make a distinction between activity segments and transition periods, the former consisting of focused behaviour patterns of a duration exceeding one minute. The remaining patterns, the transition periods, were in turn subdivided into 'pre-solution' and 'solution' phases, since she viewed the question of 'What do I do next?' posed by the child as a problem to be solved.

Stodolsky found that transitions from an activity segment directly to a solution phase tended to be associated with older children, and she suggests that this is because this form of transition requires a degree of planning. Her data also suggested that the children who tend to progress from one activity to another with dispatch are those who spend most of their time in activities. A correlation of activity length with child's age was obtained, although activity lengths were less variable in younger children. Interestingly, Stodolsky found that, in her observations, attention spans were also related to mental age and to differences in the school environments. The way in which children choose activities may therefore be a useful index of other features of their play. Consequently, we decided to inquire into the manner in which children approach and depart from nursery activities. Four nursery schools participated in the study and each was visited for two complete morning sessions.

Observations were made at a variety of different nursery activities which were categorized into four principal groups:

121

1 Free-play with materials, e.g. sand, water, clay, in which the outcome of the child's play is unpredictable;
2 Product-oriented activities, e.g. painting, collage, drawing, in which an end-product forms a predictable outcome;
3 Representational object play, e.g. play with dolls, model cars, farm animals, in which the object manipulated represents something to which it bears a resemblance;
4 Semi-structured activities, e.g. playing lotto, completing jigsaws, in which the play is constrained by the material or activity itself.

Observations were made upon children as they approached a target activity. Note was made of the child's style of approach, the number of other children or adults present at the activity and the manner in which the child departed from the activity. The duration of the activity was measured with a stop-watch and recorded at the end of the observation. When information had been obtained for a group of children at a particular activity, the observer switched her attention to a different activity where the procedure was repeated. In total, 160 observations of boys and an equal number of observations of girls were made. Most observations were made at product-oriented activities and least at representational object play, reflecting differential availability of these two kinds of activity. Girls and boys were observed with similar frequencies at each type of activity.

The data pertaining to attention spans have already been presented. For purposes of further analysis a distinction was made between activities at which adults were present for a substantial part of the time and those where adults were present briefly or not at all. Analysis revealed that girls more frequently than boys opted for activities where an adult was present. This finding was true for all forms of activity. That adults were more likely to be found at particular kinds of activity than others is one which we have already discussed. However, it may be noted here that an adult may be an important factor in determining a child's choice of activity; this may be especially the case for girls.

Children approached activities in different ways, and these were classified into four main types as shown in Appendix G. These were: own initiative, wander, request and adult-initiated. Similarly, the way children left activities was classified into the following four types: spontaneous, wander, finish product and adult intervention.

## How children approach activities

The most frequent form of approach children made to any activity was at their own initiative and in a decisive manner. When all approaches were considered, this kind accounted for nearly 80 per cent. Table 8.3 shows the proportions of different kinds of approach for different kinds of activity.

Girls tended to be less decisive than boys, except at representational play, as shown by the higher proportion of approaches in which they wandered to an activity. Adult-initiated approaches were more frequent for girls than for boys, especially for product-oriented activities and structured activities. These findings would suggest that in product-oriented activities a certain amount of negotiation between a girl and an adult may occur prior to the girl commencing the activity. However, the pattern overall is very similar across sexes

TABLE 8.3: *Forms of approach to activities*

|  | Own initiative % | Wander % | Request % | Adult % |
|---|---|---|---|---|
| **Free-play with materials** | | | | |
| Girls | 78.6 | 11.9 | 2.4 | 7.1 |
| Boys | 84.1 | 4.5 | 2.3 | 9.1 |
| G + B | 81.4 | 8.1 | 2.3 | 8.1 |
| **Product-oriented** | | | | |
| Girls | 63.9 | 9.7 | 9.7 | 16.7 |
| Boys | 81.0 | 5.2 | 6.9 | 6.9 |
| G + B | 71.5 | 7.7 | 8.5 | 12.3 |
| **Representational object** | | | | |
| Girls | 100.0 | 0 | 0 | 0 |
| Boys | 72.4 | 13.8 | 3.4 | 10.3 |
| G + B | 80.0 | 10.0 | 2.5 | 7.5 |
| **Semi-structured** | | | | |
| Girls | 74.3 | 11.4 | 2.9 | 11.4 |
| Boys | 93.1 | 3.4 | 0 | 3.4 |
| G + B | 82.8 | 7.8 | 1.6 | 7.8 |
| **Overall** | | | | |
| Girls | 72.5 | 10.0 | 5.6 | 11.9 |
| Boys | 82.5 | 6.3 | 3.8 | 7.5 |
| G + B | 77.5 | 8.1 | 4.7 | 9.7 |

and type of activity. Children usually choose their own activities decisively, and do not often make requests.

Analysis subsequently turned to the average time spent at an activity following different styles of approach. There appears to be a correlation overall between form of approach and time spent. When boys approach an activity on their own initiative, their attention spans are longer than when they approach in any other way. Girls spend longest at an activity either when they approach it on their own initiative or if they approach it at the suggestion of an adult. Girls spent least time, on average, when they wandered up to an activity. By contrast, boys spent least time when an adult suggested an activity. Not surprisingly, attention spans tended to be briefest when children wandered into an activity and longest when they entered into the activity on their own initiative.

In general, children tended to approach activities where other children were playing, which is not surprising given the relationship between the number of children in a nursery and the activities available. However, there did appear to be a difference on this measure when children requested to do an activity. In this case they were obviously more interested in the activity they wanted to do than in joining other children, as they were more frequently alone following a request approach than in a group of children. This tendency was particularly evident amongst boys.

## How children leave activities

In most instances, it would appear that children leave activities spontaneously. Frequently, it was observed, they passed on directly to another activity. Rarely did the departure from an activity appear aimless. When the style in which a child left an activity is considered in relation to the kind of activity, some interesting differences emerge. Children most frequently left free-play and representational play activities spontaneously, and in both of these activity types they left quite frequently at the suggestion of an adult – adult intervention being especially prevalent in representational play. When children were engaged in product-oriented activities, they most frequently left when they had completed that product, although this in fact accounted for only 47 per cent of occasions; in other words, for over half the time the products children were involved in were not actually completed. This finding is especially applicable to boys.

Children tended to leave structured activities spontaneously, though this accounted for a little less than half the bouts; this was the kind of activity from which children most frequently wandered aimlessly away. Incidence of adult intervention was fairly high here, at 26.6 per cent of occurrences, being higher than for product-oriented activities and free-play, but not for representational play.

Finally, from this analysis it may be seen that girls tended to wander away from activities more than boys, particularly from free-play to structured activities. Boys, however, wandered away from product-oriented activities more than girls.

Most adult interventions occurred at an overall change in the pattern of nursery activities as organized by the adult. Two other forms of intervention occurred less often but with approximately equal frequency. One form was an adult suggestion (18.2 per cent) that the child finish an activity (accompanied, for example, by taking away a painting) and/or that the child should start a new activity (e.g. that the child stop playing with cars and go on to do a collage). The last kind of adult intervention was indirect (16.7 per cent) and sometimes unintentional: the child left the activity because the adult had done so, e.g. followed the adult to another activity, or immediately stopped when the adult left the activity.

Children spent longest at activities where the departure was caused by adult intervention. When this is related to the kind of activity it becomes obvious for both boys and girls that free-play with materials and representational play give rise to the longest attention spans, which are terminated by adult intervention. An example of this is children settling down to play with small cars and blocks where they remain until an adult asks them to clear up and get ready for dinner. Wandering away from an activity tended to be associated with brief attention spans in both sexes.

Overall, it would appear that when children do become involved in an activity for a long period of time, especially a rather unstructured activity such as sand or water play, or play with representational objects, only the constraints of the nursery routine cause them to stop, i.e. they are asked to stop because it is milk time or dinner time. Short attention spans, on the other hand, seem to be related to indecisiveness; most of the shorter bouts culminated in a child wandering off rather aimlessly.

## Discussion

The picture that emerges from all the studies represented in this chapter is of generally purposeful but interrupted activity. During free-play in nursery schools, a large number of activities are usually available for children. As the name suggests, children are free to choose which activities to be involved in, and for how long and with whom. The studies were designed to discover how children exercise this freedom of choice.

On the whole, children appeared competent and decisive as evidenced by the fact that they usually chose activities on their own initiative and made the decision to leave spontaneously. It was also noted that boys' scores were higher for both these measures, which suggested that they were more decisive than girls. Children did not often request to do activities except product-oriented ones, where girls made a few more requests than boys. Wandering up to an activity occurred more frequently among girls than boys at about 10 per cent of the time, and following an adult's suggestion to do an activity was more frequent in girls than boys.

Leaving an activity was usually spontaneous, but girls wandered off more than boys and also stayed to finish a product more often than boys.

Different kinds of activities led to slight differences in the way children started and left them: approaches to free-play and representational play were more likely to be spontaneous; adult suggestions were more frequently made at product-oriented activities and structured activities.

The effect of the presence of an adult is an interesting one since it may be unintentional. From our data we cannot say that children *necessarily* chose an activity because an adult was there. However, we can say that girls rather than boys tended to prefer activities where an adult happened to be present. This would suggest that the distribution of the adults in the nursery is a key factor in the environment.

# Chapter 9

# Use of language

The importance of language development in the early years has recently been given a great deal of emphasis. Not only does language facility play a crucial role in communication but also, arguably, in conceptualization and the symbolic manipulation of the environment. The role of the nursery in promoting development of language ability has been recognized by researchers (e.g. Tough, 1973) and the previous chapters have afforded evidence of the high priority accorded to the facilitation of language development amongst the aims of staff in nursery education. As Wood *et al.* (1980) point out, encouraging children to talk about their thoughts, experiences and feelings is seen by nursery practitioners as one of their principal contributions to the overall development of the children in their care.

Several empirical studies of language usage in the nursery have been conducted over the past twenty years, producing a number of different findings. Caldwell *et al.* (1967), for example, found that the role played by the teacher in eliciting language changed with the child's age. Thus, whereas with younger children teachers tended to inform (didactic teaching), with older children, questioning assumed greater importance, suggesting a sensitivity of staff to the linguistic needs of the children. Shields and Steiner (1973), in a study of spontaneous speech in three- to five-year-olds, discovered that conversations between children were slightly longer than those between teacher and pupil. Yet episodes of communication between adults and children exploring the child's area of thought and interest tended to be of longer duration than any other category of dialogue. This suggests that where staff are able to gauge the interests of the child accurately, conversations may be extended, and the development of the child's linguistic facility enabled. However, other studies

127

focusing on the linguistic forms used by adults and children in the nursery are more critical. Thus, Thomas (1973) suggests that opportunities to extend the child's usage of language, and through it his perceptions of the environment, are neglected within traditional nursery practice. This criticism is made the more telling by the findings of two more recent studies. Tizard (1979) shows that the quality of mother–child talk at home, built on shared topics and presuppositions, is richer and much more finely tuned than dialogue in nursery school. In addition, Sylva *et al.* (1980), in an observational study of nursery classes and playgroups, found that 'coherent conversations were few and far between' (p. 92).

The findings of the studies presented above would suggest that, although development of the child's linguistic abilities does undoubtedly occur in the nursery, this may be more a result of processes of normal maturation and interaction within the home, than the consequence of a hypothetical enabling environment within the nursery. Indeed, far from enhancing the child's linguistic development, traditional nursery practice may in some instances act as a hindrance. It may be argued that although teachers are frequently well aware of some of the linguistic 'needs' of children and the means by which these may be met through the medium of discourse, the free-play setting within the nursery precludes lengthy and/or systematic work with the child. As a consequence, the outcome for the child may be rather different from the objective originally outlined by the nursery staff. In particular, the child's expectations concerning the nature and customary duration of dialogue with adults may be established at a rather low level, a point which will be elaborated upon later. Given the broad scope of the present project, it was obvious that the language environments that obtain within pre-school provision should be areas of principal concern to us. This concern is reflected in the studies discussed below.

## The interactions

Our initial aim in the examination of language in the nursery was to describe the major characteristics of children's speech within the various forms of pre-school provision. Six nurseries from each of the four forms of provision described at the beginning of this report participated in the study and the subjects were eighty children of four years of age (twenty children divided equally between the two sexes in each type of nursery). Each subject was denoted as a target child and observed unobtrusively by a member of the research team for two separate periods of ten minutes, during which time each

TABLE 9.1: *Mean number of utterances by children in each form of pre-school provision*

|  | Boys | Girls | Combined |
|---|---|---|---|
| NS | 26.9 | 26.4 | 26.7 |
| NC | 31.1 | 29.1 | 30.1 |
| PG | 19.1 | 22.9 | 21.0 |
| DN | 23.2 | 24.2 | 23.7 |
| All contexts | 25.1 | 25.7 | 25.4 |

utterance of the child was event-sampled and entered on a matrix of predetermined categories. The recording system, which is described in detail in Appendix H.1, enabled the nature of the child's utterance, its immediate antecedent and the type of person addressed (boy, girl, adult) to be entered.

The basic unit of analysis was the utterance. Initial data analysis revealed the mean number of utterances per child for the combination of the two periods of observation. Comparison of the data for children in different contexts on this measure revealed marked similarities (Table 9.1).

Children in nursery classes tended to produce most utterances in the allotted time span while children in playgroups produced fewest. Overall, however, there was much individual variation and the differences between groups of children in the different types of nursery were not significant on this measure. Children's utterances tended to be fairly simple in grammatical form and discrete, rather than complex and extended in sequence, and these characteristics applied to conversations both with adults and with other children.

Perhaps surprisingly, in view of the findings of previous research on sex differences in early childhood development, girls and boys did not differ markedly in total amount of speech as measured by the mean number of utterances produced during the observation period. The number of utterances for boys and girls were similar in each type of establishment. However, some qualitative differences in language usage between the sexes were found, as described below.

As part of the recording procedure, note was made of whether each utterance of the child appeared spontaneously or was elicited by a preceding verbalization or action of another child or an adult. The analysis of the collected data revealed that, in general, children's speech tended to be spontaneous (see Table 9.2), although spontaneity of utterance was rather more characteristic of speech addressed to peers than of speech to adults. The amount of

TABLE 9.2: *Frequency and percentage of spontaneous and of elicited children's utterances by sex of child, type of nursery and addressee*

| | | To adult | | | | To child | | | |
| | | Spontaneous | | Adult-initiated | | Spontaneous | | Child-initiated | |
| | | no. | % | no. | % | no. | % | no. | % |
|---|---|---|---|---|---|---|---|---|---|
| NS | Boy | 34 | 52 | 32 | 49 | 148 | 73 | 54 | 27 |
| | Girl | 74 | 64 | 42 | 36 | 100 | 75 | 33 | 25 |
| | Combined | 108 | 59 | 74 | 41 | 248 | 74 | 87 | 26 |
| NC | Boy | 52 | 65 | 28 | 35 | 171 | 74 | 60 | 26 |
| | Girl | 61 | 54 | 53 | 46 | 121 | 68 | 56 | 32 |
| | Combined | 113 | 58 | 81 | 42 | 292 | 72 | 116 | 28 |
| PG | Boy | 64 | 67 | 32 | 33 | 76 | 80 | 19 | 20 |
| | Girl | 76 | 60 | 50 | 40 | 82 | 80 | 21 | 20 |
| | Combined | 140 | 63 | 82 | 37 | 158 | 80 | 40 | 20 |
| DN | Boy | 51 | 73 | 19 | 27 | 97 | 60 | 64 | 40 |
| | Girl | 55 | 63 | 32 | 37 | 103 | 67 | 51 | 33 |
| | Combined | 106 | 68 | 51 | 32 | 200 | 63 | 115 | 37 |

spontaneous speech to other children was greatest in the nursery class and least in the playgroups. By contrast, the quantity of spontaneous speech to adults was greatest in the playgroup and least in the day nursery. Although these differences are not great, they nevertheless may reflect underlying trends in the different forms of provision, a point which will be returned to later.

Children's speech was normally addressed to a single individual, whether child or adult, rather than to a group, and the few instances of group address have been excluded from the following part of the analysis. As Cooper (1979) points out when commenting upon a similar finding, the emphasis on talking to an individual, whether peer or adult, may be seen as a reflection of the social level of nursery-aged children and the social climate of the nursery school.

In general, the greater proportion of the children's speech was directed to peers rather than to adults (Figure 9.1). An exception to this pattern was found in playgroups, where it should be remembered that a superior adult:child ratio obtains. In this context, children's speech was approximately evenly divided between other children and adults. A sex difference emerged in the proportion of speech addressed to different classes of individuals (Figures 9.2 (a) and (b)). In three of the four contexts, girls addressed the greatest number of their utterances to adults and fewest to peers of the opposite sex. By contrast, the boys in three of the contexts addressed

FIGURE 9.1: *Percentage of speech addressed to another child or to an adult by children in each of four nursery provisions*

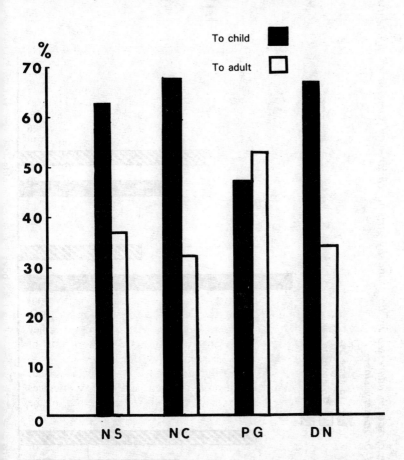

the greatest number of utterances to other boys, and fewest to girls. The exceptions to these patterns were the boys in the playgroup and the girls in the day nursery. In the former, the majority of utterances were addressed to adults. In the case of the day nursery girls, rather more utterances were addressed to boys than to other girls. In playgroups where, as already noted, there appeared to be more speech to adults than to children, the girls' tendency to speak most to adults is exaggerated. It is perhaps noteworthy that this was also the context in which the proportion of utterances directed to adults was greatest amongst the groups of boys. Girls' speech to adults was

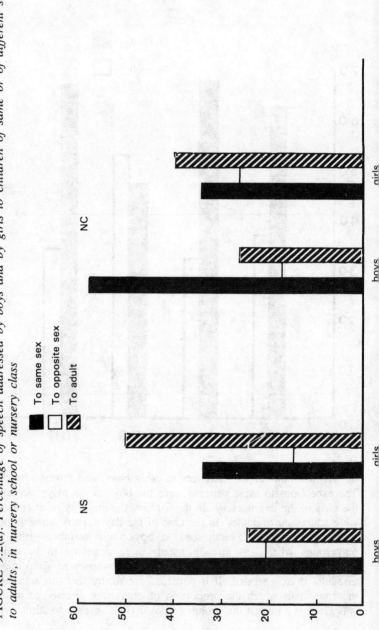

FIGURE 9.2(a): *Percentage of speech addressed by boys and by girls to children of same or of different sex, or to adults, in nursery school or nursery class*

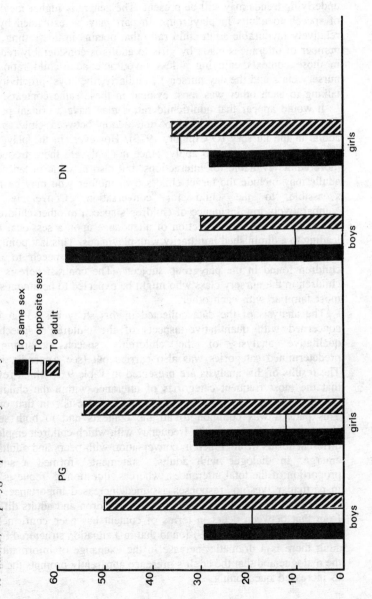

FIGURE 9.2(b): *Percentage of speech addressed by boys and by girls to children of same or of different sex, or to adults, in playgroup and day nursery*

Legend:
- To same sex
- To opposite sex
- To adult

reduced in nursery classes and day nurseries. Again an examination of the data failed to reveal significant differences on this measure between the contexts. This failure may, however, reflect large individual differences and the comparatively small sample size, and underlying trends may still be present. The generally higher incidence of speech to adults in playgroups in part may be explained by the relatively favourable adult:child ratio that obtains in this setting. The number of utterances made by girls to adults is considerably reduced in those contexts enjoying a less favourable adult:child ratio (the nursery class and the day nursery). Similarly, the boys' proclivity for talking to each other was most evident in these same contexts.

It would appear that adult:child ratios may have a crucial part to play in determining the level of interaction between children and adults in the nursery (O'Connor, 1975). However, in the playgroup special circumstances also apply, since not only are there frequently more adults available for interactions, but also in some instances the adults may include the target child's own mother who may be more accessible to the child for conversation. Conversely, the comparatively low incidence of children's speech to other children in this context may be a reflection of attendance upon a sessional basis leading to a diminished familiarity with playmates. This last point may explain partially the low levels of spontaneous speech to other children found in the playgroup subjects. The contrast here is with children in the nursery class who might be expected to be amongst the most familiar with each other.

The analysis of the data collected in this study has so far been concerned with quantitative aspects of the children's speech. A qualitative analysis of the children's speech according to predetermined categories was also carried out (see Appendix H.1). The results of this analysis are presented in Table 9.3, which reveals that the most frequent categories of utterance within the children's speech were 'statements', 'questions' and 'requests', in that order. This pattern was common to all the contexts and to both sexes. However, a difference in the frequency with which children employed different forms of utterance in conversation with peers and adults did emerge. In dialogue with adults, 'statements' formed a smaller proportion of the total utterances, whereas 'questions', 'requests' and in particular 'yes/no' responses assumed increased importance.

The finding that the dialogue between children and adults differed from that between peers in terms of content has been confirmed by other studies. Cooper (1979) found that in a situation structured by the adult there is a dramatic increase in the exchange of information in the dialogue and that the adult's presence apparently prompts the child to increased questioning.

TABLE 9.3: *Percentage of occurrence of different categories of children's utterance by addressee, sex of child and nursery context*

|  |  | Statement % | Explanation % | Request % | Question % | Yes/no % |
|---|---|---|---|---|---|---|
| **Child to child** | | | | | | |
| Boys | NS | 75.7 | 6.4 | 6.4 | 5.9 | 5.4 |
| | NC | 64.1 | 6.1 | 9.5 | 14.3 | 6.1 |
| | PG | 67.4 | 5.3 | 3.2 | 16.8 | 7.4 |
| | DN | 76.4 | 5.0 | 3.1 | 7.5 | 8.1 |
| | Combined | 70.9 | 5.8 | 6.4 | 10.5 | 6.4 |
| Girls | NS | 70.6 | 6.0 | 6.8 | 9.0 | 7.5 |
| | NC | 70.6 | 1.1 | 5.1 | 13.0 | 10.2 |
| | PG | 75.7 | 5.8 | 3.9 | 5.8 | 8.7 |
| | DN | 76.0 | 1.9 | 3.9 | 11.7 | 6.5 |
| | Combined | 72.7 | 3.5 | 4.9 | 10.5 | 8.5 |
| **Child to adult** | | | | | | |
| Boys | NS | 59.7 | 1.5 | 9.0 | 10.4 | 19.4 |
| | NC | 56.3 | 1.3 | 10.0 | 18.8 | 13.8 |
| | PG | 54.2 | 3.1 | 14.6 | 16.7 | 11.5 |
| | DN | 60.6 | 7.0 | 9.9 | 16.9 | 5.6 |
| | Combined | 57.0 | 3.8 | 11.4 | 15.8 | 12.3 |
| Girls | NS | 60.3 | 2.3 | 4.6 | 19.1 | 13.7 |
| | NC | 45.6 | 1.8 | 11.4 | 14.9 | 26.3 |
| | PG | 51.6 | 1.6 | 13.4 | 14.3 | 19.0 |
| | DN | 70.5 | 5.7 | 11.4 | 9.1 | 3.4 |
| | Combined | 56.0 | 2.6 | 10.3 | 14.7 | 16.4 |

That the nursery staff have a crucial role to play in the facilitation of the child's language development has been fervently argued for many years (e.g. Cooper, 1979). The study described above shows that although most children's speech is directed to peers (except in the playgroup) the proportion of utterances directed to adults is considerable. In addition, dialogue with an adult may assume a

TABLE 9.4: *Mean number of utterances per adult by nursery context and addressee*

| | | To children | | | To adults | Combined |
|---|---|---|---|---|---|---|
| | Boys | Girls | Group | All children | | |
| NS teachers | 23.6 | 22.1 | 0.9 | 46.6 | 10.1 | 56.7 |
| NS NNEBs | 16.8 | 21.2 | 0.0 | 38.0 | 12.0 | 50.0 |
| NC | 12.9 | 24.0 | 4.4 | 41.3 | 9.1 | 50.4 |
| PG | 18.5 | 17.1 | 1.5 | 37.1 | 15.1 | 52.2 |
| DN | 21.8 | 15.1 | 0.6 | 37.5 | 11.6 | 49.1 |

qualitatively different form from that with children. Several studies in recent years have emphasized the need to increase the linguistic interaction between nursery staff and children since, arguably, staff represent the prime resource of the nursery. Our second study, therefore, was conducted in order to examine the contribution of the adult to dialogue in the different forms of pre-school provision.

The subjects of this study consisted of fifty-four adults in the four different forms of nursery (ten teachers and ten nursery nurses in nursery schools; ten nursery nurses in nursery classes; ten playgroup supervisors; fourteen day nursery officers). An event-sampling procedure similar to that of the previous study was employed, with the utterance again forming the unit of data collection (see Appendix H.2), and each subject was observed for two separate periods of ten minutes during free-play sessions within the nursery. As with the previous parts of the project concerning the observation of adults, care was taken to make the process of observation as unobtrusive as possible.

Initial analysis focused on quantitative aspects of the nursery staffs' use of language. The mean number of utterances recorded within the twenty minutes of observation on each subject is given in Table 9.4. Most adult utterances were directed at children rather than other adults, and to individual children rather than groups. Nursery school teachers tended to produce the greatest number of utterances in the given time span, playgroup supervisors least, but individual differences within the groups of subjects were large, reflecting perhaps the importance of individual *styles* of interaction within the nursery (see Wood *et al.*, 1980). Most conversation between adults was found in the playgroup. In this context, dialogue with other adults, in particular the mothers of children who may be present, may be seen as an important aspect of the role of the playgroup supervisor. Least conversation between adults was found in the nursery classes where there are generally fewer adults present and thus available to talk to and where the pressure on adults to interact with children may be at its greatest as a consequence of the relatively poor child:adult ratios.

If, in terms of the quantity of speech, adults in the different contexts are similar, differences emerge when the quality of the patterns of speech is examined. As previously, utterances were divided into different categories by content (see Appendix H.2). The analysis of the utterances recorded is given in Table 9.5. The most frequent form of utterance employed by adults was the 'statement', followed by the 'question'. Statements may be informative and questions may be regarded as useful interlocutory devices but both forms of utterance may in certain circumstances become stereotyped, repetitive and banal, for example: 'Yes, it's a square' and 'What colour's that?'

Two categories of utterance which may be seen as having an unambiguously educational function, 'explanations' and 'options', were disappointingly limited in their frequency of occurrence. Perhaps reassuringly, they appeared most frequently in the speech of teachers but even here did not assume importance. This finding is similar to those of Thomas (1973) and Tizard *et al.* (1976a).

Inspection of Table 9.5 shows that staff in day nurseries tend to be dissimilar from their colleagues in other forms of pre-school provision in several aspects of their use of language. In general, staff language in the day nursery would seem to assume a more imperative air with a higher frequency of commands as opposed to requests. Rebukes from staff were comparatively frequent and the speech of day nursery officers shows the lowest level of approbation. In summing up these findings in the day nursery, a picture emerges of a language environment that tends to be rather more negative than the other contexts.

In general, the sex of the child addressed had little effect upon the content of the utterance. Usually, boys tended to be subject to a greater number of commands and requests from adults and, in the day nursery, to a greater number of rebukes. By way of contrast, rather more questions, explanations and options were addressed to girls. These comparatively minor differences in the dialogues between nursery staff and children of different sexes may reflect both actual and perceived differences in the behaviour of boys and girls. Teachers and nursery nurses may perceive boys as rougher and more boisterous and may tend to change their own behaviour accordingly if they consider these to be undesirable traits. Certainly, there is some evidence to suggest that boys engage in more physical activity in the nursery and this may necessitate proscription on the grounds of safety.

The tentative conclusions that have been drawn from the qualitative analysis cited above are congruent with the data obtained on the

TABLE 9.5: Mean and percentage occurrence of different categories of adult utterance to children by nursery context

| | Statement/comment | Explanation | Command | Request | Question | Yes/no | Approbation | Option | Comfort | Rebuke | Total |
|---|---|---|---|---|---|---|---|---|---|---|---|
| **NS teachers** | | | | | | | | | | | |
| Mean | 14.7 | 5.9 | 2.1 | 4.3 | 12.2 | 0.7 | 2.8 | 2.6 | 0.1 | 1.2 | 46.6 |
| % | 32 | 13 | 5 | 9 | 26 | 2 | 6 | 6 | 0 | 3 | |
| **NS NNEBs** | | | | | | | | | | | |
| Mean | 10.0 | 3.8 | 2.3 | 5.9 | 8.6 | 0.2 | 4.1 | 2.3 | 0.1 | 0.7 | 38.0 |
| % | 26 | 10 | 6 | 16 | 23 | 1 | 11 | 6 | 0 | 2 | |
| **NC NNEBs** | | | | | | | | | | | |
| Mean | 14.6 | 3.8 | 3.0 | 2.7 | 12.6 | 1.5 | 2.3 | 0.4 | 0.4 | 0.0 | 41.3 |
| % | 35 | 9 | 7 | 6 | 31 | 4 | 6 | 1 | 1 | 0 | |
| **PG** | | | | | | | | | | | |
| Mean | 14.8 | 3.1 | 1.9 | 2.4 | 11.2 | 0.6 | 1.1 | 1.2 | 0.6 | 0.2 | 37.1 |
| % | 40 | 8 | 5 | 7 | 30 | 2 | 3 | 3 | 2 | 1 | |
| **DN NNEBs** | | | | | | | | | | | |
| Mean | 9.1 | 1.6 | 8.2 | 3.7 | 8.5 | 1.8 | 0.5 | 0.4 | 0.5 | 3.2 | 37.5 |
| % | 24 | 4 | 22 | 10 | 23 | 5 | 1 | 1 | 1 | 9 | |

TABLE 9.6: *Mean number and percentage of adult utterances by nursery context and form of elicitation*

|  | Spontaneous | | Child-initiated (speech) | | Child-initiated (action) | | Mean Total |
|---|---|---|---|---|---|---|---|
|  | Mean | % | Mean | % | Mean | % |  |
| NS teachers | 20.4 | 43.8 | 14.2 | 30.5 | 12.0 | 25.8 | 46.6 |
| NS NNEBs | 19.6 | 51.6 | 7.2 | 18.9 | 11.2 | 29.5 | 38.0 |
| NC NNEBs | 17.8 | 47.3 | 14.7 | 25.3 | 8.8 | 27.4 | 41.3 |
| PG | 20.8 | 56.1 | 10.5 | 28.3 | 5.8 | 15.6 | 37.1 |
| DN | 11.8 | 31.5 | 7.0 | 18.7 | 18.7 | 49.9 | 37.5 |

spontaneity of the adult utterances (see Table 9.6). Whereas the utterances of playgroup supervisors and nursery teachers showed the greatest tendency to spontaneity, the utterances of day nursery officers tended to be elicited by the behaviour of the children and, in particular, by their actions. The finding that teachers' utterances tend to be spontaneous corresponds with the assertion that teachers in nursery schools tend to dominate conversations (Cooper, 1979). Certainly it would suggest that adults are the main instigators of conversation in the nursery. Nevertheless, children may still have an important role to play in the setting-up of dialogue, and the initial overture that the child makes may have a critical influence on the determination of whether the child manages to gain access to the adult's attention and upon the length and form of an ensuing conversation.

As a consequence, the third study of this chapter was designed to investigate the nature of the spontaneous overtures children make to adults in nursery schools and to examine adult responses in relation to them. Adults in nursery schools were chosen as the targets of this study and a sample of both nursery teachers and nursery nurses was obtained in order to establish whether children distinguished between the two roles and whether the adults fulfilling them responded in different ways. Observations on a total of fourteen teachers and fifteen nursery assistants were made by two members of the project team. Again the subjects of this study were accustomed to the presence of observers and no apparent alteration in their behaviour occurred during the course of the study.

Each subject was observed individually during sessions of free-play activity until a total of fifteen interactions between the target and an approaching child had taken place. An interaction was deemed to consist of the child's overture and the adult's *initial* response or responses in utterances. Each interaction was noted in full by the observer who remained sufficiently close to record it without distracting the participants. Each consecutive interaction recorded involved a different child. However, children within the nursery may be represented more than once in the data and allowance should be made for this when consideration is given to the results. Where further dialogue followed upon the initial overture and response its occurrence was noted but not included in the main analysis, described below, although further comments about these extended interactions will be made later. In addition to the verbatim accounts of the interactions, the total observation time for each adult subject, the activities she engaged in and her location in the nursery were recorded. A *post hoc* categorization of the children's speech and the adult's responses was made upon completion of data collection, details of which may be found in Appendix I. The duration of the observation session for individual target adults was very variable, with a range between 15 and 135 minutes (means 48.9 and 45.7 minutes for teachers and nursery nurses respectively). The data would suggest, therefore, that some adults are more sought out by children for interaction than others, but that the nominal role of the adult may not be a key factor here. Overall, the majority (74 per cent) of the interactions occurred indoors, most frequently (55 per cent) when the adult was engaged in associative activity.

## Children's overtures

A total of 210 overtures made to teachers and 225 made to nursery nurses were observed and recorded. The result of an analysis of the overtures by category is given in Table 9.7, which shows the percentages of overtures of different kinds addressed to teachers and nursery nurses. Inspection of the table would suggest that despite differences in training and in the role in the nursery, teachers and nursery nurses are the subjects of similar overtures from the children.

The conversational openings made by children to adults could be further classified into three superordinate categories by reference to their content: openings concerning aspects of the present nursery situation; openings concerning other children present in the nursery; openings related to aspects outside the nursery, especially in the child's home. The overwhelming majority of overtures (76 per cent) were concerned with aspects of the current activities within the nursery. By contrast, references to contexts outside the nursery were represented in only 7 per cent of the children's overtures. These

TABLE 9.7: *Percentages of children's overtures of different categories*

| | Teacher % | Nursery assistant % | Teacher & nursery assistant (combined) % |
|---|---|---|---|
| Request | 23.3 | 18.2 | 20.7 |
| Show | 17.1 | 17.8 | 17.5 |
| Statement | 15.2 | 14.7 | 14.9 |
| Question | 10.5 | 8.0 | 9.2 |
| Other child | 7.6 | 8.9 | 8.3 |
| Home | 7.1 | 6.7 | 6.9 |
| Observation | 5.2 | 7.1 | 6.2 |
| Personal | 4.3 | 5.3 | 4.8 |
| Intention | 3.3 | 5.8 | 4.6 |
| Domestic | 2.9 | 4.9 | 3.9 |
| Q-explanation | 3.3 | 2.7 | 3.0 |

findings are generally in accord with those made by Wood *et al.* (1980). They state that talk about on-going activities (here-and-now) occupied 70 per cent of all utterances by the adult and that the principal topics of conversation were the child addressed and objects and possessions. The findings would, therefore, seem particularly robust. Even where statements relating to situations or events beyond the immediate nursery context were made, they were sometimes prompted by the current setting as, for example, when a nursery nurse got the nursery's pet rabbit out and children started to discuss their own pets: 'I've got a rabbit'; 'We have got a yellow bird'.

Of the individual forms of overture the most frequent were 'request' and 'show'. Both forms seek adult approval, 'request' seeking consent in the choice of activity (e.g. 'Can I play in the water?', 'Teacher, can I sit by you?'); 'show', approval of action or product (e.g. 'Teacher, look'). Both forms can be seen as overt demands for attention. 'Statement' was another frequently occurring category of overture, consisting of comments about on-going activities, e.g. 'I've got some pastry', 'We are playing at cops – I'm a cop'. 'Comments about other children' were categorized separately and usually took the form of complaints (e.g. 'He's got my wheel') or tale-telling (e.g. 'Teacher, a little boy, he pinched that girl's plasticine'), although they could on occasion show *bonhomie* (e.g. 'I saw Craig, that's my friend').

About 10 per cent of children's opening utterances were in the form of questions. (In fact, more questions than appear in this category were asked, but several were more properly included under other categories; e.g. 'Can we go out now?' is a request, while 'Are you going out now?' is a question.) Questions were quite varied (e.g. 'Shall I do 5?' 'Are you going to talk to my mummy?' 'What are you making?' 'Where can I get a chair from?') but were defined by the seeking of some kind of verbal reference. Questions that sought and required an explanation (Q-Explanation) were, however, very infrequent, representing only about 3 per cent of all overtures.

The importance of fantasy play has been greatly emphasised by teachers, yet only two overtures of the 435 recorded referred to the child's play in this domain. The first example occurred when a child at model play said, 'He's going in the river for a swim – he's jumping about', apparently referring to an imaginary character and pretending the block area was a river. The adult's response was: 'Well, remember what I said, don't swing those bricks about.' The second example occurred outside when an adult went towards a shed and a child said, 'You'd better not open that because there's a big bad gorilla in there.' The adult replied, 'Oh, I see.' The section on fantasy play (Chapter 7) reveals a relative lack of involvement of adults in such play, and the paucity of overtures concerning fantasy play in the present study seems to indicate that children do not expect adults to participate in this form of activity.

### Adults' responses

Thus far we have considered the children's overtures. What then of the adult responses? In a second part of the analysis, adult responses were categorized into thirteen types as described in Appendix I. The proportions of different types of *initial* response given by teachers and nursery assistants are presented in Table 9.8. Inspection of this table reveals that the most frequently occurring response to a child's overture was a question. Three principal forms of questions were identified amongst these responses (Table 9.9):

(a)  Simple questions asked to clarify what the child had said because the adult had misheard, or did not understand what the child said (e.g. 'Do what, my love?'); or of a minimal nature (e.g. 'Has he?').
(b)  Questions to elicit further information from the child in reference to what he had just said (e.g. 'Have you done that yourself?', 'What have you done?', 'Where's the foal?').

TABLE 9.8: *Percentages of different adult responses to children's overtures*

| | Teacher | Nursery assistant | Teacher & nursery assistant (combined) |
|---|---|---|---|
| | % | % | % |
| Question | 26.8 | 29.0 | 27.9 |
| Statement | 18.2 | 19.6 | 18.9 |
| Instruction | 12.4 | 10.6 | 11.5 |
| Minimal | 11.8 | 8.8 | 10.2 |
| Approbation | 6.1 | 7.6 | 6.9 |
| Repetition | 4.5 | 4.7 | 4.6 |
| Explanation | 5.4 | 1.5 | 3.4 |
| Suggestion | 3.8 | 2.6 | 3.2 |
| Intention | 3.2 | 2.9 | 3.1 |
| Delay | 1.6 | 4.4 | 3.1 |
| Negative | 1.3 | 4.4 | 2.9 |
| No response | 1.9 | 2.9 | 2.4 |
| Scold | 3.2 | 0.9 | 2.0 |

TABLE 9.9: *Percentages of different types of adults' questions*

| Question type | Teacher | Nursery assistant | Teacher nursery assistant (combined) |
|---|---|---|---|
| | % | % | % |
| (a) | 20.2 | 18.2 | 19.1 |
| (b) | 69.0 | 79.8 | 74.9 |
| (c) | 10.7 | 2.0 | 6.0 |

(c) Questions about the properties of objects (e.g. 'What's the shape inside the triangle?').

Although individual variations existed, almost all adults exhibited the same pattern of questioning – giving responses of question type (b) more frequently than of type (a) or (c) (75, 19 and 6 per cent of all questions respectively).

The second and most frequent adult response came in the form of a 'statement' or 'comment'. There was considerable variety among responses classified in this way, but what they had in common was that each was related to what the child had just said, and was conversational in tone and subject matter, confirming the child's response or adding further information, e.g.

Child: I've finished. [milk]
Adult: So I see. You've got a white moustache.

Child: My daddy is on a train now.
Adult: Yes, he's going to be on the train all day.

Child: Look at mine.
Adult: Oh yes, you've been making patterns with the sponge.
Child: We've got two twins.
Adult: Two twin boys and two twin girls.

Child: Peter won't let Colin have a go on the pedal car.
Adult: Well, Colin looks quite happy playing in the sand.

'Minimal responses' – e.g. 'Yes' (in reply to a request), 'I see' – were relatively common and were usually elicited when an adult was involved in something which the child was interrupting. There was also quite a high frequency of 'repetitions' (4.6 per cent), e.g.

Child: Mrs B, my baby's coming here.
Adult: Your baby's coming here – what is it – a boy or a girl?

or

Child: I can do a cockerel.
Adult: You can do a cockerel.

It may be worthwhile considering both these findings in relation to the studies of adult attention spans which were found to be highly fragmented by children's interruptions. The place of the 'minimal response' in this context is fairly obvious. It may be argued that the repetition of part of the phrase used by the child in this overture also represents a leading choice, allowing the adult greater time to contemplate a more elaborate response or to return to continue with her original activity or conversation. It is interesting that children were seldom ignored completely. 'No response' was included as a response category in order to see how often children failed to gain the adult's attention. This category was infrequent (2.4 per cent of all responses) but occasionally a child would have to ask two or three times before receiving a response, which again reflects the demands constantly made upon adults which they cannot always meet.

Arguably, some of the adults' responses could be interpreted as being more informative and stimulating to the child than others. Thus, in the former category one might place 'questions' (types (b) and (c)), 'statements', 'explanations', 'instructions', 'suggestions', 'intentions' and 'negatives'. This group would then contrast with that composed of 'questions' (type (a)), 'minimal responses', 'approbations', 'repetitions', 'delays', 'scolds' and 'no response' which might be termed uninformative and unstimulating.

According to this categorization the adults' responses to children's overtures were usually reasonably stimulating and informative (70 per cent of all utterances). Moreover, no real difference between teachers and nursery nurses was found. However, the 30 per cent of uninformative responses is still quite high and probably reflects the demands made on adults, as previously noted, and the fact that many overtures were simple and did not require a more elaborate response. In addition, although 'approbations' may be seen as being relatively uninformative utterances it may be argued that they encourage children and create a warmer atmosphere, if not used in a superficial manner.

Thus far, we have considered the child's overtures and the adult's responses to them separately. It remains to consider the relationship between the two sets of utterances. Table 9.10 shows the most frequently occurring responses to each kind of overture.

The most frequently occurring child overture was a 'request' to do some kind of activity. The most common adult response was a 'statement' about what the child had just said, e.g.

Child: I want to carry the clay there.
Adult: There you are then, it's heavy though.

'Instructions' were also frequent, e.g.

Child: Mrs Jones, can I make my aeroplane now?
Adult: You go on to the woodwork bench then.

as were 'questions', e.g.

Child: Can I do that?
Adult: You want to do some finger painting?

Other fairly frequent responses were 'delay', or a 'minimal response', usually affirmative, such as 'Yes, dear'.

Children frequently showed adults objects or pieces of work with a comment (Show), and the most frequent response to this kind of overture was a 'question' about what the child was showing, e.g.

145

TABLE 9.10: *Relationship between child overtures and adult responses*

| Child Approaches | Percentages of most frequently occurring adult responses | | | | No. different types response | Total no. responses |
|---|---|---|---|---|---|---|
| Request | Statement | 19.4 | Delay | 11.1 | 12 | 124 |
|  | Instruction | 18.5 | Minimal | 10.4 |  |  |
|  | Question | 17.7 |  |  |  |  |
| Show | Question | 31.2 | Statement | 11.6 | 12 | 138 |
|  | Approbation | 23.2 |  |  |  |  |
| Statement | Question | 22.7 | Minimal | 15.5 | 11 | 97 |
|  | Statement | 21.6 | Instruction | 11.3 |  |  |
| Question | Question | 32.2 | Minimal | 11.9 | 9 | 59 |
|  | Statement | 25.4 |  |  |  |  |
| Other child | Statement | 30.6 | Instruction | 10.2 | 11 | 49 |
|  | Question | 24.5 | Suggestion | 10.2 |  |  |
| Home | Question | 61.9 | Statement | 14.3 | 5 | 42 |
|  |  |  | Repetition | 14.3 |  |  |
| Observation | Question | 33.3 | Statement | 19.0 | 12 | 42 |
|  |  |  | Negative | 11.0 |  |  |
| Personal | Question | 40.0 |  |  | 8 | 25 |
| Intention | Question | 32.1 |  |  | 8 | 28 |
| Domestic | Minimal | 34.6 |  |  | 8 | 26 |
|  | Instruction | 26.9 |  |  |  |  |
| Q-explanation | Statement | 39.1 |  |  | 6 | 23 |
|  | Question | 21.7 |  |  |  |  |

'What's that all about?' or an 'approbation', e.g. 'Oh, that's beautiful'. Fairly frequently adults would make a 'statement' or 'comment' about what was being shown, e.g. 'Oh, you've stuck it on upside down'.

When children made 'statements' about on-going activities in the nursery, the adults most frequently responded by questioning the child about what he had said, or made a 'statement' or 'comment' in response. Interestingly, the most frequent response to a child's 'question' was for the adult to pose another question, e.g.

Child: The lights are upside down now, aren't they?
Adult: You like them upside down, do you?

Most children's overtures elicited a wide variety of different kinds of responses but when children talked about their home or experiences outside the nursery, only five different kinds of adult response were made. In most instances, the children were questioned about what they had said, e.g.

Child: We have got a yellow bird.
Adult: Is it a canary or a budgie?

Sometimes adults made 'statements' or 'comments' about what the child had said, or simply repeated the child's words, e.g.

Child: My daddy's got some white roses in the garden.
Adult: Some white roses?

In either instance it is clear that the adult has difficulty in elaborating the conversation through shared experience.

Finally, when children asked questions seeking explanations, they usually received a 'statement/comment' in response, e.g.

Child: Why don't they put them in here?
Adult: I don't think they want to.

or another 'question', e.g.

Child: What is this?
Adult: What does it look like?

Only rarely did children receive explanations that could be termed elaborate. Indeed, a lack of elaboration could be said to characterize nursery discourse, as evidenced by the fact that the majority of children's overtures elicited a single adult response in the first instance and that it was rare for more than two types of response to be given in the initial reply.

It should be remembered that the analysis above deals only with the child's overtures and the adult's initial response or responses. Analysis ceased when the adult ceased speaking and/or a further child speech occurred, since it was not always possible to record *further* speech accurately. However, seventy-two examples of extended conversations are noted and were classified according to the form of the adult response preceding the extended dialogue. Thus, for example, if a child made a statement and was followed by an adult making a statement and then asking a question to which the child replied with another statement, the extended interaction would be classified under 'question'. Table 9.11 shows the proportion of extended interactions grouped in this way and reveals that extended interactions occurred most frequently after questions when preceding adult responses are examined. No other form of response seems very likely to elicit further conversation.

TABLE 9.11: *Percentages of extended interactions grouped according to the preceding adult response*

| | | | |
|---|---|---|---|
| Question (b) | 58.3 | Question (c) | 2.8 |
| Question (a) | 11.3 | Explanation | 2.8 |
| Statement | 7.0 | Scold | 2.8 |
| Instruction | 5.6 | Request | 1.4 |
| Minimal | 5.6 | Delay | 1.4 |
| | | Negative | 1.4 |

**Discussion**

The importance of the adult's contribution to dialogue in the nursery should not be underestimated. Indeed, it has received a great deal of emphasis, notably through the work of Joan Tough and her colleagues (see Tough, 1976; 1979). However, the present series of studies shows little evidence that staff within various forms of provision are extending the children's use of language in the manner prescribed by researchers; and this finding is in accord with those of other projects which have addressed themselves to this area (e.g. Wood *et al.*, 1980). Although it should be stressed that within each group of adults there was a variety of individual styles of language use, a general picture of the language environment of the nursery may be built up. Perhaps the most noteworthy features of this environment are the tendency to limit speech to references to current events and the overall paucity of elaboration and complexity in dialogue. Complex conversations involving explanations, projections into the future or detailed accounts of past events are comparatively (and perhaps disappointingly) rare. This state of affairs would seem to be independent of the training of the staff and may result from factors that are common to all forms of nursery context adhering to extended sessions of free-play. In many ways these characteristics of the typical nursery language environment may be seen as appropriate to the age and ability level of the children. Children between the ages of three and five tend to be involved with the concrete here-and-now, rather than the abstract future or past and to have limited language-related abilities. However, they may well be capable of pursuing a dialogue at a higher level than is typically seen in the nursery and factors other than the children's overall ability level may be of greater consequence in determining the nature of the speech between nursery staff and the children in their care. For example, Wood *et al.* (1980) have shown that the management of tasks allocated to a particular adult and the design of the building and grounds in which these tasks have to be performed may have an important effect upon the adult's style of discourse. In addition, the training that the members of staff have received may have repercussions upon their language usage. For example, in the present series of studies, nursery teachers tended to produce rather more speech that might be considered enabling (i.e. explanations, options) than their colleagues from different forms of training. However, differences between the groups of adults were comparatively small and the major influence upon dialogue in the nursery may be the nature of the free-play period itself and the style of interaction between member of staff and child that this period may encourage. Previous studies (e.g. Thomas, 1973; Tizard *et al.*, 1976a) have been either explicitly or implicitly critical of the language employed in dialogue in the nursery. By implication at least, deficiencies in the form and style of speech employed may be laid at the door of the members of staff of the nursery. However, simple denigration of the expertise of nursery staff in fostering dialogue with children would, we believe, be both an unwarranted simplification and an injustice to the many efforts of the staff. Certainly, there is evidence to suggest that nursery staff are well aware of the importance of fostering children's language facility and of the means by which this may be carried out (e.g. Tough, 1976). The reason why it is difficult to put into practice ideas about extending children's language usage may lie in other features of the environment.

As previous studies in this volume have shown, the adult in the nursery represents a primary focus for the attention of children and is, as a consequence, subject to numerous overtures, both verbal and physical, during the course of the free-play session. It would seem to us that major difficulties faced by the adult who wishes to extend a child's overture into a conversation are the determination of the form which her initial response to the child's overture should take and the choice of method for dealing with the almost inevitable interruptions from other children that occur during the course of the conversation.

Few adults in the nursery would consciously wish to deny any children the opportunity to converse with them. However, there is a danger that by responding to all overtures made to her the adult will be unable to pursue a conversation with a particular child to a satisfactory conclusion. As Wood *et al.* (1980) point out, if the teacher or playgroup worker is going to acknowledge every opening from a group of children, no idea or experience is going to be elaborated in depth. As a consequence, discourse between adult and children may take on a rather disjointed, superficial quality. Evidence of this was given in the findings of a pilot study carried out on the present project in which teachers and nursery nurses in nursery schools were equipped with a radio-microphone in order that their conversations during free-play periods might be recorded in detail. An example of an adult attempting to respond to numerous overtures is given below:

Adult: Put your name card there, Simon.
Child 1: Look what I'm making.
Adult: Don't forget to leave a big space in between.
That was it, Sean?
Child 1: That's the sky.
Adult: That's the colour of it. Is it a windy day?
Child 1: Yes.
Child 2: Mrs Lewis, Mrs Lewis.
Adult: Oh, that looks interesting.
[To other child] On the tray.
Child 2: That's a flower. That's a flower.
Adult: Is it, Andrew?
Child 3: Mrs Lewis.
Adult: Have you got some flowers in your garden?
Have you? What sort?
Child 2: Lots of big 'uns.
Adult: A big flower.
And what's it called?
Child 2: A wasp-flower.
Adult: A wasp-flower? Do lots of wasps land on it?
Child 3: I've made a big duck. I've made a big duck.
Adult: Oh, yes, you're good at drawing ducks, aren't you?
Mm? Don't forget to put his beak on.
That's a good try, Simon.
What about putting some colours on, Mark? Make it nice and bright.
Child 4: Mrs Lewis, I've done that.
Adult: Good.

This and similar examples of discourse have an underlying air of superficiality. That adults attempt to respond to the majority of the overtures of nursery children is evident from the relative infrequency of the 'no response' category in the study of interactions described above. Yet in free-play the overtures tend to persist. An alternative for the adult is to employ a fending technique such as a 'minimal response', but even this may have deleterious consequences for the current conversation.

As already stated, conversations with children tend to be focused upon present activity. Adults in the nursery frequently see it as an objective to encourage the child to talk about events that have occurred in the past and to predict future occurrences, and the need for such an extension of the discourse is frequently promulgated by researchers. Tough (1973) cites a conversation between a mother and child which includes recall of an excursion by train that they made together as an example of a dialogue between actors who share a common environment and history. The nursery worker is perhaps more limited in the extent to which she can share the child's world. Perhaps partly as a consequence, much of the dialogue between adult and child may take the form of requests for, and provision of, information that in other circumstances might be available to both participants. Evidence of this may be seen in the frequency with which adults ask questions of the children. As previously stated, questions may be useful interlocutory devices when used in proper proportion, but too great a frequency of questioning may lead to stereotyped and programmatic exchanges. As Wood *et al.* (1980) found, adults who ask lots of questions tend to get answers but little more. In contrast, adults who offer children lots of their own personal views ideas and observations tend to receive a more elaborate and less predictable response from the child. In a later experimental study Wood and Wood (1983) investigated different styles of talking to a small sample of young children and found that the more questions a teacher asks, the less likely children are to take up opportunities to show initiative, to respond with unrequested information, to elaborate upon answers or to produce longer utterances. Moreover, the study showed that any attempt simply to increase the frequency of demanding questions in a session did not result in a significant increase in the amount of hypothesizing, remembering or describing which went on. By contrast, children did respond well to their teacher's attempts to reason and to speculate in their presence.

These studies do not deny the importance of skilful and sensitive questioning in discourse with young children. Rather they point out that alternative styles may be available which are as effective and which do not result in the adult assuming control of the dialogue. It has been shown (Wood and Wood, 1983) that in the experimental setting the teacher could change her style of talking to the children. Whether such a change is readily capable of being effected in the free-play setting remains conjectural. Indeed, it may be argued that a paradoxical state obtains in the nursery during free-play sessions. Although adults are eager to develop language facilities in children, their very enthusiasm may cause them to dominate the children in conversation and preclude certain forms of discourse. Moreover, even where the adult may dominate a particular dialogue she may not be in overall control of the setting in that she may be subject to interruptions to which she may find it difficult not to respond, even if only to a minimal degree.

To conclude this chapter, let us quote another passage from the pilot project mentioned above. Even where adults attempt to enter the child's world in a wholehearted way, difficulties abound:

Teacher: Is it a cowboy game you're playing?
Thomas: Er, it's more like space to me.
Teacher: Oh, I see, a space game.
          So Richard would be Darth Veda, would he?
Richard: Darth Veda?
Thomas: No, but Darth Veda's a baddy too. You can't kill him.
Teacher: Well, you said Richard was the baddy.
Thomas: I mean space – but not Star Wars space.
          Ordinary space.

# Chapter 10

# Adjustment of new children

## The first six months at nursery school

Entry into a nursery is likely to be the first time a child will have left, for any considerable period of time, the relative familiarity and security of the home and family. This is the first transition in a sequence which will take the child from one educational setting to another until ultimately he leaves school. Arguably, it is also one of, if not the, most important transitions for the child and his parents. As Blatchford *et al.* (1982) point out, the popular view is that the first major transition is at the time when the child is approaching the age of five and entering infant or first school. Yet for the many children who have already attended a pre-school, the magnitude of this step may be somewhat diminished since they already have intimate experience of an environment outside the home. In addition, they will be familiar with many aspects of the role of teachers and with some of the activities to be found in the reception class (Cleave *et al.*, 1982). Perhaps as importantly, their parents' feelings about separation from the child and their attitudes towards the receiving school may already have been coloured by their contacts with the pre-school.

This first transition from home to pre-school is thus an important one for all concerned. For the child it is his first step alone in the outside world. For the pre-school staff, it represents a fresh responsibility, since it is they who are to continue the process of introducing the child to his cultural heritage and in some instances to commence his formal education. Nor should we underestimate the importance of this step for the child's parents. For many parents, the entry of their child into the pre-school is the first time that they

153

have placed his care and development into the hands of another person, even if there is an understanding that this is a new partnership that they are entering into. This step marks a change in their relationship with their child and a fresh relationship with a group of adults, the pre-school staff. For both parents and child, it would seem that the response of the pre-school to the delicate and sensitive initial period of entry into the new environment is potentially of critical importance.

How, then, is the introductory period handled by pre-schools? What is the reaction of the child to this new, busy, stimulating and, perhaps in some ways, frightening environment? The first question is obviously an important one and has been the subject of recent research (Blatchford *et al.*, 1982). As has been pointed out, entry into pre-school is a complex process which subsumes a number of different events and points of view, and for a full understanding each of these needs investigation. However, within the scope of this book we shall confine ourselves to consideration of the second question, noting only that most of the nurseries described in this chapter employ a fairly typical staggered entry procedure for the admission of new children. During the last weeks of the term prior to the term of admission, the children visit the nursery in the company of their mothers on two or three days of the week, each visit lasting approximately one hour. After several such visits, the mother may be encouraged to go into a room adjoining the playroom, allowing the child to explore the nursery on his own while secure in the knowledge that mother is not far away. Upon official admission, too, the mother may remain with the child for short periods during the first few days, the length of time without contact with the mother being gradually extended until such time as the child is attending the nursery alone for the complete session. In our experience, most nurseries were fairly flexible about the length of time the mother stayed during the early period of the child's career in the nursery, attempting thereby to meet the needs of the individual parent and child.

Arguably, by the time maternal support is withdrawn for the whole session, the nursery environment is fairly familiar and the child has come to place a considerable degree of trust in the pre-school staff. Nevertheless, the child may still appear somewhat apprehensive. As McGrew's observations suggest, new children's reactions at entry vary greatly (McGrew, 1972). Of the sixteen children he observed, four cried when their mothers said goodbye or within a few minutes of their departure, and two had to be restrained by the nurse from running after them. However, other new children quickly entered into play activities and ignored their mothers, who usually left after a few minutes. Even in the case of overtly confident children, however, their behaviour in the initial period may be different from that which occurs later. McGrew found conspicuous changes in the new children's behaviour during their first five days in the nursery. Notably, children tended to exhibit less 'automanipulation' and less glancing and looking around on the fifth day when compared to the first. They also tended to become more mobile during this period.

But do behavioural changes continue to occur over longer periods of time? In order to answer this question, we felt that systematic observation of the behaviour of such new children would be desirable. Accordingly, twenty children (ten boys and ten girls) were observed over a six-month period, initial observations commencing during the children's first week in school. Each child was observed for two sessions, each of thirty minutes, and the data were then averaged. Pairs of observations were made on each child at monthly intervals except during the first month when observations were made during the first and second fortnights of the month (see Figure 10.1). A checklist of the kind used in a previous study (Chapter 5) was used for recording the child's behaviour, making the data collected in the two studies comparable.

During the first months, the predominant activities observed in the new children were *play with materials* and *look/watch*. The level of the first activity was maintained during the six-month period. However, following an initial rise, the level of looking/watching declined significantly between the second and the sixth month to levels similar to those seen in the previous study of children acclimatized to the nursery environment. Physical play and fantasy play were initially present at low levels and tended to increase with time but the trends failed to reach significance. The incidence of gestures, a behaviour category similar to McGrew's (1972) 'automanipulation', decreased significantly from a fairly low level to almost nil at the end of the six-month period. Several comments may be made about these data.

First, since the level of play with materials is rather greater in the present study than in the previous studies reported here (Chapter 5), it would appear that this kind of activity has a particular attraction for new children. The activities available present novel stimuli for many children who are free to explore the possibilities of their new environment. By contrast, the level of fantasy play is initially low. This finding is in accord with what we said about play in Chapter 1. Novelty in the child's physical environment usually elicits an exploratory response provided that other aspects of the environment are not overwhelmingly threatening. The sand tray, the collage table

155

FIGURE 10.1: *Changes during the first six months at nursery school in the five most common categories of behaviour*

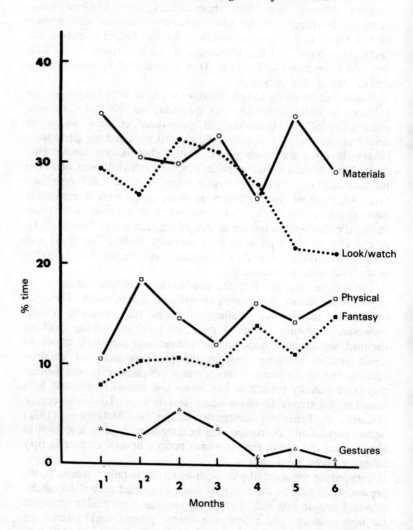

and other equipment, attractively presented, call out to be visited and examined. Often play at materials does not have to be accompanied by interaction with other children. The new child may absorb himself without the necessity of having to deal with the more volatile element of the new environment – people. Fantasy play, however,

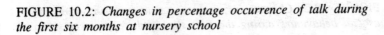

FIGURE 10.2: *Changes in percentage occurrence of talk during the first six months at nursery school*

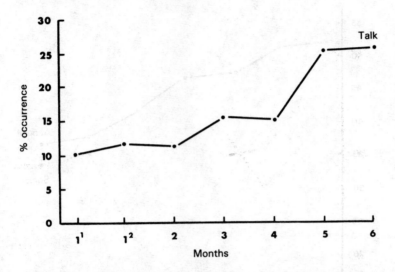

frequently requires the child to co-operate with other children, to negotiate over roles and to share both equipment and ideas. Such play, we believe, is unlikely to be observed when a child is somewhat anxious, and from some of the other data we may infer that the new child indeed is under some stress for the first few weeks.

The behaviour patterns of looking and watching initially occur quite frequently. Perhaps this is a natural response. Even adults frequently stand back and observe before actively joining in when confronted with a new situation. McGrew (1972) found levels of looking and watching to be very high initially, followed by a significant decrease in the proportion of time spent in this activity five days later. Blatchford *et al.* (1982) anticipated such a decline but did not find it in their study of the behaviour of children during their first month in the nursery. In our study, an initial decrease in the level of looking and watching was followed by an upswing in the second month before declining once more. All three studies, however, show this pattern to be quite prominent and it remains a major feature of children's behaviour in nurseries.

During the first six months the new children gradually begin to interact with their peers with increased frequency, as reflected by the increased amounts of talk and social play (Figures 10.2 and 10.3).

157

FIGURE 10.3: *Changes in percentage time spent in social and asocial behaviours during the first six months at nursery school*

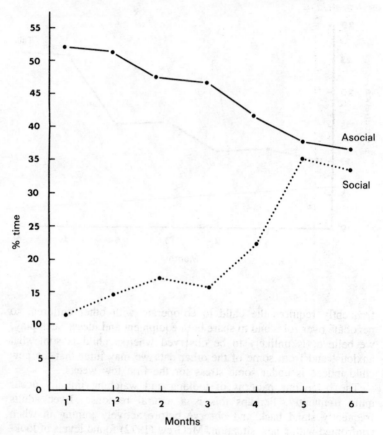

In a classic study, Parten (1932) categorized play into Solitary, Parallel, Associative and Co-operative. For the purposes of this study we utilized Parten's categories but combined the first two as being essentially *asocial* in nature, while behaviour of the second pair of categories was considered to be *social*. The distinction between *social* and *asocial* behaviours rests upon the amount and type of social communication involved in the play. Figure 10.2 shows that there is a marked and significant increase in the amount of talk directed towards adults and children in the nursery over time. Figure 10.3 shows that there is a significant decline in asocial behaviour accompanied by an even more marked rise in the levels of

158

FIGURE 10.4: *Changes in percentage time spent in gestures during social and solitary play during the first six months at nursery school*

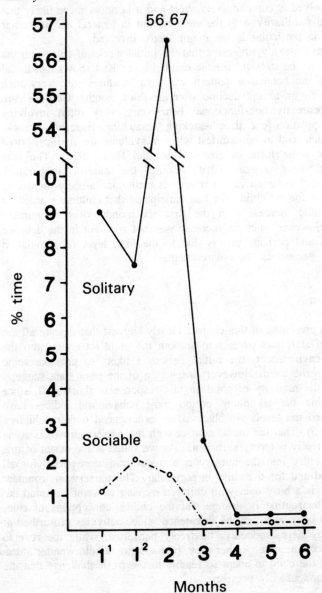

social behaviour. Nevertheless, it should be noted that even after six months, asocial behaviour still predominates. It is possible that these findings are attributable to increasing maturity. However, the time scale involved is comparatively short and it is rather more likely that increased familiarity with the environment in general and the other children in particular is the major factor involved.

We have already suggested that the initial weeks of entry into the nursery may be stressful for the child. Figure 10.4 shows that initial levels of the behaviour pattern we term 'gestures' are very high followed by an abrupt decline after the third month. 'Gestures' are those apparently non-functional behaviours, very often involving self-manipulation (e.g. thumb-sucking, scratching, fingering or rocking), which tend to be manifest when individuals are anxious, bored or under some form of stress (Hutt and Hutt, 1970). The data presented here suggest that despite the careful preparatory procedures, commencing nursery is still an anxiety-provoking experience for the child. We had anticipated that children's attention spans would increase over the first six months of their nursery career. However, such an increase was not apparent in the data we collected and perhaps this is due to the high level of stimulation normally present in the environment.

## Discussion

The data presented in this chapter clearly suggest that despite all the efforts of staff and parents to smooth the child's passage into the nursery environment, the initial period is likely to provoke some anxiety in the child. However, inspection of the same data suggests that for the majority of children this response is short-lived, since well within the six-month period most behavioural indices have approached the levels we observed in experienced nursery children (Chapter 5). That the initial contact with the nursery provokes some stress is really not very surprising. As we stated at the outset of this chapter, entry into the nursery is a major transition period for all concerned and for the child in particular. The nursery environment we know is a busy one, with children moving constantly around the room. The routine is strange and the child's conceptions of rule-governed behaviour may be threatened, since activities proscribed at home may here, suddenly, be freely permitted, while the reverse may also be the case. Rather then, perhaps, we should wonder at the ability of the child to adapt so readily to the fresh challenge that the nursery undoubtedly presents.

# Chapter 11

# Part-time and full-time pre-school attendance

The 1972 White Paper (Department of Education and Science, 1972) proposed far greater provision of part-time than of full-time education for three- and four-year-old children. Though this differential provision was largely determined by economic considerations, implicit in the document was the expectation that for most children part-time pre-school education will be as effective as full-time education. Yet, what little evidence there is suggests that the intellectual benefit derived from pre-school is proportional to the time spent in school. In an early study by Wellman (1943) it was found that children who attended pre-school for half a day gained 4.7 IQ points whereas children who attended for the whole day gained 10.5 points over a two-year period. Whilst this study has been roundly condemned on methodological grounds (Swift, 1964), surprisingly, there appears to be no recent replication of the study, nor any investigation of the relative benefits of part-time and full-time nursery education.

It seemed desirable, therefore, to test the assumption implicit in the White Paper and to examine the social and intellectual performance of children attending school on a part-time or a full-time basis. It seemed important, too, to know how full-timers and part-timers allocated their time over the various activities available in the nursery environment. Such information would also help in the interpretation of the results obtained in the cognitive and social tests. Thus a complementary study of free-play activities was carried out. Owing to the differing time spans of the two studies, only a few children were common to both.

161

TABLE 11.1: *Percentage of time spent in different play activities*

| Education | | Material play % | Physical play % | Fantasy play % | Other % | 'Transit' % |
|---|---|---|---|---|---|---|
| FT | Boys | 49.0 | 2.5 | 13.5 | 4.0 | 27.8 |
| | Girls | 22.5 | 9.4 | 15.8 | 8.3 | 34.0 |
| | B + G | 35.8 | 5.9 | 14.7 | 6.2 | 30.9 |
| PT | Boys | 40.1 | 8.6 | 5.6 | 9.7 | 28.0 |
| | Girls | 42.8 | 12.6 | 5.7 | 8.1 | 22.2 |
| | B + G | 41.5 | 10.6 | 5.7 | 8.9 | 25.1 |

*Note* The difference between FT and PT children in the amount of fantasy play was highly significant, as was the difference between FT boys and girls in the amount of time spent in material play. Not all these add up to 100%. This is because children were sometimes out of the room seeing the teacher or going to the toilet.

## Play in part-time and full-time children

Forty-eight children were observed at play. The sample was obtained from three nursery schools, one of which was a Social Priority School, and consisted of twenty-four full-time (FT) children and twenty-four part-time (PT) children, each group having twelve boys and twelve girls. The mean age of the FT children was three years eleven months and of the PT group four years.

Two observations, each of fifteen minutes' duration, were made of each child, using predominant activity time-sampling procedure with a fifteen-second sampling frame. Periods of organized activity, such as story-time, were not included in the observations. Observations of the FT children were made both in the morning and in the afternoon.

The activities were grouped as follows:

1 Play with materials – sand, water, clay, collage, etc.
2 Physical play – climbing, walking on plank, in hides, on vehicles, etc.
3 Fantasy play – 'pretend' or imaginative play (as defined in Appendix F).
4 Other activities – book, music, woodwork.
5 'Transit' activities – look/watch; walk/run.

The time spent in these activities is shown in Table 11.1. Boys overall engaged in more play with materials than did girls, but whilst the difference was considerable in the FT group, boys and girls were very similar in the PT group, with the value for girls being very slightly

TABLE 11.2: *Percentage of time spent in play activities in the morning and the afternoon*

| | Material play | | Fantasy play | | Physical play | | Other | | Transit | |
|---|---|---|---|---|---|---|---|---|---|---|
| | a.m. % | p.m. % | a.m. % | p.m. % | a.m. % | p.m. % | a.m. % | p.m. % | a.m. % | p.m. % |
| FT | 36.5 | 35.6 | 22.5 | 13.2 | 5.7 | 1.7 | 8.6 | 15.5 | 25.6 | 34.0 |
| PT | 36.1 | 46.8 | 8.5 | 2.8 | 11.2 | 10.0 | 18.8 | 11.6 | 21.5 | 28.6 |

higher. FT children engaged in significantly more fantasy play than PT children. There were no significant differences between FT and PT children on any of the other categories.

Material play, physical play and other activities may legitimately be grouped together as 'nursery activities', i.e. activities which utilize equipment and materials characteristically provided by nurseries. Fantasy play, on the other hand, is not necessarily dependent on props. When the categories are collapsed in this way, the FT group were found to spend 47.8 per cent of their time in nursery activities and the PT group 61.0 per cent. Thus, there is a clear tendency for the PT children to spend proportionately more of their time in exploiting the resources of the nursery.

**Morning versus afternoon activity**

The involvement in different activities in the morning was compared with that in the afternoon for both FT and PT groups, and the allocation of time is shown in Table 11.2. It will be seen that for the play activities, the difference between morning and afternoon were small, except for fantasy play where the difference for the FT group was statistically significant. Again, if material, physical and other play are grouped together as 'nursery activities', then the involvement in the mornings and in the afternoons is remarkably similar: 50.8 (a.m.) and 52.8 (p.m.) for the FT group and 66.1 (a.m.) and 68.4 (p.m.) for the PT group (all figures being percentages).

**Activity spans**

Activity span was measured by ascertaining the average bout length in terms of successive time intervals. A bout was considered terminated if there was a change in activity or if, within the same activity, there was a break of two or more time intervals. The differences between FT and PT groups were not statistically significant, though on the whole, part-timers engaged in activities for longer periods of time.


## Sociability

This characteristic was examined by looking at the relative amounts of solitary, parallel and associative play. Although PT children displayed more solitary play than did the FT children and, conversely, the FT children engaged in more co-operative and associative play, the differences were not statistically significant. The more solitary play of the PT children may, in part, be due to the fact that they knew each other less well than did the FT children.


## Psychological changes in part-time and full-time children during the school year

The second study was undertaken in collaboration with one of our postgraduate students, Margaret Dash, Headteacher of the Social Priority School (for further details of the study see Dash, 1980). Children on the waiting list were allocated to either full-time or part-time attendance. Each child in the FT group was matched for age and sex with its counterpart in the PT group; the groups were also matched for size of family, position in the family and, as far as possible, socio-economic circumstances. There were forty-two children in the study, twenty-one full-time and twenty-one part-time attenders, with twelve boys and nine girls in each group. The ages on admission ranged from three years seven months to four years one month with a mean of three years eight months.

Each child was tested on admission and again towards the end of his last term in school. The interval between test and re-test was on average ten months, i.e. one school year. The Peabody Picture–Vocabulary Scale was used as a measurement of intellectual ability, and the Vineland Social Maturity Scale for social competence. In addition, the Social Assessment section of the Gunzburg (1972) Chart was used since this permitted competence in more specific areas to be ascertained. The Gunzburg scales were as follows: (a) *Self-help*, consisting of assessments on table habits, mobility, toilet and washing, and dressing; (b) *Socialization*, assessed on language discrimination and home activities; (c) *Communication*, assessed on

TABLE 11.3: *Test performance of full-time and part-time nursery children*

| Tests | Subjects' education | Sex | Pre-test scores | Post-test scores | Gain scores |
|---|---|---|---|---|---|
| Peabody | FT | Boys | 85.4 | 99.5 | 14.1 |
| | | Girls | 93.1 | 104.2 | 11.1 |
| | PT | Boys | 97.0 | 108.3 | 11.3 |
| | | Girls | 90.0 | 105.8 | 15.8 |
| Vineland | FT | Boys | 87.5 | 112.0 | 24.5 |
| | | Girls | 96.8 | 120.6 | 23.3 |
| | PT | Boys | 97.5 | 119.3 | 21.8 |
| | | Girls | 101.3 | 119.2 | 17.9 |
| Gunzburg (Self help) | FT | Boys | 24.3 | 73.5 | 49.3 |
| | | Girls | 31.1 | 76.6 | 45.4 |
| | PT | Boys | 30.6 | 72.4 | 41.8 |
| | | Girls | 33.0 | 79.7 | 46.7 |
| Gunzburg (Socialization) | FT | Boys | 5.4 | 24.3 | 18.8 |
| | | Girls | 6.4 | 32.9 | 26.4 |
| | PT | Boys | 6.8 | 25.2 | 18.3 |
| | | Girls | 8.4 | 35.4 | 27.0 |
| Gunzburg (Communication) | FT | Boys | 9.8 | 39.0 | 29.3 |
| | | Girls | 14.0 | 53.2 | 39.2 |
| | PT | Boys | 14.2 | 53.5 | 39.3 |
| | | Girls | 17.2 | 55.7 | 38.4 |
| Gunzburg (Occupation) | FT | Boys | 6.9 | 28.7 | 21.8 |
| | | Girls | 6.3 | 46.3 | 40.0 |
| | PT | Boys | 7.3 | 39.2 | 31.8 |
| | | Girls | 7.0 | 42.1 | 35.1 |

language discrimination, number work, and paper and pencil work; (d) *Occupation*, assessed on dexterity and agility.

The pre-test, post-test and gain scores for each type of assessment are given in Table 11.3. Since the two groups were not matched on ability it was necessary to test whether they differed on pre-test scores. In fact it was found that the groups did not differ either on pre-test or post-test scores. The time factor (pre-test score minus post-test score) was highly significant in each case showing that there was improvement on all measures during the time at nursery school. Girls reached a significantly higher level of performance than the boys, irrespective of FT or PT attendance.

## Discussion

The failure to find any differences on the cognitive and social measures between full-timers and part-timers at first sight seems surprising. But the results must be considered in context. All the schools were fairly traditional in their outlook: they followed no set curriculum nor were there any specific objectives which determined a particular programme of action. The prevailing ethos may be described as 'the provision of an enabling environment in which the child played, learned and developed at his own pace' (Cass, 1975a). In such an environment all children improved quite significantly and full-time schooling conferred no particular advantages upon boys or girls. While the improvement on the Gunzburg scales may be attributed to maturational factors, the improvement on the Peabody and Vineland scales, which use standard scores, reflects a genuine increase in competence in these domains. It is perhaps surprising that the improvement in both dexterity of fine movements and agility of gross movements was so much greater for girls than for boys. The girls' advantage on the socialization scale is less surprising in view of the different demands that are made of girls and boys, particularly within the home.

The complementary study of play activities revealed that the full-time attenders spent more of their time, compared with the part-timers, in fantasy play, while the latter occupied themselves more with 'nursery activities'. Thus, the part-time children appeared to be making more intensive use of the nursery's resources and to 'busy' themselves more. This seemed to be true whether they were morning or afternoon attenders.

Webb (1963) has stated that there is no apparent difference in the play of part-time children in the mornings and the afternoons. On the other hand, it is often argued that children are likely to be tired in the latter part of the day and hence unable to make as much use of the materials and opportunities available. The data of the first study, however, offer no support for this latter argument: the effect of such 'tiredness' might be expected to be most evident in the full-time children who have had neither a rest nor a change of environment, yet their involvement in material and other forms of play was as active in the afternoon as it was in the morning. It was only with fantasy play that any afternoon decrement was observed, and this was so for all children. Thus the decrease in activity was a differential one. On the other hand, there was a higher incidence of 'transit' activity in the afternoon, particularly in the full-time group, suggesting that play was more interspersed with non-purposive activity.

These apparently perplexing results may be explained by reference to the distinction drawn between *epistemic* and *ludic* activities (Chapter 1). We argued that the behaviours commonly termed 'play' were of two distinct kinds: *epistemic*, concerned with the acquisition of information (e.g. problem-solving, exploration), or *ludic*, whereby such information may be utilized in a creative, idiosyncratic manner (e.g. symbolic or fantasy play). There clearly is a limit to the amount of information which can be extracted from the materials available in a nursery school during (say) a single week. (We are well aware that teachers make a determined effort to vary the materials and intellectual problems confronting their charges on a regular basis.) It might be supposed, therefore, that this finite amount of information will be acquired more quickly by full-time than by part-time children. Thus, the switch from epistemic to ludic behaviour, which, as we indicated in Chapter 1, occurs only when objects have become familiar, may occur more readily in full-timers than in part-timers. In an early study (Hutt, 1967) employing the novel object described in Chapter 1, we compared the effects of spacing encounters with the object at intervals of forty-eight, twenty-four and twelve hours. Whilst the amount of epistemic behaviour shown on successive occasions was almost identical under the three different regimes, the amount of ludic behaviour was not: the more closely spaced the exposures, the greater the amount of ludic behaviour shown. This would support the argument, then, that full-timers have twice the opportunity of exhausting the epistemic possibilities of the nursery school than part-timers and thus are more prepared to exploit the ludic possibilities of the environment than their part-time peers. This effect seems to be stronger than that of time of day.

# What do children learn from pre-school?

# Chapter 12

# Intervening in fantasy play

In Chapter 7 and Appendix F we saw that fantasy play may be divided into five main categories ranging from representational play to immaterial fantasy. It seems not unreasonable to suppose that during representational play a child is expressing knowledge of particular events (or sequences of events) and during fantasy object or immaterial fantasy is using that knowledge in original and creative ways. Since standard intelligence tests require a child both to express information and to use his knowledge, it might be thought that intervention in children's fantasy play, so as to increase its thematic diversity, would enhance performance on this type of test. However, whether fantasy play is uniquely useful is in doubt; the evidence from the Headstart programmes in the US suggests that children's IQ can be enhanced by a variety of intervention procedures (Zigler and Trickett, 1978), and that the degree of benefit is greatly dependent on the commitment and emphasis of the staff (Beller, 1973).

The study by Smith and Syddall (1978), which had not been published by the time our own studies were undertaken, strongly suggested that increased adult interaction with pre-school children on a day-to-day basis may be sufficient to bring about changes in their performance on tests of cognitive ability; the precise form of these interactions (whether they do or do not employ stimulation of the children's fantasy play) may be less important.

The following two studies were an attempt to assess the effects of different kinds of intervention technique, with specific reference to the hypothesis that through fantasy play children acquire appropriate cognitive skills which optimize their performance on intelligence tests. Because the nature of the interventions described (working with small groups of children on symbolic play themes) was similar to that in a study by Saltz, Dixon and Johnson (1977), an attempt was also made to confirm their findings that intervention in fantasy play enhances creativity and social responsibility.

Although the experimental design of the two studies was similar – pre-test measurements, fantasy play interaction, post-test measurements – they differed considerably in detail. Most important was the nature of the thematic material employed in the fantasy intervention. In the first study, carried out by our former colleague, Dr Miranda Hughes, children were introduced to a number of novel real-life situations and these provided the thematic material for subsequent fantasy play. In the second study, carried out by a teacher colleague, Mrs Norma Anderson, the themes employed in the fantasy play intervention were already familiar to the children and were taken from fairy stories and everyday life.

## Fantasy play with novel thematic material

The subjects of Hughes's (1981) study were twenty-eight children (age range three years six months to four years six months at the time of pre-testing). They were drawn from three different pre-school establishments (two nursery schools and one day nursery), and each experimental group contained a representative cross-section of social class groups.

The intervention took place during the course of the spring and summer school terms and within the pre-schools' timetables. This comprised a total of sixteen weeks intervention (allowing a fortnight for testing at the beginning and end), during which time each group received an average of one and a half hours of specialized adult contact per week.

Group A (ten children) were taken on fortnightly outings to places of interest (a pottery, a fire station, a hospital, a garage, a wildlife park, a quarry and a shop). During these outings the children's attention was drawn to the type of work that the adults were doing, and the materials with which they worked. These outings were intended to provide the children with novel information which was then followed up in three fantasy play sessions. The play sessions were fifteen minutes long; the play tutor used the first of these to encourage the children to imitate the roles they had seen, and in the subsequent sessions encouraged them to develop fantasy themes around these roles. Group B (ten children) were taken on the same outings, but subsequent sessions, while related to the outings, were based on general pre-school activities (collage, painting, etc.). The adult made specific efforts to draw the children's attention to the properties of the materials they were working with, and to discuss issues related to the outing. Group C (eight children) had an equivalent amount of adult contact divided between symbolic play sessions (which were similar to those of Group A) and intervention in general pre-school activities. The mode of intervention was deliberately 'child-centred' (Hughes, 1981).

Saltz and Johnson (1974) have documented the difficulty of sustaining a fantasy play theme with a group of children and the intervention sessions were therefore usually conducted with small groups of children (two to six). All children were tested on measures of general cognitive ability and creativity before the initiation of the intervention. General cognitive ability was measured using the McCarthy Scales of Children's Abilities. The General Cognitive Index (GCI) on this scale provides separate scores on verbal ability and perceptual performance/quantitative ability scales. Creativity was assessed by fluency and originality scores on the Alternative Uses (five items) and Pattern Meanings (four items) tests of the Wallach and Kogan (1965) test battery. Creativity scores were derived by giving one point for each response, and an additional one point for each unique response. Teachers provided measures of sociability and imaginativeness by using Herbert's Social Behavioural Rating Scale (SBRS) (Herbert, 1974). A rating of sociability was derived from teachers' responses to seven questions (each on a five-point scale) and has been validated in other studies (Herbert, 1974). The imaginativeness measure was derived from the practicality/imaginativeness question which was also rated on a five-point scale: from 'shows little imagination especially in creative activities' (1) to 'very imaginative' (5). All children were also observed for one hour (three twenty-minute sessions on different days). An instantaneous scan sampling convention (Tyler, 1979) was adopted whereby each child was observed at intervals of thirty seconds and a note was made of whether she was engaged in fantasy play. The percentages of observations with fantasy play were used as an estimate of the percentage of the total time each child spent in this type of activity. These tests were administered again at the end of the summer term.

The pre- and post-intervention means for each set of scores are given in Table 12.1. All groups showed a significant improvement of about four points on the GCI of the McCarthy Scales, but there

TABLE 12.1: *Summary of pre- and post-intervention measures in study employing novel thematic material*

| Test measures | Group A pre- | Group A post- | Group B pre | Group B post- | Group C pre- | Group C post- |
|---|---|---|---|---|---|---|
| GCI | 111.6 | 115.6 | 107.5 | 112.1 | 104.0 | 108.4 |
| Verbal ability | 53.9 | 56.4 | 53.7 | 55.3 | 51.1 | 53.9 |
| Perceptual skills | 115.8 | 117.4 | 107.6 | 114.7 | 105.8 | 109.4 |
| Creativity | 10.5 | 16.4 | 10.7 | 18.1 | 18.1 | 22.1 |
| Imaginativeness | 3.0 | 3.0 | 3.4 | 3.9 | 2.8 | 3.6 |
| Extraversion | 26.6 | 25.5 | 26.7 | 29.2 | 25.1 | 26.7 |
| % fantasy play | 7.6 | 20.9 | 19.5 | 23.3 | 9.6 | 12.4 |

were no significant differences between groups. The improvement on the verbal subscale was not as marked as the improvement on the perceptual abilities subscale. Creativity scores improved for all three groups, but the differences between groups were not significant. The teachers' ratings of imaginativeness in the children remained constant for Group A, but increased in Groups B and C. Again, there were no significant differences between the groups. There were no significant changes in the teachers' ratings of sociability. Although the data in Table 12.1 indicate a general trend of increased time spent in fantasy play, only Group C show a statistically significant increase.

The relationships between the measures were evaluated by calculating their inter-correlations. The amount of time spent in fantasy play at post-testing was positively correlated with the amount of fantasy play at pre-testing. . . . [Fantasy] play did not correlate significantly with any other measures. The remaining measures all showed the expected correlations between pre- and post-test scores, and the McCarthy Scales also showed significant inter-correlations. The only other significant correlations were between the teachers' ratings of imaginativeness and the GCI and verbal ability scores (Hughes, 1981).

Note that we have inserted the term Fantasy where Hughes (idem) uses the term Symbolic, the terms having been employed synonymously by other writers (Hutt, 1981).

## Fantasy play with familiar thematic material

The second study, carried out in association with our colleague,

Norma Anderson, set out to compare children's performance on tests of general cognitive ability, social skills and divergent thinking, before and after periods of tutoring in 'imaginative play'; tutoring in 'perceptual skills'; or an equivalent period of conventional nursery school activity. The imaginative play condition entailed the enactment of themes already familiar to the children (see below). A full account of the study has been written up by Anderson (1980).

The subjects were eighteen children from an inner-city nursery school, who were divided into triads, the children in each group being matched by sex, age and intelligence, as measured by the GCI of the McCarthy Scales. The mean age of the three groups thus formed was four years two months. The experimenters were the teacher normally involved with the children in school, and Norma Anderson herself, a former primary teacher who was used to visiting nursery schools, and who was conversant with the behaviour of young children and with general educational practice in nursery schools. The experimenters met with both experimental groups for eighteen sessions of fifteen to twenty minutes each, over a period of ten weeks. Each experimenter spent the same amount of time with the two experimental groups, so that the groups were treated alike with regard to the individual attributes of the adult and the amount of adult–child interaction. For the first nine sessions the imaginative play group was seen before the perceptual skills group. For the latter nine sessions the order was reversed.

Each group withdrew into a group into a small staffroom, or into an entry hall, where there was space to set up a 'bus', a 'space rocket', the 'bridge' (for the 'Three Billy Goats' fairy story), chairs, climbing boxes or tunnels. The experimental treatments were as follows: Group A were exposed to a programme of activities designed to promote role playing, to encourage make-believe with regard to objects, actions and situations, and to stimulate interaction between children.

Each theme was enacted at least twice. On the first enactment of the theme the children often needed much guidance from the adult, but on the second occasion the ideas from the first were remembered by the children, and more ideas were added both by them and by the adult. Well known and well loved stories which involved role play like the 'Three Billy Goats Gruff', were enacted. Sometimes the whole group together played each role in turn, in the sequence of the story, but more often, each role was played for the whole story by the individual children, who would change roles in the next enactment. In this way they would get 'the feel' of the different roles, which required very different responses.

175

Children who were known not to exhibit many imaginative play skills were particularly encouraged to play more elaborately. A child would be given imaginary icecream, and encouraged to lick it and enjoy it, or the adult would have a telephone conversation with a child when they pretended to play a visit to India. A variety of themes was chosen to facilitate imaginative play. As well as the enactment of stories, children and tutor played imaginatively with pipe-cleaner people in a doll's house, and with play people on a village plan. Everyday events were acted out, but new ideas were also introduced, like lost possessions or naughty children. A hospital theme afforded social role play when accidents and illnesses were treated by doctors and nurses. Journeys by bus and aeroplane, and a space rocket trip to the moon were simulated.

Some props were always provided, but apart from the more structured situations with the furnished doll's house and pipe-cleaner people, these were planned so as to be sufficient to encourage and contribute to the imaginative play, without distracting from the play by being an interest and novelty in themselves. They were intended to act as pivots in enabling the child to ignore the stimulus of the real world, as he played in the world of pretence. Thus hats (which teachers had mentioned as often helpful in cementing a role) were provided: a peaked cap for the bus driver or pilot; space helmets to go to the moon. Play boxes were arranged to make the Pigs' house of sand, twigs and bricks; and to make the rocket stage with steps up to it, and with seats inside. Moreover, the children often assembled and dismantled these concrete symbols, thus acknowledging both their real and symbolic use. Chairs and a wooden steering wheel were combined to make an aeroplane. Many objects were imagined as well: for example pretend telephones were used, and pretend tickets for fares on the bus. Large cardboard boxes and hats and puppets were provided on two occasions towards the end of the study, when children were encouraged in free imaginative play, and the experimenter followed the children's ideas when interacting. A quick review of pictures in a book, or of a current theme or study was sometimes provided to help the children with their representation (Anderson, 1980).

Group B took part in a wide range of activities selected for their enjoyment and to ensure a considerable amount of adult interaction and involvement. The activities were carried out with attractive materials, many of which were new to the children. The adult interacted by arranging the materials, talking to, praising and questioning the children, taking up their ideas, and joining in the activities herself. Non-fiction books and pictures were looked at for similarities and differences, labelling and comment. Through a variety of games perceptual skills were exercised, when children matched colours, shapes and objects; built up parts of the body to make a person; and used balances. Children clapped and used musical instruments along with the adult, to make and copy rhythms. The names of the instruments were used by teacher and children, and there was general discussion of the activity as it developed. Classification skills were encouraged when, for example, children cut out pictures of different foods and stuck them on cardboard dinner or tea plates. The teacher interacted with each child individually and with the group as a whole. The children made patterns, used logic blocks, and counting was often involved.

Prior to, and subsequent to, the intervention programme, cognitive ability was measured by the McCarthy Scales of Children's Abilities; creativity by the Alternative Uses (five items) and Pattern Meanings (four items) of the Wallach and Kogan test battery; and sociability by the Herbert SBRC. Observations of fantasy play were made twice for each child in Groups A and B in the ten days prior to the interactive programme. Total observation time was twenty minutes, behaviour being observed at intervals of fifteen seconds using predominant activity scans (Tyler, 1979). Fantasy play was categorized according to the definitions of Davie *et al.* (1984). A matched control group (C) was subjected to psychological testing before and after the intervention programme, but otherwise engaged in the usual day-to-day activities of the nursery.

The means of the various measures are shown in Table 12.2. Both the interaction groups increased their fantasy play, the fantasy intervention group more than the perceptual skills group, but the differences were not significant. On the McCarthy GCI both intervention groups showed a significant improvement between pre- and post-test; the difference in change scores between the two groups was not, however, statistically significant. Group C obtained almost identical scores for pre-test and post-test. Although Group B obtained a higher score on the SBRS post-test, the magnitude of the improvement in Group A was significantly greater. On the Wallach and Kogan test the changes pre- and post-test were not statistically significant.

TABLE 12.2: *Summary of pre- and post-intervention measures in study employing familiar thematic material*

| Test measures | Group A pre- | Group A post- | Group B pre- | Group B post- | Group C pre- | Group C post- |
|---|---|---|---|---|---|---|
| GCI | 101.7 | 112.5 | 101.7 | 107.7 | 103.3* | 103.5* |
| Verbal Index | 50.5 | 57.7 | 46.8 | 51.2 | | |
| Perceptual Index | 51.3 | 57.3 | 54.8 | 57.5 | | |
| Quantitative Index | 51.3 | 55.5 | 54.7 | 56.7 | | |
| SBRS | | | | | *† | *† |
|   Competence | 36.8 | 38.5 | 37.7 | 39.2 | | |
|   Anxiety | 12.6 | 13.0 | 10.7 | 10.6 | | |
|   Behaviour problems | 45.2 | 45.3 | 46.5 | 46.5 | | |
|   Dependency | 5.0 | 24.2 | 23.2 | 21.3 | | |
|   Extraversion | 24.3 | 25.2 | 25.0 | 24.2 | | |
| Wallach and Kogan | | | | | *† | *† |
|   Pictures (frequency) | 6.5 | 8.3 | 6.2 | 5.7 | | |
|   Pictures (originality) | 3.2 | 4.0 | 3.5 | 1.8 | | |
|   Alternative uses (frequency) | 7.5 | 8.0 | 6.5 | 8.0 | | |
|   Alternative uses (originality) | 3.2 | 2.3 | 2.0 | 2.0 | | |
| % fantasy play | 20.8 | 28.3 | 19.5 | 20.1 | *† | *† |

* Regrettably, Anderson was unable to provide detailed information on the McCarthy performance of Group C.
† Not measured.

## Discussion

As we have already noted, there were several methodological differences between the studies of Hughes (1981) and of Anderson (1980). In Hughes' study, a series of novel inputs from outside the pre-school provided a continual source of fresh thematic material for fantasy play. In Anderson's study, the thematic material was already relatively familiar, though it was not possible to control 'familiarity' with anything like the same rigour as was 'novelty' in the previous study. In practice, it appears that the nature of the thematic material is not itself a crucial variable. In both studies, the 'interactive' groups, A and B, showed a substantial increase in cognitive performance, as measured by the McCarthy Scales, compared with the control groups who were exposed merely to the usual nursery school routine – mainly free-play.

Although the brief of these two studies was somewhat narrower than that either of Saltz, Dixon and Johnson (1977) or of Smith and Syddall (1978) the results do tend to support those of the latter authors, thus lending credence to the contention that increases in standardised test scores, particularly IQ, can be achieved equally successfully by any type of adult intervention in the pre-school. The difference between educational techniques appears to be far less important than the difference between intensive educational intervention and no intervention at all. Thus, the data add further support to the conclusions of earlier chapters that a key factor is neither the nature of the materials, nor of the activities to which the child is exposed, but whether or not an adult is actively involved in their exploitation.

Ironically, adults in pre-school are sometimes embarrassed at taking an active part in fantasy play, an activity upon which they lay great store (Anderson, 1980). However, the benefits of fantasy intervention – which, of course, may well be short-lived – do not appear to be a consequence of the imaginative nature of the play, but of the enforced interaction with materials, other children and the caring adult. Such interaction does seem to increase the occurrence of immaterial fantasy, which, by definition, involves greater involvement of language usage than (say) representational object play. But increased language usage may also be involved in those other interactions considered here – discussion of outings (Hughes, 1981) or perceptual skills training (Anderson, 1980) – with which adults feel more comfortable. In short, fantasy play can be employed to increase children's exploration of the properties of materials or to heighten the quality of verbal intercourse, but it is only one of many activities in the pre-school which can provide these experiences. The key to the quality of children's learning experiences is adult participation. Just as the presence of adults may increase a child's attention span (Chapter 8) and may present a greater conversational challenge than that of other children (Chapter 9), so the adult's participation is an essential ingredient in any programme aimed at enhancing cognitive performance.

# Chapter 13

# Play and learning

The McCarthy Scales, which were employed to measure behavioural changes following adult intervention in children's play (Chapter 12), are fairly gross measures of cognitive ability, even though they may be divided into subscales and yet further divided into individual subtests. Moreover, the type of intervention reported in the previous chapter, which might be termed a total 'enrichment' programme, gives only an indirect answer to the question of *how* the complex set of events which comprise the intervention programme are related to the changes effected. It is a matter of conjecture why stimulating a child (say) to participate in the enactment of fairly stories (Anderson, 1980) or in visits to places of interest (Hughes, 1981) should have an effect upon the Verbal Scale of the McCarthy. It may be presumed that fantasy and perceptual skills training have a poten-tiating effect upon certain cognitive processes (such as verbal expres-sion) which are similar to, or the same as, those which the McCarthy Scales purport to measure. It seems to be the case, however, that the McCarthy Scales are a better indicator of the *outcome* of adult intervention than of the *processes* which are responsible for changes in performance. In this chapter, therefore, we examine four studies in which special play experiences were devised for pre-school children and their effects tested, but where there was a much more direct relationship between the intervention procedure and the method of evaluating its effects. In each case there was a specific hypothesis concerning what psychological process was likely to be affected by the intervention and the evaluation procedure was devised to test this process directly. Wherever possible, the post-test incorporated materials from the intervention itself. The studies were carried out by two former colleagues, Ms Gay Wilson and Dr Miranda Hughes. Taken together, the four studies all point towards the same general conclusion, namely, that the oft-repeated proposition, 'children learn through play' (e.g. Cass, 1975a) cannot be sustained without important qualifications. Rather, we must distinguish between different types of play, each of which may have its own particular motivation and psychological function. In the present chapter we look at the role of imaginative play in memory, the role of exploratory behaviour in problem-solving and the role of imaginative play both in stimulating conservation skills and in engendering creativity.

## Play and memory

The first study to be reviewed in this chapter was carried out by our colleague, Ms Gay Wilson. Wilson's study (1980) was concerned with the effects of 'play tutoring' upon children's recollection of what she entitled 'a novel experience' – in this case, a visit to a farm. Her sample consisted of sixteen four-year-olds, eight boys and eight girls from a nursery school serving both a council house estate and a private estate. The study comprised four phases: (i) an initial observation phase in which children's spontaneous behaviour, especially their fantasy play, was recorded; (ii) the visit to the farm; (iii) two sessions devoted either to 'play tutoring' or to 'passive tutoring'; and (iv) a final observation phase in which observations similar to those of the initial phase were made.

The categories of play activity recorded by Wilson were in effect the same as those employed in our descriptive study of fantasy play in Chapter 7. Each child was observed for nine daily sessions, each of ten minutes' duration, over a period of two weeks. The sessions were organized so as to cover all times of day. Behaviour was recorded at intervals of fifteen seconds using a predominant activity scan (Tyler, 1979). In the third week the children were taken on a visit to a dairy farm. The visit took about one and a half hours. The children were shown a variety of animals, including birds; were allowed to feed the cows; rode in tractors; and saw various processes in operation, such as milking and purification. In the week following the farm visit each child was allocated at random to one of three groups: a 'play tutoring' group (N = 6); a 'passive tutoring' group (N = 6); or a control group (N = 4).[1]

The first group was given two sessions, of twenty-five minutes

[1] The subgroups began with equal numbers, but attrition occurred in the control group owing to illness.

each, of tutoring in 'socio-dramatic play' (Smilansky, 1968), set two days apart.

> Sociodramatic play was defined as the physical interpretation of an event during which the child takes on a role either of himself or another person or thing in a different situation, imitating the person or thing in action or speech, with the aid of real or imagined objects. The play becomes sociodramatic when the theme is elaborated in co-operation with at least one other player, here the rest of the tutoring group and the teacher. Verbal interaction involved imitation, substitution of verbal description for objects and actions and planning of the play. In the first session the teacher played through the visit with the children in an active imaginative way. A row of chairs was arranged to represent the minibus which took the children to the farm, but no other props were used. The teacher prompted the children's recall by asking them to imagine they were at the farm, to point to the various animals they could 'see' and to imagine that they could feed and stroke these. In this way the whole visit was explored, in chronological order. In the second session the children were encouraged to take on the roles of the animals they had seen on the farm, prompted by a tape-recording of animal noises. In particular, the teacher asked the children how they thought the animals might have felt, what the animals did when they saw the children, what they wanted to eat, etc. (Wilson, 1980).

The 'passive tutoring' group received the same amount of adult interaction as the play tutoring group, but the form of the intervention was different:

> The children were given paper and boards and were seated at the start of the first session. The teacher talked to them about the visit, referring to the events again in chronological order, using a book with some relevant pictures. When she talked about the cows, she suggested that the children should begin to draw and the session continued with the drawing and crayoning while the teacher talked and prompted recall, following the same themes as those explored with the play tutoring group. In the second session the teacher used the tape-recording of animal noises, a farm layout and various figures and animals to once again explore the details of the farm visit. Once again the same content was adhered to as in the play tutoring session (Wilson, 1980).

The tutoring in each case was carried out by the child's own

TABLE 13.1: *Percentage of time spent in fantasy play*

|  | Phase (i): before tutoring | Phase (iv): after tutoring |
| --- | --- | --- |
| Play tutoring | 7.82 | 17.18 |
| Passive tutoring | 13.5 | 18.89 |
| Control group | 6.39 | 8.33 |

TABLE 13.2: *Attention spans for fantasy play (seconds)*

|  | Phase (i): before tutoring means | Phase (iv): after tutoring means |
| --- | --- | --- |
| Play tutoring | 41.7 | 73.65 |
| Passive tutoring | 37.65 | 62.25 |
| Control group | 34.95 | 37.5 |

teacher. The observer was not present, but each session was tape-recorded and subsequently checked by the observer to ensure that the agreed procedures were being followed. The control group received no special treatment following the farm visit. In the week following the intervention sessions all children were again observed at free-play. The procedure was the same as that employed in the initial phase of the study. After all observations had been completed each child was given a recall test of the details of the farm visit; this was carried out exactly four weeks from the time of the visit. Children were taken individually into the room in which the play tutoring had taken place and were shown a toy farm. They were then asked a series of questions, such as: 'What sort of birds were there?' 'What did the cows have on their ears?' 'Where does the cow's milk come from?' 'What do we call baby cows?' There were twenty-eight such questions in all.

A large number of behavioural variables were recorded, but we will consider just two which are of especial interest in the present context. Table 13.1 shows the mean percentage of time spent in fantasy play in phases (i) and (iv) respectively. The control group showed a small (2 per cent) and statistically non-significant increase in fantasy play, whilst the passive tutoring and play tutoring groups showed increases of 5 per cent and 10 per cent respectively. Unfortunately, the baselines of the two intervention groups in the first phase were different from each other, so that we cannot directly

TABLE 13.3: *Percentage of time spent in play with materials*

|  | Phase (i):<br>before tutoring | Phase (iv):<br>after tutoring |
|---|---|---|
| Play tutoring | 30.55 | 32.59 |
| Passive tutoring | 22.59 | 29.07 |
| Control group | 30.76 | 49.93 |

TABLE 13.4: *Attention spans for play with materials (seconds)*

|  | Phase (i):<br>before tutoring<br>means | Phase (iv):<br>after tutoring<br>means |
|---|---|---|
| Play tutoring | 68.55 | 85.55 |
| Passive tutoring | 55.95 | 88.05 |
| Control group | 55.5 | 103.2 |

compare the percentage gains of the two groups. Nevertheless, they clearly are different from the control group. A similar picture is seen if we compare the attention spans of the three groups in phases (i) and (iv) (see Table 13.2). Whilst again differing in their pre-intervention baselines, the changes following intervention are quite clear-cut and consistent with the changes in amount of fantasy play. A small but statistically non-significant increase in attention span is observed in the control group. The attention spans of the experimental groups after intervention were almost double their values before intervention. The increase in the attention span of the play tutoring group is somewhat greater than that observed in the passive tutoring group, though the difference is not statistically significant.

Interestingly, when Wilson examined a second main behavioural category, 'play with materials' – that is, using materials in a conventional manner and specifically excluding their use in fantasy – a different picture emerged (Tables 13.3 and 13.4). The control group in this case showed a marked increase both in percentage time spent in play with materials and in activity span, whilst the two experimental groups showed much smaller increases. These findings suggest two things. First, the study appears to have had an effect upon the behaviour of all children, not only upon those in the experimental groups. (This 'Hawthorne' effect (Roethlisberger and Dixon, 1939) is often found when a group of people, because they are the subjects

TABLE 13.5: *Mean number of items recalled (maximum twenty-eight) about visit to farm*

| | |
|---|---|
| Play tutoring | 25.5 |
| Passive tutoring | 22.7 |
| Control group | 16.75 |

of an experiment, are paid special attention and show a change towards what they believe to be the behaviour expected of them.) Second, the change in the amount and duration of fantasy play shown by the two experimental groups cannot be accounted for merely by an overall increase in activity, since the increase in play with materials shown by the control group is not accompanied by a corresponding increase in fantasy play. Both the increase in fantasy play shown by the experimental groups and the increase in play with materials shown by the control group were achieved at the expense of watching/looking. It thus appears that, at least within the short time span of this study, fantasy tutoring and, to a lesser extent, passive tutoring does have specific effects upon the occurrence of fantasy in free-play.

However, does such tutoring have a corresponding effect upon recollection of the so-called novel experience? Table 13.5 shows the number of items from the recall test appropriately answered by each group. The control group, four weeks after the farm visit, were able to give appropriate answers to just over half the recall items. In contrast, the play tutoring group achieved about 90 per cent and the passive tutoring group about 80 per cent appropriate responses respectively. The score of the play tutoring group differed significantly from that of the control group and the difference between the combined scores of the two experimental groups and the control almost reached statistical significance.

It must be admitted that the Wilson study is not without flaws: no account was taken of the children's pre-intervention knowledge of farms; and it would have been desirable to match the groups by pre-intervention activity rather than allocate children randomly to the experimental and control groups. Nevertheless, taking the findings at face value, a fairly clear picture emerges. Tutoring children in fantasy play, incorporating ideas from a novel experience, does not aid encoding of such an experience significantly more than talking and drawing related to that experience. Either of these practices will facilitate learning relative to children who engage in neither.

## Play and problem-solving

The notion that opportunity to 'play' with materials leads to learning of their properties is implicit in nursery practice. Moreover, experiments by Sylva *et al.* (1974) and by Smith and Dutton (1979) have shown that prior opportunity to manipulate sticks and a clamp by which the sticks can be joined, may indeed facilitate the solution of a problem in which an out-of-reach object may be retrieved by a long stick constructed from two shorter ones clamped together. However, it is not clear from these reports what was the nature of the 'play' in which the children engaged with the sticks and clamp prior to being confronted with the problem. It would be predicted that activities of the type we categorized (Chapter 1) as 'epistemic' or exploratory *would* lead to learning of the properties of the sticks and clamps, whereas 'ludic' activities, including fantasy play, would produce poorer learning. In a study by our colleague, Dr Miranda Hughes (1981; 1983), children were presented with a problem similar to that used by Sylva *et al.* (1974) and by Smith and Dutton (1979). The children were given an opportunity to manipulate the materials for a short period prior to attempting their solution. In Hughes's study, however, the children were divided into two groups: in one group the component materials were presented in a plain functional form; in the other group the materials were decorated in such a way as to invite ludic behaviour. The basic material consisted of three sticks which could be connected by inserting the end of one stick into a joint at the end of another; the connection could then be secured by inserting a metal key through the joint. For one group (A) the sticks were brightly painted but otherwise unadorned, for the other group (B) each stick was constructed to appear like one of three doll-like figures – a policeman, a Red Indian and a woman holding a baby. The keys were designed to look like a truncheon, a tomahawk and a baby's rattle respectively.

There were twenty four-year-olds in each group, all children coming from the same playgroup in a predominantly middle-class area. The children were taken singly to a small room within the playgroup. Hughes told the children that she had brought some special toys with her and that she wanted to see what the children would do with them and whether they might be useful to have in the playgroup. Each child was then observed for five minutes and a record made of his amount of exploration and the number of functional properties discovered, e.g. whether the child inserted one stick into another, or inserted a key to secure. Non-exploratory behaviour was also recorded. From these observations an 'exploration score' was devised ranging from zero (no attention to slots, keys or inserts) to five (full construction appropriate to the task). The mean score of Group A was 3.2 and that of Group B 2.1 (a statistically significant difference), showing that the ludic possibilities of the figures presented to Group B did inhibit exploration. Indeed, as Hughes notes, one child in this group spent part of the time making a wigwam for the Red Indian, another mutilating the policeman with the tomahawk.

The children were then presented with the problem-solving task. A jelly baby was placed in a plastic cup with a handle; the cup was on the far side of a white tape stretched down the centre of the room; the child's task was to obtain the jelly baby without crossing the line. The children were told that they might use the sticks if they wished. The solution, of course, resided in being able to join together the three sticks to produce one long enough to reach the cup and then draw it in. Each child's performance was scored in terms of the numbers of 'hints' he required to complete a correct solution. The hints were given in sequence and were arranged in an ordinal scale, higher-level hints having a higher value than lower-level ones. It was found that Group A children required significantly fewer hints to solve the problem than Group B children. Thus, it would appear that 'play' with materials in a general sense does not necessarily lead to appropriate employment of the properties of those materials in a problem-solving task. The type of play is important: children who engage in a greater amount of exploratory behaviour during prior exposure to the materials perform better on the problem-solving task than do children who engage in less exploratory behaviour (and complementarily in more ludic behaviour). The greater amount of ludic behaviour in Group B appears to have been elicited by the relatively greater familiarity of the doll-like figures as compared with the sticks. The study provides further empirical evidence for the view we expressed in Chapter 1 that in some instances ludic behaviour, far from being a facilitatory influence in children's learning, may actually impede learning.

## Play and conservation skills

In a television series on Einstein's theory of relativity several years ago, Professor Sir Herman Bondi surprised his audience by announcing that three-quarters of what a theoretical physicist needs to know is learned before he enters primary school. By this, presumably, he meant that much of a child's knowledge of the real world – of cause and effect, of time, of number, of seriation, of conservation – is acquired by the time he reaches the phase of what Piaget (1952) calls 'concrete operations', at around seven years of age. The intellectual skills encompassed by the term 'concrete operations' are themselves the results of the child's discoveries in his interaction with the physical and social world during the preceding 'pre-operational' phase of development (Piaget, 1952). A number of studies of the influence of children's play upon the development of intellectual skills have been formulated within a Piagetian framework, the aim being to examine how processes within the pre-operational phase may be related to the acquisition of concrete operations. One of the most recent of such studies is that of Golomb and Cornelius (1977) on the effects of training in 'symbolic' play upon conservation skills.

Golomb and Cornelius observed that, in fantasy play, children have a clear notion of the fantasy and reality components of what they are doing. In playing a role (e.g. Superwoman), the child is able to step out of the role if she wants to go to the lavatory, or is called by her mother. Similarly, the child may pretend that a piece of clay is a cake, but is careful not to bite into it. Thus, the child appears to manifest a kind of 'pseudo reversibility' in which the identity of the play object (including the child herself) and its temporary transformation in make-believe is intuitively recognized. Golomb and Cornelius argue that this 'pseudo reversibility of thought' in symbolic play may be related to the 'reversible thought operations' which characterize the attainment of conservation. Thus, if the child is made aware of the 'pseudo reversibility' shown in her spontaneous fantasy play, this knowledge may be carried over into more formal situations requiring reversible operations, such as conservation tests. Moreover, if 'the reversibility seen in play is indeed a spontaneous precursor of the process that characterises successful conservation, then training in symbolic play may facilitate the attainment of conservation' (Golomb and Cornelius, 1977, p. 247). The play training employed by the authors was a periodic 'challenge' to the child during the enactment of a fantasy role regarding the incompatibility of the real and the imaginary features of the situation. After three twice-daily play sessions involving such challenges, Golomb and Cornelius demonstrated an improvement on conservation tasks involving 'reversible thought operations'.

Our attempt to replicate this important, if somewhat surprising, finding was carried out by Dr Miranda Hughes (1981). Hughes employed the design used by Golomb and Cornelius themselves, but with two important modifications. First, in the original study, the same adult had both administered the tests of conservation and carried out the play training; in Hughes's study, two different adults were involved, one to carry out the conservation tests, the other to carry out the play training. Second, as well as the comparison group included in the original study, who engaged in an equivalent amount of fantasy play but without challenge, Hughes included a third group who spent a similar amount of time in play with materials but not in fantasy play.

There were forty-two children in Hughes's study, aged three years nine months to four years nine months and drawn from nursery schools in Area A. The children were allocated to one of three groups: E1 (fantasy play with challenge group); E2 (fantasy play, no challenge group) and C (control group). The groups were balanced for age and sex. The study took five days, the first and last being devoted to testing on conservation skills and days 2 to 4 to the fantasy intervention. On the first day, children were examined on two well-known Piagetian conservation tasks. The first required children to indicate whether or not two equal balls of clay contained the same amount, after one had been deformed; the second whether or not two equal quantities of liquid remained the same after one had been poured into a different sized container. In each case, children had not only to give the correct judgment, but also had to give an appropriate explanation for their judgment. An example of an appropriate explanation involving reversibility would be 'If you poured it back it would be the same', or 'You didn't add any clay or take any away, so they must be the same'. Following Golomb and Cornelius (1977), a score of 0 was assigned to each answer indicating a failure to conserve; a score of 1 to each judgment which was correct but which was not accompanied by an adequate explanation; a score of 2 for each correct judgment accompanied by an appropriate explanation.

The experimental stage of the study required two periods of fantasy play on each of three successive days. On days 2 to 4 each child in the two experimental groups was seen twice for about fifteen minutes. Equipment was introduced by the experimenter, who suggested the initial theme of play. During play the children's suggestions and ideas were followed, but the experimenter ensured continuation of the basic themes. Hughes's (1981) procedure is best described in her own words:

On day 2, playdoh was used to make a picnic; the players drove to the mountain or seaside in a car made from chairs. On day 3, a set of soft toys picked strawberries (pebbles or beads), and then went horse-riding on empty egg-boxes. On day 4, the same soft toys went boating and shopping; the adult took the role of shopkeeper and sold an assortment of objects (woolly hat, sponge, socks) as either food or pets.

TABLE 13.6: *Summary of conservation scores showing the number of children in each scoring category*

|       | Pre-test scores | | | Post-test scores | | |
|-------|:---:|:---:|:---:|:---:|:---:|:---:|
|       | 0 | 1 | 2 | 0 | 1 | 2 |
| E1    | 10 | 3 | 1 | 9 | 4 | 1 |
| E2    | 10 | 3 | 1 | 10 | 2 | 2 |
| C     | 11 | 2 | 1 | 11 | 1 | 2 |
| Total | 31 | 8 | 3 | 30 | 7 | 5 |

Children in the E1 group were challenged at appropriate moments during play about the dual nature of the objects being used. For example, during the picnic scene, the adult might ask for some food, and when offered playdoh would enquire how it could be food and playdoh at once. On each day there were two such challenges. Children in the E2 group played the same games, but without the challenges. The control group continued with normal nursery activities during days 2 to 4 (Hughes, 1981, p. 123).

On day 5, the children were again tested on the conservation task. Table 13.6 shows the number of children in each group who obtained conservation scores of 0, 1 or 2. The scores of the groups post-intervention did not differ significantly from their scores pre-intervention, thus indicating that intervention in fantasy play had no effect upon conservation judgments.

## Play and creativity

The study by Hughes (1981), reported above, showed that exploration of the properties of materials aided children in the solution of a problem incorporating the use of those materials. Her study provided no support for the notion that playful behaviour of an imaginative kind with the materials was as effective as this exploration. Moreover, in those cases where the clearest evidence of playful behaviour was observed – making a wigwam or roadway with the sticks or the invention of an imaginary confrontation between the Indian and the policeman – subsequent solution of the problem was especially impaired. Are there, then, no greater cognitive benefits to be gained from imaginative play than can be derived from other activities? Should we simply accept that activities which are most clearly 'playful' have no cognitive benefits, but are, as we suggested in Chapter 7, primarily concerned with regulating a child's mood state? In fact, Hughes in a subsequent study was able to demonstrate one possible cognitive benefit of imaginary play – it *may* enhance creativity.

The subjects of Hughes's (1981) study were thirty children from the reception class of a primary school, their ages ranging from four years nine months to five years nine months. The children were divided into three groups of ten. Each child in the first group (Play condition) was seated at a table on which was an array of objects such as paper towels, wet cups, paperclips. The child was encouraged to play with these objects for six minutes, during which time her behaviour was observed from a distance. At the end of this period the observer went over to the child and asked her to think of all the things that can be done with a paper towel. The reason for selecting the paper towel as the test of 'alternative uses' was that, in an earlier study, Dansky and Silverman (1973) had found that this item had elicited most responses from their subjects. When the child had finished responding she was shown one of the pattern-meaning cards of the Wallach and Kogan (1965) test battery and asked to think of all the things it could be. Each child in the second group (Imitation condition) was introduced to the objects used in the Play condition and then the observer spent six minutes performing actions with the objects which had to be imitated by the child. She was told to 'watch what I do and then you do the same'. The observer then wiped the cups with the towels, filled and emptied the matchboxes, pushed pipe-cleaners through cotton reels and clipped and unclipped cards with paperclips. At the end of the six minutes devoted to imitation, the child was asked to think of as many uses as possible for the paper towel and was then given the pattern-meaning card employed to test the Play group. Each child in the Control group spent the same amount of time in the room with the observer as children in the other two groups, but the six-minute session was devoted to crayoning and drawing. At the end of the session the children were asked the same questions as the other two groups about the paper towel and the Wallach–Kogan card.

The responses to the 'paper towel' question were divided into two categories. Standard uses were ones for which ostensibly paper towels were invented, e.g. wiping, cleaning. All other uses were categorized as non-standard. It was found that whilst there were no significant differences amongst the three groups with regard to the number of standard uses for the paper towel, the Play group produced significantly more non-standard uses than either the Imitation or Control groups. Moreover, the Play group scored significantly higher on the Wallach and Kogan pattern-meaning test than either of the other two groups. It was also found that in the Play group the amount of time spent playing with the towel during the initial six minutes and the number of instances in which the towel was combined with other objects was significantly correlated with the number of alternative uses suggested for the towel in the subsequent test. Unlike the play observed in Hughes's previous experiment with the interconnecting sticks, the children's manipulations were ludic in character. For example, the child who obtained the highest score for what she called 'play richness' during the pre-exposure period 'dried the cups, then wrapped them up and put pipe cleaners round to hold the paper on; she then put the matchboxes on top and covered them with another towel'. Thus, from this study it would appear that play with materials which is of a ludic character may have a 'priming' effect upon the child's imaginative processes, which leads to a greater availability of responses involving the potential use of the materials.

**Discussion**

In Chapter 12 we argued that such benefits as may accrue from tutoring in fantasy play are probably the result of the increase in guided interaction with materials and of the increased linguistic input provided by the caring adult during fantasy play. These factors, rather than fantasy *per se*, seemed to be the important ones, since children who were given extra training in 'perceptual skills' showed increases in performance on the McCarthy Scales which were comparable with those of children who took part in the fantasy sessions. At first sight, Wilson's (1980) study seems to invite a similar interpretation. Children who talked about and drew pictures of a farm visit were only slightly poorer at remembering details of the visit than children who engaged in fantasy enactment of the visit. This perhaps is not surprising when we read Wilson's description of the fantasy sessions. Children clearly were being encouraged to recall, rehearse and recall again the various events of the farm visit; the fantasy provided a vehicle for the memorization processes. It might be argued, however, that fantasy could have played a part in the children's learning processes, though this was not through the fantasy intervention itself. Rather, it may be claimed that the spontaneous fantasy play which took place *between* the intervention sessions and the recall test enhanced consolidation of the material.

It will be recalled that *both* the interaction groups in Wilson's study showed an increase in their spontaneous fantasy play after the two types of play intervention. According to this argument we might expect to find a correspondence between the amount of post-intervention fantasy play and the number of items recalled. Examination of Tables 13.1 and 13.5 shows this to be the case. The play tutoring group which increased its fantasy play by approximately 10 per cent compared with its pre-intervention baseline, obtained a higher recall score than the passive tutoring group which increased its fantasy play by only 5 per cent. The differences are not statistically significant, but it would be wrong to reject them out of hand, if they could be corroborated in other ways. The most relevant comparative data, probably, are those of Hughes (1981) which were reviewed in the previous chapter. From Table 12.1 it may be seen that fantasy play, as in the present case, increased in all three of Hughes's groups following play intervention. However, the size of this increase was not correlated with changes in any of the other measures of behaviour, such as McCarthy scores. We are, therefore, led to the conclusion that the case for *cognitive* benefits of fantasy play remains unproven.

Our view is supported by the results of Hughes's study (1981; 1983), reported in this chapter, examining play and problem-solving. This study indicates that imaginative play may actually impede, rather than facilitate, discovery of properties of materials which are necessary to the subsequent solution of a problem employing those materials. Again, Hughes's (1981) study of conservation failed to demonstrate any improvement in conservation skills following a period of fantasy tutoring in which reciprocity between the fantasy properties of materials was periodically challenged, i.e. in which the 'ludic' and 'epistemic' possibilities of materials were juxtaposed. As we have indicated, the original findings of Hughes's study are at variance with those of Golomb and Cornelius (1977) who claimed to have found a facilitatory effect upon conservation by the 'fantasy play with challenge' paradigm. We have noted that Hughes employed a methodology slightly different from that of Golomb and Cornelius (1977) themselves: the person who tested for conservation before and after the play tutoring sessions was not the person who carried out the play sessions. This by itself would not be sufficient to account for the difference between her findings and those of Golomb and Cornelius. Guthrie and Hudson (1979) did employ the same person to test for conservation and to run the play sessions, but still failed to replicate the earlier findings. Hughes herself, in attempting to account for the differences in outcome of the three studies, implicates the likelihood of there being differences in the style of 'prompting' the children during fantasy play:

In this study, children were required to state both the 'real life' and the 'pretend' nature of the object, and then to give some explanation of how it could be 'two things at the same time'. A common answer was of the type that we were *pretending* that the box was a boat, and the child was not then prompted further. However, it can be conjectured that if the child were asked 'does the box change when we pretend it's a boat?', the child would be more likely to focus on the idea of invariance of the properties of objects despite a symbolic transformation. The idea that transformation can preserve the identity of objects might then be more easily generalized to conservation of substance despite transformation of shape. That is, a child confronted with an adult who had insisted on the articulation of the invariance of an object during 'pretend' play, would generalize this type of response when being tested by that adult subsequently (Hughes, 1981, p. 126).

In contrast with the above findings, Hughes's (1981) study on play and creativity seem to suggest that 'ludic' behaviour may have a priming effect upon children's imaginative processes. However, this may not be the only possible interpretation of her findings. We have already seen (Chapters 1, 7, 10 and 11) that ludic behaviour occurs only when children are in a relaxed mood state. Moreover, in the case of day nursery children (Chapter 7) we saw that when they were engaged in fantasy behaviour they were likely to produce language whose variety was much greater than that produced during non-fantasy behaviour. Intuitively, it seems reasonable that the more relaxed people are – e.g. when in the company of family or close friends – the greater variety of behaviour they are prepared to deploy. Conversely, when people are mildly anxious – e.g. in the presence of people more powerful than themselves – their behaviour is likely to be more stereotyped. Thus, what may have occurred in the present study is that pre-exposure to materials and the absence of any initial adult interference with the children produced a relaxed physiological state which facilitated the free association processes later demanded by the alternative uses test. This interpretation does not invalidate the findings of the study – unquestionably the 'Play' group did show a greater variety of responses on the alternative uses test – but what it suggests is that the priming effect may not have been a direct one upon cognitive processes, but may have been mediated by motivational changes.

If there is one single message which comes through this chapter, it is the importance of the caring adult both in directing the child's

play in an appropriate way at the appropriate moment, and in gaug-
ing the child's mood state and deciding in which circumstances it is
inappropriate to intervene. In short, adults' activities cannot be
merely monitorial if they are to make the best use of the pre-school's
resources. The adult must be clear in her objectives, that is, what
are the developmental processes which are to be potentiated. The
adult must be sensitive to the child's mood state and know what
developmental processes are most likely to be facilitated in that
particular state. It is clear that 'play' – and the purest form of play
to most caring adults (Chapter 7) appears to be fantasy play – by
itself is not the most direct route to understanding; adult intervention
is essential. Wilson's (1980) study shows, as did the studies by
Anderson (1980) and Hughes (1981) reported in the previous
chapter, that whether the adult uses fantasy or not in her interaction
with the child is not important. What is important is that the child
is stimulated by the adult to interact with materials and to engage in
conversation. Leaving the child to 'do her own thing' has limited
value. As we have seen in the case of problem-solving, allowing the
child simply to 'play about' may actually inhibit learning of the
possibilities of materials. Even children's creativity, which requires
a relaxed mood state, is enhanced when the adult engages in
activities which are both more likely to engender such a mood state
and are gently directive. Finally, we saw in the case of the attempted
replication of the Golomb and Cornelius (1977) study that the precise
way in which adults talk to children during fantasy play may have
crucial effects upon the outcomes of such studies.

# Chapter 14

# From nursery to reception class

In Chapter 3, we noted that both the parents of nursery school children and nursery school teachers themselves saw nursery attendance as a 'preparation' for primary school. In discussion, teachers frequently claimed that former nursery school children would be expected to adjust to the demands of primary school much more readily than children who had come straight from home. It was suggested, for example, that children with nursery experience would be superior to their inexperienced peers in applying themselves to school work, i.e. their concentration would be greater. It was also suggested that the social competence of the former nursery children would be greater in terms of their ability to deal with teachers; for example, such children would be more effective in attracting and holding the attention of teachers when they (the children) required help. This chapter describes two studies addressed to these suppositions regarding the performance of nursery school children when they reach primary school. The behaviour is compared, during the first term of reception class, of children who have attended nursery school with that of ones who have no nursery experience. The variables chosen for study were: their attention spans; their relative ability to elicit adults' attention.

## Attention spans in reception classes

It is sometimes argued that pre-school experience enables a child to settle into a school regime more easily than if he had not had that experience. It may be that a child at nursery school learns to concentrate in spite of other activities going on around him. Some evidence supporting this supposition was obtained in a study of children in their own homes, who were found to be more distractible than their peers in nursery schools (Davie *et al.*, 1984). We examined the hypothesis, therefore, that the nature of pre-school experience has some effect on children's ability to attend when they commence primary school.

Forty-nine children from the reception class of six primary schools were observed during their second week of school: twenty-six children (fourteen boys and twelve girls) had previously attended a nursery school or class and twenty three (eleven boys and twelve girls) had been at home.

Each child was observed during the second week of term on two occasions, each lasting fifteen minutes. Observations were made in the morning during normal school activity when the child's behaviour was usually task-oriented, and excluded breaks for milk and lunch. Two similar observations of each child were made again in the three weeks prior to the end of term. The child's behaviour was monitored by an observer using a four-channel event recorder, each channel of which was used to record a different aspect of behaviour as follows:

Channel 1: attention to task or activity – recorded duration of the child's orientation to a task;

Channel 2: look/watch – duration of periods when the child looked elsewhere (e.g. at picture or wall), or watched other children;

Channel 3: peer interaction – duration of any encounter with another child;

Channel 4: adult participation – duration of a child's attention to adult's speech or to activity in which adult was also involved.

Channels 3 and 4 could record simultaneously with Channel 1, or independently. Absence of record on all four channels during the session denoted that the child was 'looking around, with no point of focus'. For all channels, the child's visual orientation was taken as determining the focus of attention. After the observations every entry on each channel of a recording was measured and the distances translated into time.

Attention spans were longest when children were involved in tasks or activities (Channel 1, mean = 15.9 seconds) as opposed to looking and watching (Channel 2, mean = 7.7 seconds) or interacting with other children (Channel 3, mean = 6.9 seconds). Simultaneous analysis of Channels 1 and 4 yielded the durations of attention when an adult was present with the child at a task and the

TABLE 14.1: *Attention spans (in seconds) for activities in the reception class according to pre-school experience*

| Pre-school experience | | Start of term | | End of term | |
|---|---|---|---|---|---|
| | | Alone | With adult | Alone | With adult |
| Nursery | Girls | 16.1 | 20.2 | 17.4 | 24.1 |
| | Boys | 11.0 | 22.8 | 18.0 | 17.2 |
| | Both | 13.5 | 21.5 | 17.7 | 20.7 |
| Home | Girls | 16.5 | 13.8 | 20.5 | 24.5 |
| | Boys | 10.6 | 14.0 | 17.2 | 18.7 |
| | Both | 13.0 | 13.9 | 18.8 | 21.6 |

spans achieved when the adult was absent. The mean spans for attention to task at the beginning and at the end of term, with and without an adult, are given in Table 14.1. The influence of the adult was a statistically significant factor, while the time spent at the primary school was a factor that approached significance. Neither sex nor type of pre-school experience proved to be significant.

Analysis of Channel 3 revealed that periods of peer interaction were shorter at the beginning of term (mean = 6.2 seconds) than at the end (mean = 7.6 seconds), but the difference fell short of statistical significance. However, in terms of frequency of interaction rather than duration, the children with nursery experience had significantly higher scores, both at the beginning and at the end of term.

The most important factor in the study appeared to be the involvement of the adult in focusing the child's attention. Surprisingly, in view of claims previously made, the nature of pre-school experience had little effect on the child's ability to attend. By the end of the term, children who had entered reception class directly from home were indistinguishable from children who had attended nursery school, with regard to their attention spans both when alone and when with an adult.

## Children's bids for attention

Because of their previous experience in the nursery of attempting to elicit an adult's attention in competition with others, nursery school or nursery class children may be more effective in gaining the teacher's attention in the reception class than their peers with no nursery experience. Children were therefore observed during their first term in the reception class in order to ascertain what types of bids and how many bids or approaches to adults they made, and how successful they were in gaining a response from the adult. Half the children had previously attended a nursery school or class, and half had remained at home.

Thirty-two children were observed in eight reception classes of infant schools. From each of these classes four children were selected: one boy and one girl who had been to a nursery school or class, and one boy and one girl who had not previously attended a nursery. Thus there were eight children in each group. The children were each observed during the second or third week of their first term at infant school for a session of forty-five minutes during normal school activities in the morning. Milk breaks and sessions such as music and movement were not included in the observations.

Children's bids for attention and the adults' responses were monitored by the observer who recorded these according to pre-selected categories. Types of bids noted were either verbal or non-verbal as follows:

Verbal speech (VS): child asks a question or makes a comment to an adult.

Verbal call name (VCN): child calls an adult by name to elicit attention.

Verbal call other (VCO): child calls out, not using the adult's name.

Non-verbal approach (NVA): child approaches adult without speaking, e.g. child walks up to the adult holding a book to be marked.

Non-verbal symbol (NVS): child seeks attention by using a symbol according to the custom of the school, e.g. raises hand or puts hands on head.

Non-verbal direct contact (NVD): child makes direct contact with the adult to gain her attention by, for example, patting her arm, tugging at her clothes without speaking.

On some occasions, verbal and non-verbal approaches might be combined, e.g. child puts hand up and calls out simultaneously, in which case both were recorded.

Adult responses were also recorded according to whether they were verbal or non-verbal, and also where there was no response, as follows:

TABLE 14.2: *Number of bids made*

|     | Total | Mean no. of bids/child | SD | Non-verbal | Verbal | Non-verbal + verbal |
|-----|-------|------------------------|------|--------------|-------------|----------------------|
| HB  | 45    | 5.63                   | 5.24 | 25 (55.5%)   | 13 (28.8%)  | 7 (15.5%)            |
| NB  | 95    | 11.98                  | 5.44 | 48 (50.5%)   | 37 (38.9%)  | 10 (10.5%)           |
| HG  | 40    | 5.00                   | 2.33 | 30 (75.0%)   | 3 (7.5%)    | 7 (17.5%)            |
| NG  | 34    | 4.25                   | 2.38 | 17 (50.0%)   | 10 (29.4%)  | 7 (20.6%)            |

Verbal response (VR): adult responds with a comment, explanation or other speech.

Non-verbal response (NVR): adult responds without speaking, e.g. by nodding, or marking work which has been presented.

Ignore (I): adult ignores, or fails to notice, a child's bid, and does not respond to it.

### Number of bids

Boys and girls who had come straight from home (HB and HG), and girls who had attended a nursery school or class (NG), all made a similar number of bids for the adult's attention. Boys who had attended a nursery previously (NB) made rather more bids than the others (see Table 14.2) but the difference was not significant, partly because the greater number was largely accounted for by two particular boys in a sample of eight.

### Types of bid

The bids were divided into non-verbal bids (i.e. NVA, NVS, NVD) and verbal bids (VS, VCN, VCO). Bids which contained both non-verbal and verbal elements were combined with verbal bids. Table 14.3(a) shows the percentages of the different types of bids. Slightly more non-verbal bids were made than verbal bids, except in the case of girls from home, who made very few verbal bids. The difference between groups was not significant. However, when children from home were compared with children from nursery regardless of sex, the nursery children made significantly more verbal bids compared with the home children.

200

TABLE 14.3(a): *Comparison of verbal and non-verbal bids:*
*percentages*

|    | Non-verbal (%) | Verbal and combined (%) |
|----|------|------|
| HB | 55.5 | 44.4 |
| NB | 50.5 | 49.4 |
| HG | 75.0 | 25.0 |
| NG | 50.0 | 50.0 |

TABLE 14.3(b): *Comparison of verbal and non-verbal bids:*
*numbers*

|         | Non-verbal | Verbal and combined | Total no. of bids |
|---------|------|------|------|
| Home    | 55   | 30   | 85   |
| Nursery | 65   | 64   | 129  |

TABLE 14.4: *Success of bids*

|    | No. of bids | Success | Fail |
|----|------|------|------|
| HB | 45   | 30 (66.7%) | 15 (33.3%) |
| NB | 95   | 63 (66.3%) | 32 (33.7%) |
| HG | 40   | 28 (70.0%) | 12 (30.0%) |
| NG | 34   | 23 (67.6%) | 11 (32.4%) |

TABLE 14.5: *Successes and failures of nursery and home*
*children's bids*

|            | Success | Fail | Total |
|------------|------|------|------|
| Non-verbal | 69   | 51   | 120  |
| Verbal     | 75   | 19   | 94   |
|            | 144  | 70   | 214  |

*Success of bids*

(i) The bids were examined to see which were successful, i.e. received a verbal or non-verbal response from an adult, and which were unsuccessful, i.e. received no response from an adult. Overall, the success of bids was evenly distributed between the children (see Table 14.4). (ii) When the bids were subdivided into verbal and non-verbal bids and the data pooled for all subjects, it was found that bids containing verbalizations were more likely to be successful than non-verbal bids, and that the difference was significant. The overall figures for this comparison are shown in Table 14.5. (iii) Finally, the data were examined to see if any particular children were more successful than the others at gaining the attention of adults. Since verbal bids were more successful than non-verbal bids at gaining the attention of an adult, it was thought that boys from nurseries, having made more verbal bids, might exhibit more success than the other children. However, this was not the case as there were a large number of unsuccessful verbal bids made by just two of the boys out of a sample of eight.

## Discussion

Measures of attention span, especially with the adult present, and of children's success in bidding for teacher's attention, may be seen as two facets of the social controls of the reception class. Children with nursery experience differed only very slightly from children without such experience. Children from nurseries did, however, make more verbal bids for attention than children straight from home, though this finding hides a large sex difference, the girls making relatively few of the bids. The only other statistically significant finding was that the verbal bids were more successful in attracting attention than non-verbal bids.

Our findings are not unlike those of Jowett and Sylva (1986) who compared performance on the Boehm (1970) Test of Basic Concepts and the Adjustment to School Scale (Thompson, 1972) in two groups of working-class children, first when they entered reception class and again six months later. One group had attended a local authority nursery class; the other were 'graduates' of local playgroups. Performance on the Boehm Test was not significantly different between the two groups, but the children who had attended nursery class were reported as showing better concentration when alone, they were more independent and they approached teachers as 'resources for learning'. In other words, the former nursery school children seemed to be more confident and more successful in attracting the attention of teachers than children from playgroups. (It may be noted that many of the children in our 'home' sample had, in fact, attended a playgroup for several hours a week.)

Initially, we were somewhat surprised to find that in the reception class children with nursery experience were so similar to those without. One possible explanation for our findings is that we might have been unfortunate in our choice of measures. However, not only did our measures intuitively seem reasonable, they had been selected in collaboration with nursery teachers. If, as our teacher colleagues suggested, nursery school is a 'preparation' for primary school, children having experience of nursery school might have been expected to show superior powers of concentration (as measured by attention span) and greater adroitness in handling contacts with adults (as measured by ability to attract and hold their attention).

If fact, reasons for the similarity of the two groups were not difficult to find. When we examined in detail the regimes of the various reception classes employed in this study, we realized that the classes chosen were very conventional in their teaching style. The demands of the teachers for children to 'pay attention' and to 'speak when spoken to' seemed to impose a consistency of behaviour which quickly supervened any differences between groups which initially may have been present. As we saw in Table 14.1 the two groups, children with nursery experience and those without, became more similar as the term progressed. What this suggests is that the ethos of the primary school is different from that both of the home and of the pre-school. As Cleave *et al.* (1982) indicate:

> Routines and patterns of appropriate behaviour, such as how to move from place to place in an orderly manner, and when to keep still and silent, have to be learned for specific events like assembly, PE, and music and movement which take place away from the classroom (p. 206).

Children have to learn to 'toe the line' in a way which is as unfamiliar to the ex-nursery school children as it is to the children who come straight from home.

The homogeneity of behaviour imposed upon children in the reception class is at variance with the expectations of nursery teachers who clearly believe that their work with pre-school children in some way may equip their charges better to cope with the primary school. This gap between the expectations of nursery teachers and the reality of primary school is also touched upon by Cleave *et al.* (1982). Drawing from their own experience of the transition from pre-school to primary school, they point out that gaps in understanding may arise from:

*What do children learn from pre-school?*

Pre-school staff who do not know what goes on in other provisions, who would like more contact with schools and who feel their opinions are not valued.

Infant staff who know nothing of their new entrants' pre-school experience, who regard pre-schools with suspicion, who seem unapproachable to parents and non-professionals, and who are unaware of the cultural customs of their pupils (Cleave *et al.*, 1982, p. 210).

What the studies reported in this chapter show is (i) the effectiveness of the social controls of the reception class; (ii) the mismatch between the expectations of nursery school staff and those of primary school staff. We would thus fully endorse the conclusion of Cleave *et al.* (1982):

there is a need for everyone concerned with young children to learn about each other's work and visit each other's provision. Barriers of suspicion, professional jealousy and entrenched attitudes must be broken down in the interests of co-operating together for the benefits of the child (pp. 211–12).

# The findings and
# implications of the study

# Chapter 15

# Summary of findings

In this chapter we need to bring together some of the main points from each of our areas of inquiry to see if there are any generalizations which may be drawn regarding either the organization of pre-school activities or their significance in psychological development. Before doing so, however, we perhaps should ask to what extent our findings may be regarded as having a reasonable degree of generality. During the course of the project we studied the behaviour of about one thousand children who passed through fifty or more pre-school establishments. The various nursery schools and classes, the day nurseries and the playgroups were located in the two areas we designated Area A and Area B: respectively, the city of Stoke-on-Trent with the adjacent municipal borough of Newcastle-under-Lyme; and the three South Cheshire towns of Crewe, Winsford and Macclesfield. In the companion volume to the present one, Davie *et al.* (1984) have compared the demographic characteristics of Stoke-on-Trent with those of seven other urban areas. The main difference between Stoke-on-Trent and the other areas resides in its chief manufacture, pottery. Because so many of the jobs performed within the pottery industry are categorized as Social Class III Manual in the Registrar General's Classification, there tends to be an over-representation of this category in Area A compared with our nearest major cities, Birmingham and Manchester. Compared with these cities also there is an under-representation of people in Social Classes I and II. Ethnic minority groups are also somewhat under-represented in comparison with our nearest large cities, Birmingham and Manchester. In terms of most of the indices of what may be termed 'the quality of life' – home ownership, sanitation, curtilage, etc. – Stoke is roughly intermediate between an inner-city area such as Lambeth and a relatively prosperous city of equivalent size such as Nottingham. Overall, however, we have no reason to suppose that the social and economic *milieu* of the children in our studies was markedly different from that of children from other urban areas. Moreover, the fact that Area A and Area B children and adults within the same type of provision (e.g. nursery school or playgroup) were so similar to each other in terms of attitudes and behaviour, but equally were different from people within a different type of provision in terms of attitudes and behaviour, suggest that our findings should have a reasonable degree of generality. That is, the type of *provision* attended is a more important determinant of behaviour than is its geographical location.

The one feature of the pre-school provision in Stoke-on-Trent which is different from that of other areas is that nursery classes are generally staffed by nursery nurses rather than by nursery teachers, the overall directive responsibility for the class being taken by the primary school head teachers. We think it unlikely that this regional anomaly should seriously distort our findings on nursery classes for, as we saw in Chapter 4, in their views about pre-school, nursery nurses in nursery classes are much more like nursery teachers than they are like fellow nursery nurses in day nurseries. With this caution in mind, we will now attempt to draw out what seem to be the salient features of our findings.

## Organization of pre-school environments

A wide variety of activities was potentially available in all nurseries but, on average, the greatest number actually available was found in playgroups. This was because playgroups tended to put out all their equipment at once. Fewest activities were found in day nurseries, especially where children were family grouped. Nursery schools and nursery classes had more materials than other provisions, but were selective in setting them out. They were also more diligent than the other provisions in organizing, structuring and directing children's activities with the available materials. Nursery schools both engaged in a wider variety of *organized activities* and showed greater variability of content than other provisions. The organized activities generally comprised story and singing sessions, assembly, playing musical instruments and use of audiovisual aids such as a record player or television. In contrast, organized activities were observed less frequently in playgroups and tended to be much more stereotyped in the way they utilized materials than was the case with nursery schools. This may perhaps reflect an undue reliance in playgroups upon the course materials of the Pre-School Playgroups Association.

During free-play in all provisions children were most frequently seen using representational objects (e.g. dolls, cars) and in the 'home corner'. Sand and water, though often provided, were played with comparatively infrequently. The range of activities engaged upon by children with sand and water was small and activities tended to be stereotyped, such as pouring from one receptacle to another. Adults were most frequently seen at potentially 'messy' activities such as clay, collage and painting. Adult participation in sand and water activities was low except in day nurseries where the presence of younger children necessitated adult presence to mop up spills.

## The staff of the pre-school

There were some marked differences amongst the adults in charge of the various pre-school provisions. Nursery assistants in day nurseries tended to be younger, less experienced and less likely to have children of their own than nursery assistants in nursery schools/classes or than nursery teachers. In general, however, adults involved in the care of children in the various forms of pre-school provision shared more similarities than they displayed differences. The adults in all forms of provision gave strongly vocational reasons for their choice of occupation, with nursery nurses emphasizing helping the disadvantaged child. They were also quite surprisingly in accord regarding the benefits of pre-school attendance. The three most important benefits were seen as: (i) the opportunity for children to mix with others; (ii) the enhancement of language development; and (iii) the opportunity to discover and employ their potential. In general, the staff of nursery schools and classes emphasized language development more than mixing and the playgroup staff vice versa. Day nursery staff tended to stress the importance of the child's emotional development.

When asked to rank six putative nursery programmes in order of priority, all pre-school staff chose the one allowing the child 'to develop his potential at his own rate in a caring environment'. Thus, despite the differences of ethos of the various provisions and the differences in training of the adults who administer them, the practice of the various provisions is remarkably similar. The staff of all types of pre-school provision emphasize 'free-play' and place relatively little emphasis upon organized activity. However, as we indicated in the previous section, nursery teachers show more concern about organization than other caring adults, and even when they adopt a *laissez-faire* approach, it is informed by ideological assumptions regarding the presumed manner in which children gain from their experiences in the nursery. A somewhat sad finding of this part of the study was the low importance accorded to the role of parents as a complement to the work of the pre-school. In the recent study by Ward (reported in Chapters 3 and 5) it was found that the expectations and aspirations of parents and nursery teachers were often at variance, if not diametrically opposed. The notion of parents and adults acting as partners in the 'institutionalized' care of children clearly has a long way to go. Even so, we found (Chapter 4) that nursery staff in nursery schools/classes considered the home–school link to be of paramount importance, emphasizing the need to know about the child's home background. What seems to be amiss is the unilateral notion of partnership often adopted by nursery staff – a point made by Gordon (1968) – such staff having the right to request knowledge and aid of parents, but not vice versa. It was found that nursery nurses in particular accorded parental involvement the lowest priority, a finding noted also by Watt (1977) who found that nursery nurses were unwilling to concede to parents a role in the nursery which might pre-empt their own.

Overall, both the attitudes of nursery staff and their practice are centred on the child and the need to provide an environment in which he can develop in his own way and at his own pace. Adults comprise the most important resource of the pre-school. In all types of pre-school more children are present at a task when an adult is present than when no adult is present. Thus, although in principle a child is free to choose his own pursuit during the greater part of the nursery session (formally 'organized' activities, as we saw above, accounted for only 30 per cent of the session), in practice this choice may be greatly influenced by the way in which adults choose to distribute their time. Thus, the ratio of children to adults, and the adult's contribution to the child's play activity, are important factors in determining the play sequences that occur in the pre-school, and consequently the learning that occurs. In general, about 20 per cent of the time of the adults in all types of pre-school was spent in monitorial activities and about 10 per cent in tasks which took them away from the main area of the children's activities (though because of the special physical needs of their younger age group, in day nurseries the percentage was higher). The remaining time was divided between 'associative' and 'non-associative' activities. It is with regard to these two activities that the greatest differences are observed in the behaviour of the various pre-school provisions. The adults (teachers and nursery assistants) of the nursery school and nursery class (predominantly nursery assistants in the North

Staffordshire area) spent a significantly greater amount of their time on associative activities – active participation in the child's play – than upon non-associative activities. The latter activities – tidying up, putting out materials, talking to other adults – occur most frequently amongst playgroup staff. Moreover, we found that the activity spans – that is, the time spent upon individual activities – within the general category of associative activity were on average longer per child for nursery school/class staff than for day nursery or playgroup staff, the latter having the shortest activity spans of all. However, again it is the similarities amongst the four pre-school provisions which assume importance rather than their differences. It was noted in Chapter 5 that the activity spans of the adults – that is, the *average* amount of time continuously devoted to a single activity – in the various provisions never exceeded one minute. When we examined adults' attention spans with individual children, the period of time that an adult was able to attend to a child before her attention was diverted to another child, the figure was even lower – about forty-five seconds. The fluidity of the 'free-play' situation and the constant interruptions – which, whether from children or from other members of staff, are largely adventitious – often serve to terminate involvement with a particular child. That most adult attention spans are of less than one minute should be a matter of concern since it implies that periods of concentrated work with a single child who may particularly require attention are often precluded. Given the child:adult ratios observed in pre-school settings and the fragmentation of attention which this leads to, it is remarkable that the adults are able to maintain a coherent sequence of guidance and stimulation for so many children.

## Children's activities in the pre-school

Activities in the four contexts were fairly similar overall, most time being spent in activities with materials, especially in nursery classes. Physical activities were highest in playgroups. Most fantasy play was seen in nursery schools and nursery classes. Quite high amounts of 'transit' activities – that is, looking and walking around – were seen in all contexts, approaching 30 per cent of the time. Children's activity spans were found to be longest in nursery schools and nursery classes, and shortest in day nurseries. In all cases they increased when an adult was present, the effect of the adult being most marked in day nurseries where the child's attention was otherwise most fragmented.

In general, children were incisive in their choice of activities, which usually they both chose and left of their own volition. Moreover, they attended for longer periods to activities which they themselves chose than to ones to which they had been directed. However, a particular activity having been chosen, the quality of the child's play often fell far short of the caring adult's expectations. Examination of the interview and questionnaire data (Chapters 6 and 7) reveals a diffuseness of view amongst the caring adults as to the purpose of particular materials and activities. (This was particularly notable in the case of imaginative play – see below.) For example, in the case of play with dry sand, adults frequently suggested that it assisted imaginative play, whilst others suggested that through play with this material children would learn to share and co-operate. In practice, the activities of the children with dry sand were highly stereotyped and repetitive, comprising largely of pouring sand from one receptacle to another and the children had little or no interaction either with each other or with adults. Similarly, in the case of water play, adults frequently stressed its value in the development of children's cognitive processes. Yet, although some exploratory activities were observed, such as pushing objects under water and watching them bob up again, the predominant activities again were stereotyped and repetitive, the most frequently occurring pattern of behaviour being moving objects out of the way. Indeed, it is difficult to see how what Sylva *et al.* (1980) have entitled the 'cognitive challenge' of materials and activities can be realized without the active participation of adults. As we have seen, the sand and water troughs tend to be places where children go to be alone, perhaps to retreat for a time from the hustle and bustle of the nursery. Where several children appear simultaneously at these activity areas they tend to play in parallel rather than interactively. It is perhaps unsurprising, therefore, that so much of the child's time at the water trough has to be devoted to moving other children's objects out of the way. The interest of adults in these areas is often merely monitorial, preventing or clearing up spills.

The sand and water troughs are examples of what we have termed 'micro-environments'. We can see that there are good practical reasons for creating and preserving such micro-environments for special purposes. However, to do so creates a paradox. Adults in the pre-school, especially nursery teachers, constantly reiterate the special importance of imaginative play. Yet, when children create an episode of particularly imaginative activity by attempting to link two micro-environments, e.g. by taking 'cakes' of sand and water into the Wendy house, their action results in disapproval – they are 'messing up' the Wendy house. In short, children are often thwarted in one of the psychological processes about which teachers presumably are most concerned, i.e. making new cognitive connections. Of all the caring adults, nursery teachers would be the most incensed were we to suggest that they are actively discouraging their charges from a most important learning experience; but this indeed appears to be the case.

One feature of the pre-school which particularly interested us was the use made of physical play. We saw that indoors such play was most prevalent in playgroups, especially amongst boys. We inferred that the other provisions tended to discourage physical play indoors, no doubt with good reason, because of its potential safety hazard. However, there may be another reason for the relatively low occurrence of physical play even outdoors amongst at least two of the other provisions. Nursery teachers place a relatively low value upon physical play as a medium for anything other than 'letting off steam'. Its potential for inculcating cognitive skills is seldom realized. In consequence, outdoor activities in nursery schools and classes are even more stereotyped than indoor ones. Just as nursery teachers seem loath to make connections indoors between different micro-environments – the products of the easel, the sand tray or the water trough are not for use elsewhere – so they seem loathe to attribute functions of 'indoor' activities to outdoor ones, such as physical play. Thus, the teacher's role outdoors becomes more monitorial than educative.

When full-time and part-time children were compared, only slight differences in behaviour were observed. Part-time children tended to spend less time looking and watching, and more time in exploratory activities, than full-timers. Full-time children spent more time in fantasy play than part-time children, especially during the afternoon sessions. The activity spans for part-time children were longer than those for full-time children. It appears that both part-time and full-time children give precedence to exploratory activities. Fantasy play is only engaged upon by the full-timers when a certain amount of exploratory activity (equal to that of the part-timers) has been accomplished.

## Fantasy play

Teachers were interviewed in order to ascertain their views on fantasy play. Almost all of them felt that this kind of play was very important for pre-school children. However, there were marked differences of opinion as to its attributes or its exact benefits. The most frequently quoted benefits (in order) were that fantasy play served emotional needs, aided language development and promoted reasoning. Our studies of fantasy play strongly suggested that fantasy play did indeed *reflect* both a child's emotional state and its linguistic competence (see below) but there was no evidence to suggest that either was *aided* by fantasy play. As for promoting reasoning, the study by Hughes (1981) quoted in Chapter 13 indicated that the solution of a problem using materials to which the child had previously been exposed was the more readily solved if he did *not* engage in fantasy play.

A study of fantasy play revealed that much of this type of play was fairly simple, using small replicas of adults' objects, and occurred in the home corner based on domestic themes. Elsewhere in the nursery more variety was found and themes included pretending to be well-known characters such as police officers and television stars, while objects were used to represent different things, such as blocks becoming guns or buildings in the child's imagination. Quite complex themes developed where props were most flexible. Girls tended to concentrate on domestic themes more than boys.

New children at nursery school did not engage in fantasy play during their first two weeks, and only a little in subsequent weeks. Only after the first month did these children manifest 'normal' levels of fantasy play. Fantasy play and social play increased over the six months as children became more relaxed and got to know one another better. Thus a child's emotional state may be inferred from the presence of fantasy play. Such play occurs only in positive affective states.

A number of studies were carried out to examine the extent to which fantasy play could be boosted by 'play tutoring' and whether such tutoring had any beneficial effects upon the child's cognitive abilities. Although the aims and methods of the studies differed in detail, the overall picture is quite clear. Fantasy play can be increased by play tutoring but its enhancement does not appear to confer any intellectual benefits which cannot be attributed to other factors. For example, if children were encouraged to engage upon fantasy play incorporating themes from special events (e.g. a visit to a diary farm), their subsequent knowledge of the event was no greater than that of children who had merely discussed the event with a teacher, made drawings and looked at relevant pictures. In two studies, the development of children tutored in fantasy play was compared with that of children given tutoring in 'perceptual skills' and with that of a control group who were given no special tutoring. Short-term improvements in cognitive ability, as measured by changes in the General Cognitive Index of the McCarthy test, were obtained in both tutored groups relative to the control group, but the fantasy-tutored group did not differ from the perceptual skills group.

This series of studies on fantasy play is on-going, but so far we would regard the case of the intellectual or social benefits of fantasy play to be unproven. Moreover, the amount of fantasy play manifested by children in our four pre-school settings (the case may not be the same for the home) was uncorrelated with any of the variables which might be thought to reflect variations in cognitive style: IQ, social class or personality (Hughes, 1981).

Examination of fantasy play may reveal a competence in the child which otherwise is not apparent. Having noted that the speech of many day nursery children was limited or primitive, recordings were made of their ordinary discourse and of their discourse during fantasy play. An interesting finding was that of four measures of linguistic complexity, three were significantly greater in play than in normal discourse. Moreover, there was a tendency for statements of intention and speech acts associated with announcing, regulating and planning activities to occur more frequently during fantasy play. Children appear to be able to use two linguistic codes, fantasy play betraying a linguistic competence beyond that evident in their day-to-day speech. We were thus driven to regard fantasy play not so much as an aid to learning, but as an aid to 'diagnosis' of the child's mood, past experience and hidden talents.

## Child–adult interaction

A study was made on adult responses to children's overtures in nursery school. The most frequent approaches made by children were requests (to do certain activities) and statements (about activities), in that order. Adult responses tended to occupy the child rather than to seek from or offer information to the child, and there were no differences between teachers and nursery assistants. Most adult responses (nearly 30 per cent) were questions, often in the form of turning the child's statement into a question. Other frequently occurring responses were statements of a general nature about the activities, minimal responses (e.g. 'Yes, dear') and instructions (e.g. 'Put it there'). Responses which gave explanations were infrequent, but were slightly more common by teachers than by caring adults in other pre-school provisions.

Observations of adults were made in all four types of pre-school. The frequency of occurrence of different types of adult utterance was recorded. Adults spoke more to children than to other adults in all contexts and this trend was more noticeable in nursery schools and nursery classes. In playgroups the incidence of adults speaking to other adults was greater than in other types of nursery. Spontaneous utterances were more frequent than other types of utterance (e.g. response to child's action) in nursery school, nursery class and playgroup. In day nurseries, however, most adult speech occurred in response to children's actions. Adult speech in response to child speech was highest in nursery classes compared with other forms of nursery. Overall, teachers in nursery schools talked most to children, followed by nursery assistants in nursery classes. The lowest mean number of utterances was made by day nursery staff.

Similar records were made of children's speech. Children talked more to one another than to adults except in playgroups, where there was a higher ratio of adults to children. When speech was divided into four categories ('spontaneous', 'response to child speech', 'response to child action' and 'response to adult') differences were found between children in different establishments. Children in nursery schools used most spontaneous speech, followed by child-initiated speech. In nursery classes and playgroups response to child speech was highest, followed by spontaneous speech in nursery classes and by response to child action in playgroups. In day nurseries child speech tended to be initiated by the actions of other children. Overall, girls preferred to talk to adults, and boys to boys, though there were some variations according to the type of establishment.

Our overall impression of the verbal interaction of children and adults in the pre-school is similar to that of Wood *et al.* (1980). Adults are anxious not to deny children the opportunity to converse with them. However, the efforts of adults to give equal attention to the fragmentary verbal gambits provided by children (the significance of which is often not understood by the adults) may result in verbal exchanges which are anything but conversation.

**After pre-school**

As we saw in Chapter 1, implicit in any proposal to extend provisions for the under-fives is the assumption that children who enjoy such a provision are benefited in some way, either in the short term or in the long term, relative to the children who do not. However, we are entitled to ask: What benefit? For which children? From which provision? In Chapter 3 we saw that rather similar benefits were claimed for pre-school attendance by the caring adults in the four very different provisions we studied, but these benefits were shrouded in language of such generality that this was hardly surprising. When, however, attempts have been made to measure directly differences between children who have attended a pre-school provision compared with others who have not, the results have often been disappointing. The findings of the Headstart programme (Cicirelli, 1969) have already been mentioned, the early benefits upon cognitive measures 'washing out' in the primary school. However, the benefits of pre-school experience need not be only, or primarily, cognitive. In our own studies we examined the effects of nursery experience upon two somewhat different skills – the ability to concentrate, and success in bidding for the attention of an adult. In the first study, attention spans of children were measured in reception classes at the beginning and at the end of the first term. Children who had had nursery experience were compared with ones who had had no nursery experience. Attention spans to school activities, to adults and to peers were measured, as well as the duration of visual scanning. Children attended longest to school activities, then to adults, and lastly to peers. Visual-scanning attention spans were extremely short. Attention spans for all children increased over the term, and were greater for boys than for girls. Adult participation improved all children's ability to concentrate at any time. There were, however, no significant differences in attention span between nursery and non-nursery groups.

Because of their previous experience of attempting to elicit an adult's attention in competition with others, it was thought that nursery school children would be more effective in gaining a teacher's attention in the reception class than children with no nursery experience. Children with and without nursery experience were compared in terms of their number of bids for attention, their types of bid, verbal or non-verbal, and the success of their bids. It was found that children who had come straight from home and ones who had attended a nursery school all made a similar number of bids for the attention of the adult. Children with nursery experience made significantly more verbal than non-verbal bids than children straight from home, but in terms of success of bids – that is, whether or not a bid attracted the attention of an adult – the two groups were not significantly different. In short, it would appear that children straight from home may be less ready to use verbal means of attracting the teacher's attention, but they are ready to use other means at their disposal, and overall are just as successful in attracting attention as children with nursery experience.

## Conclusions

All four types of provision which we examined were happy, busy places; places where, as we were constantly reminded, children were

217

able to 'realize their potential'. Nevertheless, in terms of their objectives, their organization and their activities, the different provisions remained quite distinctive and it would be foolish to envisage one type of provision taking over the role of the others. In addition we have noted that although there have been some changes, most notably with the introduction of computers into early education, the basic curriculum obtaining within the nursery remains based on the same material foundations as we witnessed at the outset of our studies (Curtis, 1986; Abbott and Fairbrother, 1986). Greater changes have occurred in the processes involved within an activity as the research message implying the desirability of increased structure in children's play has spread. However, most aspects of nursery practice would appear to remain unaltered.

The day nurseries have a wide age range of children including ones under three years, many of whom require a great deal of personal attention purely in terms of their physical needs. It is not surprising, therefore, that the adults caring for such children both perceive and perform their roles in a manner very different from those of adults in other provisions. In comparison with these other provisions, the day nursery adults spend a considerable part of their time in monitorial activities, or outside the immediate purlieu of the children, emptying potties or washing clothes. Even when in immediate contact with the children, the day nursery staff frequently have to devote considerable time to individual children with pressing emotional problems, with a corresponding dilution of their attention to other members of the group. What impressed us in our observations of the day nurseries was how much this area of public sector provision would benefit from a greater input of resources. Where so much of the caring adults' time is spent in looking after a child's physical needs, is it reasonable to expect them to devote an adequate amount of time to their avowed aims of potentiating the child's social and emotional needs?

The physical and emotional privation which often characterized children in the day nurseries was less evident in the playgroups and nursery schools and classes. There were, however, marked differences between the DHSS-supported playgroups and the DES-supported provisions. In general, the playgroups catered for younger children than the nursery schools and classes. Both the parents of children in the two provisions and the caring adults had little doubt that their functions were quite different. The playgroups were seen as an important first step between home and the wider social environment and the skills to be developed by this step are the ability to mix and to gain social poise. In contrast, both parents and the adults in the nursery schools and classes see the skills to be inculcated as cognitive ones, as preparation for the more 'serious' business of the primary school. This difference between playgroup and nursery school is indicated in a number of ways: in the emphases placed by the staffs upon the different aspects of the child's development; by the emphasis upon materials made available to children in the two provisions – sand, water and physical play apparatus as opposed to pre-maths, pre-reading materials; but most of all by the attitudes to playgroups of parents and of playgroup supervisors themselves. Parents clearly saw a distinction between roles of playgroups and nursery schools – the former providing a first step in social competence, the latter a preparation in terms of cognitive skills, differences which they translated into practice. Often, children would be sent to playgroup at age three and then be withdrawn and sent to nursery school at age four. Playgroup supervisors were usually clear that their role was not that of 'preparing' the child for primary school and they indicated that they did not wish to pre-empt the role of the nursery teacher.

In our view, the playgroup supervisors, the nursery teachers and above all the parents, have shown a wisdom of judgment not always evident in discussions of the merits of playgroups (Plowden, 1982). If we are to accept that pre-school is to provide not only an initial training in social skills, but a preparation for the more formal skills of the primary school, we are demanding a level of understanding of cognitive and social development which it is unreasonable to expect adults to derive from sporadic courses, excellent though these may be, such as those run for supervisors by the Pre-School Playgroups Association. This is not to say that we do not have criticisms to make of the training of nursery teachers. The sometimes *laissez-faire* organization of nursery schools, the failure to distinguish the effects of ludic as opposed to exploratory activities, the demeaning of the cognitive potential of outdoor activities and the reluctance of adults to join in children's fantasy play are all matters to which attention should be paid. However, they are all matters which could best be considered as part of the training of teachers. There is scope for considerable improvement in nursery teacher training: teacher trainers could benefit from a more thorough understanding of recent theories of play in relation to cognitive development and of the practical effects of intervening in children's play (Chapter 12). However, these improvements can be brought about only by a continuing investment in teacher training. The training courses of organizations such as the PPA are valuable, but they are no substitute for a teacher training course with its intensive theoretical and practical basis. One matter upon which teacher training courses *can* learn from the PPA is the satisfaction to parents provided by realistic involvement in the development of their children. We have noted (Chapter 3) that nursery teachers acknowledge the importance of home background in influencing early development, yet at the same time they accord a low priority to parental involvement in their child's early education. Moreover, the term 'parental involvement' may have many meanings, spanning the roles of merely admiring observer of the teacher's efforts to joint policy-maker (Gordon, 1968). The latter possibility is hardly known to teachers, but it is in this domain that the PPA scores its most signal success: the parents *are* the policy-makers as far as their children's welfare is concerned. If nursery teachers are to retain their unique role in the preparation of children for primary school, this is a nettle they necessarily must grasp.

The most important resource of all pre-school provision is the adults in charge of them. We have seen that when an adult is present at any activity, children's activity spans are increased by as much as 100 per cent. Conversely, not merely the duration of the children's activities, but also their quality is affected adversely by the absence of an adult. For example, ubiquitous activities, such as play with dry sand or with water, are highly stereotyped when no adult is present to guide the child's activities. In contrast, we saw in Chapters 12 and 13 that where adults are able to work intensively with small groups of children, or even on occasions with individual children, quite remarkable changes may occur in scores on cognitive tests. There may be differences of opinion as to what are the processes affected by such intervention, but there can be no doubt that close child–adult interaction may result in 'magical' changes. What this suggests is that a high child:adult ratio is essential if the type of cognitive benefit we have indicated may ensue. This points to the need for continuing commitment to investment in the public sector, at least at its present level, if the present benefits are to be maintained. Nursery schools and classes provide the most suitable entrée to the ways of the primary school. Their provision should be of the utmost educational priority.

# Chapter 16

# Some implications of this study

## Play in theory and in practice

In Chapter 1 we described some of our own early experiments upon the reactions of nursery school children to a novel toy (Hutt, 1966), over a six-day period. We showed that children's behaviour towards the toy could be divided into two categories. During the first few days of exposure the predominant group of behaviours was concerned with the inspection and exploration of the object, behaviour being stereotyped in form and accompanied by a facial expression of concentration. During the last three days, a group of behaviours emerged which were innovative, idiosyncratic and unpredictable and were accompanied by a relaxed posture and facial expression. The first groups of behaviours, which we suggested were concerned with the implicit question 'What does this *object* do?', we labelled 'exploration'. The second group, which we suggested were concerned with the implicit question 'What can *I* do with this object?', we labelled 'play'. Although the distinction between exploration and play was made initially on morphological grounds, we also suggested that the two categories could be distinguished in terms of their motivational antecedents and their functions (Hutt, 1970). At the time, we thought we had made a useful contribution in identifying the occasions upon which the description 'playful' could properly be applied to the behaviour of children. As we have already indicated, however, we had underestimated the tenacity with which others, especially nursery staff, would adhere to the term 'play' to describe any or every activity of young children (excepting biological necessities such as eating, sleeping and elimination). We therefore conceded that if every activity of the child in the nursery

221

was to be labelled 'play', two other terms would be required to cover our original distinction between discovering the properties of objects and putting these discoveries to use in a diversive manner. We thus found ourselves thrust back to the terminology employed by Berlyne (1960), who labelled activities concerned with discovery 'epistemic behaviour' and others concerned with diversion 'ludic behaviour'.

After studying the activities of children in pre-school environments we are persuaded that a considerable variety of such activities – not only our original ones directed to the novel toy – can be encompassed by these two main categories. We therefore attempted to develop a taxonomy to account for all those intrinsically motivated, self-chosen activities which occur in the pre-school and which generically we call 'play'. The complete taxonomy is presented in Figure 16.1. It is not regarded as being in any way a definitive classification of children's activities. It is presented here simply as a means of helping to systematize the material presented in Chapters 5 to 12.

The chief subdivisions are *epistemic* behaviour, which is concerned with the acquisition of knowledge and information, and *ludic* behaviour, whose function is essentially diversive, that is, concerned with self-amusement. These two categories of behaviour differ first in their focus of attention, epistemic behaviour being cued by an external source of stimulation, whereas ludic behaviour lacks such a specific focus. Second, while epistemic behaviour is relatively independent of mood state, ludic behaviour is highly mood-dependent – the child plays because she wishes to and simply for the fun of it and if she is anxious it is hardly reasonable to expect her to 'have fun'. Third, there are constraints imposed upon epistemic behaviour which stem from the nature of the focus of attention, whereas any constraints in ludic behaviour are only those which the child imposes upon herself.

These two major categories of play may be further subdivided. On the extreme left of Figure 16.1, we have most task-like to work-like forms of epistemic behaviour, namely *problem-solving* activities – puzzles, jig-saws, formboards, mazes, etc. To a certain extent the objective is inherent in the task itself: even a two-year-old does not need to be told what to do with the formboard, for as it is placed before her she reaches out to pick up the pieces and promptly inserts them. The desire to achieve solution wholly constrains the child and the particular behaviour patterns shown are determined only by the nature of the problem. An equivalent of this category for the adult might be the solution of crosswords.

A second subdivision of epistemic activity, whose objectives

222

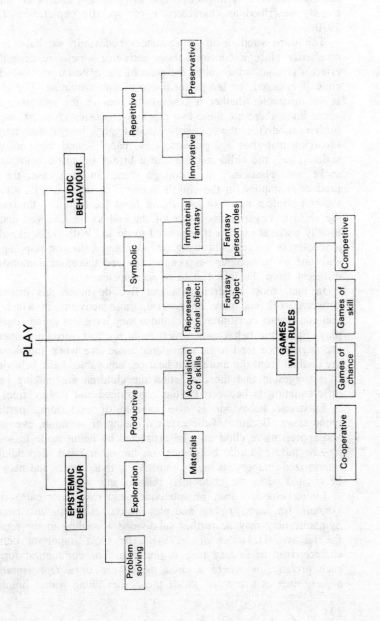

FIGURE 16.1: A proposed taxonomy of children's play

are only a little less explicit, is that of *exploration*: here again, the particular manipulatory movements depend upon the object or material being explored, but the behaviour will be recognized by its attentive features of inspection and investigation and other features already described as characteristic of 'specific exploration' (Hutt, 1970).

The third subdivision of epistemic behaviour we have termed *productive* since it concerns those activities which are designed to effect a change, which alter the state of the material with which the child is engaged, or the performance of the individual. The change is demonstrable whether it concerns actions or the substance acted upon. Since there are these two types of processes involved, we may further subdivide the category accordingly: into those activities involving materials – e.g. sand, clay, paper – and those involving skills. Thus, the child might make a bridge or castle with sand, a snake with plasticine, or a collage scene. In each case, the end-product is implicit in the child's activity; in other words, although the end-product may not be evident from the activities themselves, the child is nevertheless aware of the end to be achieved and can usually make it explicit if requested to do so. With skills like riding a scooter or bicycle, throwing and catching balls, or skipping, the end-state to be achieved is *competence* and therefore demonstrably different from the initial state of incompetence.

In fact, most children of about five do make this distinction between work and play. In general, those activities in which they feel constraints constitute work, those they have fun doing constitute play. Epistemic behaviours which require effort, sustained attention and persistence tend to be considered more like work and therefore are distinct from the more light-hearted, enjoyable, ludic behaviours. It is suggested that the distinction the children are making in this differentiation is between feeling constrained and feeling free.

Epistemic behaviour is also capable of over-riding particular mood states. Because of the external cueing of attention, even a shy and apprehensive child may be distracted by being made to solve a jig-saw puzzle. Ludic behaviour, on the other hand, depending on interiorized imagery, is highly sensitive to mood states and may only be elicited when the child feels relaxed and well.

Ludic behaviour may be subdivided into two major categories – *symbolic* (or fantasy) play, and play which has a *repetitive* element. Symbolic play may be further subdivided according to the focus of the fantasy (Davie *et al.*, 1984). The most important defining characteristic of fantasy play is pretence. The commonest form of such pretence is where a child makes use of a *representational object*, such as a toy car which she pushes along whilst simulating motor noises. The pretence may concern some change in the character of an article or object, as when a stool serves as a hospital trolley or a plate as a steering wheel (*fantasy object*); it may involve the child becoming another character (*fantasy person*) such as a fireman, Dr Who, or a doctor; or it may involve something entirely conjured out of the imagination with no material props at all (*immaterial fantasy*) as when a child claims to be taking Black Beauty for a walk.

Repetitive play may contain new features admixed with the repetition of certain patterns, as in the game where a child runs round the room ringing the bell of our novel toy each time she passes it, but each time doing so with a different part of her anatomy – palm, elbow, head, shoulder and even foot. Again, a child may rehearse an acquired skill like catching a ball bounced off a wall, but it may bounce off different parts of the wall – high, low, far left, far right, etc. Play that involves the repetition of certain actions but also introduces some novel elements may be called *innovative*, and in such play the child may be considered to be consolidating some skill or knowledge, while introducing some novelty to prevent the execution of such a skill from becoming monotonous, as well as perhaps to extend 'combinatorial flexibility' (Bruner, 1976). Where actions are repeated without any novel features they become *perseverative*. The most extreme examples of such activity are the stereotypies of autistic children, where the same sequence of actions is repeated in unvarying form over and over again (Hutt and Hutt, 1968; 1970). Although such extreme manifestations of perseverative behaviour are rare in normal children, we may regard thumb-sucking, rocking or some such repetitive mannerisms as falling in this category.

The categories of epistemic behaviour are defined primarily in functional terms whereas the categories of ludic behaviour are defined more in morphological terms. These relative emphases are the inevitable consequence of the salient features of the behaviours involved: epistemic behaviours are distinguished by the salience of their objectives or goals whereas what characterizes all ludic behaviour is its repetition, its exaggeration, its lack of economy (Loizos, 1967), its 'galumphing' quality (Miller, 1973), or its pretence. Whereas epistemic behaviour is *obligatory*, in some sense, ludic behaviour is *optional*.

The present taxonomy appears to take account of the behavioural distinction which characterizes different forms of play. It may be noted that games with rules occupy a special intermediate position between epistemic and ludic behaviours. This is because games have their own determinants and conventions and are usually highly socially constrained and often ritualized. Whether they can be classified as play at all depends upon their context – for a professional footballer the game of football constitutes work but it is play for the child on the street.

Finally, it should be pointed out that behaviour in the epistemic category may also be performed playfully, in which case the enactment takes on some of the attributes of ludic behaviour. As Miller (1973) argues: 'A child can use a tool or skill for clearly utilitarian purposes – or he can play with it' (p. 92); or as Piaget (1951) in a more general statement proclaims: 'A schema is never essentially ludic or non-ludic, and its character as play depends upon the context and on its actual functioning' (p. 90).

Our brief description of different forms of 'play' probably encompasses all, or almost all, the activities of the pre-school. We contend that the many different types of activity carried out in the nursery depend upon two distinct motivational systems, one of which, epistemic behaviour, directly promotes learning; whilst the other, ludic behaviour, may promote learning only indirectly, or indeed may serve some quite different function. (A more detailed description of the motivational concomitants of epistemic and ludic behaviours is contained in a review by Hutt (1981).)

If we re-examine the activities of the nursery (Chapters 4–11) in the context of this proposed taxonomy, a number of interesting points emerge. Pre-school environments are structured in such a way as to encourage primarily ludic rather than epistemic activity. There are, of course, differences in emphasis between the various pre-school provisions: ludic activity is greatest in day nurseries and least in nursery classes. Nevertheless, the general point stands. This emphasis upon ludic activity may have several origins. In the first place, undoubtedly it is administratively easier in a situation where (say) two adults may be striving to care for twenty or thirty children to allow some children to 'do their own thing' whilst concentrating upon the needs of a selected small group. In the second place, as we saw in Chapter 3 many teachers are committed to the view that free-play is the most important ingredient of early learning. In the light of our studies in Chapters 13 and 14, we see that this view is not self-evidently correct. Free-play, or ludic activity, clearly has an important role in psychological development, but it requires appropriate counterbalancing by epistemic activity. We have indicated (Chapter 1) the optimal conditions under which exploratory activity takes place: the child, in a familiar environment and with a familiar adult present, is confronted with a novel toy whose properties she is to ascertain through her own endeavours; her knowledge of these properties is consolidated by subsequent incorporation into a game or fantasy exploit. Such conditions are difficult to bring about in most pre-school environments, primarily due to the sheer pressure of numbers. The opportunity to provide an environment conducive to evincing epistemic behaviour in individual children or in small groups depends in large part upon the adult:child ratio; the higher the proportion of adults, the more likely it is that an adult will be able to foster the appropriate conditions. However, we would still agree with Tizard *et al.* (1976a) that the quality of the individual member of caring staff's style ultimately is more important than the adult:child ratio. For, even where adults do find themselves in a situation more conducive to the encouragement of epistemic behaviour, they frequently do not exploit it. More often than not adults, in interacting with either a single child or a small group of children, tend to dominate the interaction. We showed this most forcibly in Chapter 9 in our descriptions of conversations between adults and children. Clearly, it is administratively easy to provide for the kinds of activity we have incorporated into the general category of ludic activity. It is also easy to promote those categories of epistemic behaviour (e.g. productive activities) in which the trans-action is dominated by the adult. Moreover, some adults find a 'managerial' style easier to adopt than a ludic participatory one, a point which was made by Anderson (1980) (Chapter 12). In conse-quence, children's activities in the pre-school may tend to lurch from almost totally *laissez-faire* to almost totally adult-dominated. It is an important matter of the training of caring adults in the different pre-school settings that they are made aware of the consequences of, and the alternatives to, these two main approaches.

## Ideology of the pre-school

The studies contained within this volume are essentially descriptive in nature. However, certain inferences may be drawn from the data presented. An explicit component of our brief was to examine and compare the different forms of pre-school provision available to the under-fives in the United Kingdom. Inspection of the studies presented here reveals a distinct similarity between the different contexts notwithstanding historical differences in the underlying reasons for their foundation. A uniformity of approach at several levels may be detected.

First, the contexts of the nursery school, nursery class, day nursery and playgroup may be said to share a common ideology. A nursery represents a recognizable social world which is clearly differentiated from the social worlds of the home and of the infant school. This social world of the nursery may be distinguished with

227

reference to the ideas held by the nursery practitioners about the nature of young children and their learning process. These ideas are seldom explicitly expressed since they are so fundamental and central to work in the nursery as to make their expression unnecessary. Only when the nursery workers were questioned about their beliefs did these ideas become explicit. Examination of the ideas of the nursery staff suggests that they form a coherent body of thought or ideology.

The expressed ideology is essentially child-centred and as such mirrors the Plowden Report. It stresses the importance of early childhood both in its own right and as a critical stage in the child's development. Perhaps the most important quality of the child of pre-school age is his essential innocence. Although it was recognized that children could be 'naughty', blame for naughtiness is not centred on the child but on external factors from which the child should, if possible, be protected. King (1978) describes the ideology of the *infant* teacher thus:

> The child is seen as passing through a naturally ordered
> sequence of physical, physiological, psychological, and social
> development, although each child possesses a unique
> individuality. Young children are naturally curious, exploring
> and discovering things around them, learning best through their
> play and when they are happy and busy and free to choose to
> do what is of interest to them (p. 11).

The ideology of the *nursery* teacher is clearly similar. However there are certain important differences. First, the nursery teacher places an even greater emphasis on childhood innocence. Second, whereas the infant teacher's ideology may reveal a degree of ambivalence towards play, contrasting it with the implicitly more worthwhile 'work', no such ambivalence exists in the ideological framework of staff in the nurseries. In the infant school the range of didactic methods is comparatively great, encompassing both formal instruction and discovery learning. In the nursery, although a certain element of structure may obtain this tends to be covert; the emphasis is clearly upon play as *the* method of knowledge and skill acquisition.

The ideology of pre-school staff is of practical as well as theoretical importance since its influence is both widespread and pervasive. Only a comparatively small minority of staff would appear not to be in accord with the ideological structure as a whole, and these may be staff who have been influenced by contact with other areas of the educational or welfare systems. The effect of the ideology is reflected in the comparative liberty allowed to the nursery child during periods of free-play and in the roles customarily adopted by staff.

The studies reveal that for the greater part of each session pre-schools tend to provide numerous different kinds of activity simultaneously. The reasons for this may be related both to philosophical and to practical considerations. The former would dictate that since the child is the primary determinant of his own needs, a considerable range of different activities is required so that he may seek out a particular activity according to his momentary cognitive and affective requirements. More practically, since usually a considerable number of children are present within the same environment and since it is deemed undesirable that more than a small number should be together at a single activity or resource, numerous sites for activities are required. This policy is not necessarily ideal, however, since it may be a major contributory factor in the brevity of attention and activity spans of both child and adult. Tizard *et al.* (1976b) found no effect of child:adult ratios, but the total number of children present in a room and the amount and variety of equipment available to them may be of importance in determining certain aspects of the behaviour of both children and staff.

If there is general agreement on the underlying ideology of the pre-school, then, so too is there concordance in matters of the form that the actual provision should take. Some facilities for particular kinds of play are ubiquitous.

However, certain forms of play which have traditionally been the subject of considerable attention, e.g. sand and water play and fantasy play, although obvious in terms of provision, assume diminished importance when the temporal aspect of children's play in the pre-school is considered. Play in these areas may be particularly stereotyped and is loaded heavily towards the ludic end of the play spectrum. This is not to deny their possible value. Rather it is to suggest that further consideration should be dedicated to these forms of activity and in particular to the role of the adult.

Indoor play contrasts markedly with outdoor play in most pre-school settings in terms of both the children's behaviour and the adults'. Obviously certain constraints operate upon play in the indoor environment which may preclude particular forms of gross motor activity. Moreover, when the children are outside it is evident that the increase in level of motoric activity requires a greater degree of monitorial behaviour from the adult on the grounds of safety. However, it is disturbing that the contrast between the two types of environment should be so great, and more adult participation in some outdoor activities might be felt to be desirable.

Each of the previous two paragraphs has ended by suggesting a need to reconsider the role of the adult in the pre-school. We regard the caring adult as the most vital element of the pre-school's resources. Equipment of the appropriate kind is important but the quality of the staff is paramount. The picture of the pre-school that emerges from these studies suggests that there is a need for a greater degree of planning in provision in terms of materials, of staff roles and of time.

As Wood *et al.* (1980) point out, staff should be aware of their operational styles. The language studies of the present volume suggest that adults tend to dominate conversations, which are essentially superficial. This tendency, we feel sure, is not intentional and a variety of factors contribute to its existence. It may be seen as a consequence of the combination of the environmental factors already discussed and the staffs' belief that it is incumbent upon them always to respond to children's overtures. A degree of structure in the nursery environment clearly is desirable, but the form that this structure takes may vary considerably. Structure should not necessarily be equated with formality or inflexibility. In fact, our recommendation would be for the adoption of a 'transparent' structure rather than an 'opaque' structure.

## Implications for the training of the caring adults

The training of adults concerned with the care of pre-school children presents numerous problems. The successful training of nursery teachers may prove especially difficult, since the role of the good nursery teacher contains numerous facets each of which needs to be developed in the student. By implication, the points we shall make with regard to the training of nursery teachers apply to the training of all adults involved in pre-school provision. Not only must the nursery teacher be able to deal with the young child in a sympathetic manner, handling his early social and emotional development, guiding his cognitive awareness, and stimulating him to greater physical accomplishments, but she must also be able to communicate and empathize with parents. As we have previously indicated, the nursery represents the first point of contact with the educational system for parents, and the nursery teacher is often the first person to be entrusted with the child's welfare outside the family home. It is of great importance, therefore, that a rapport is established between nursery and home at an early stage, and it is obviously desirable that the nursery teacher is skilled in dealing with the family as a whole as well as the child in particular.

Work with adults is indeed a key component amongst the attributes required in the making of a successful nursery teacher since she is frequently in close contact with them throughout her working day. Whereas teachers in other parts of the educational system customarily work in a quasi-autonomous fashion within their own classroom, seldom is this the case for the nursery teacher, who usually works in close partnership with another teacher or a nursery nurse. The nursery teacher therefore needs to be able to communicate and co-operate with other workers in the provision of a structure for the child's play. We have argued that two forms of structure may be provided. Opaque structure impinges directly upon the child in that it constrains and organizes his activities. Transparent structure is provided by planning and combination between staff in the nursery. Traditionally, opaque structure has been marked by its absence in nurseries and it may be that some forms of opaque structure are undeniably counterproductive within the nursery setting. However, our observation would suggest that the transparent structure provided is not always adequate. As Woodhead (1976) has pointed out, the informality of the traditional nursery programme presents certain problems. Informal methods are very easily open to misuse since they make special demands upon the child's ability to take full advantage of the activities provided and correspondingly upon the teacher to ensure that each child is gaining the maximum benefit from the activities. For Woodhead, the success of informal methods is dependent upon the ability of the teacher to maintain implicitly in the quality of her organization of activities and inter-action with the children, the structural sequence and control which are maintained explicitly in a formal programme. Such a dependency makes great demands upon the staff and is something of which all teachers of nursery aged children should be aware.

We have highlighted above two particular areas of concern to nursery staff – the relationship with parents and the provision of a detailed, transparent structure – upon which we believe our research throws light. Interpretation of our findings also suggests particular implications in these areas for the training of nursery staff.

The studies reported in Chapter 3 suggest that staff in all forms of nursery provision accord little priority to the implementation of a programme which involves the active participation of parents. Although playgroups frequently emphasize the important role of parents in the running of the session, it was surprising to note that they gave this aspect of the nursery programme lowest priority of all. This result was disappointing in the light of other research conducted over the last decade which suggests that nursery programmes are most successful in terms of both the gains made by the child and the persistence of these effects in those instances where parents have been actively involved in the running of the programme. We feel that it would be desirable for trainee nursery staff to be made aware of the need to work closely with parents and to be assisted in the development of the skills required to communicate effectively with adults as well as children.

The would-be nursery teacher should also be aware of the detailed planning, evaluation and record-keeping that a successful nursery programme should entail. All staff in nurseries plan the children's day to a certain extent. However, it is the depth to which this planning extends that is our concern. At any one time, the nursery provides a variety of activities for the young child during a free-play session. As Patricia Ward's (1982) study shows (Chapter 6), nursery staff are aware that each activity provided may yield a variety of benefits. The difficulty arises in ensuring that the child derives the benefits appropriate to his level of development. For the three-year-old, the dry sand provides a novel experience in its own right. At a later stage, the adult will need to vary the equipment and her initiatives with the child in order to ensure the child continues to learn through contact with the medium. In setting out activities, therefore, staff need to be aware not only of the range of activities they provide but also of possible developmental sequences in the use of particular toys and materials. Trainee teachers, we feel, should be given more instruction in ways of examining the spectrum of their provision and the detail of its use. The model of play presented in this volume suggests a means by which the former may be accomplished. In any particular week, we would argue, staff should be attempting to ensure that a balance is struck between primarily ludic-based activities and activities loaded towards the epistemic end of the spectrum.

Within this structure, staff need to plan for the individual child. In order to do this a detailed examination of the development of the child is required. At the inception of the project described in these pages, four nurseries practised such an evaluation in a systematic manner. Consequently we developed a guide to assessment and record-keeping for nursery staff, which is published as the Keele Pre-School Assessment Guide (Tyler, 1980). Other researchers have made similar attempts to aid the development of a transparent structure for nurseries (e.g. Bate *et al.*, 1979). We feel that it is important that students should be encouraged to consider the practicalities of evaluation in the nursery and actively assisted to develop their own skills in this area by working through some of the published materials with a group of children, before developing their own approaches to pre-school assessment.

Although the distribution of time to different types of activity by staff appears generally satisfactory (Chapter 4), we were concerned by our observation that staff frequently adopted similar rather than complementary roles during the same period of time. As a consequence we feel that staff working with children may be put under unnecessary and undesirable pressure through adventitious advances from children beyond the immediate group with which they are working. Planning of the transparent structure of the nursery should take this into account. Thus, during free-play sessions, adults in the nursery should be adopting roles which differ in their approach to the children, thereby ensuring that some adults are free to interact with the children in depth while others adopt a monitorial role to deal with children requiring routine assistance. We are, therefore, arguing that a form of 'room management', as currently being implemented in special education, may have advantages for the nursery (Sturmey and Crisp, 1986). In the training of staff we feel it is desirable that students should be made aware of the different roles which they may adopt during the course of the session and the implications these carry for the transparent structure of the nursery.

# Appendix A

# Definitions of categories of activities employed in study of resources in the nursery and checklist

## Categorization of available activities

| Activity category | Description |
|---|---|
| Wet sand | Wet or moist sand, or other granular material, available for play within a pit or trough. |
| Dry sand | As for wet sand, but material should be dry and capable of being poured. |
| Water | Provision for play requiring water as an essential element other than facilities usually employed for washing, etc. |
| Clay | Provision for play with any pliant substance having no predetermined shape, e.g. clay, dough, Playdoh. |
| Brush painting | Activity involving the application of paint to paper or to an object by means of a brush. |
| Finger painting | Activity involving the spreading of paint or similar material with the fingers. |
| Object printing | Printing with paint, ink or similar material involving use of an object whether commercially manufactured or prepared in the nursery, e.g. potato cuts. |
| Collage/cutting | Activity involving the sticking of materials onto paper or card with glue and/or the cutting out of shapes of pictures with scissors. |
| Large construction | Provision of objects for use as construction toys requiring comparatively gross motor movements for their manipulation, e.g. large Lego, large wooden blocks. |
| Fine construction | Provision of objects for construction requiring fine and precise motor movements for their manipulation, e.g. Lego, Sticklebricks, small wooden cubes. |

| | |
|---|---|
| Modelling | Activities involving the use of materials (e.g. cardboard boxes) and glue to construct realistic or abstract three-dimensional models. |
| Woodwork | Activity involving the use of wood and carpentry tools. |
| Puzzles | Provision of materials requiring arrangement of pieces into a pattern or the sorting of objects by shape or colour, eg. conventional jig-saws, picture-trays, sorting tasks. |
| Drawing | Activities involving colouring or drawing on paper or card with materials other than paint, e.g. pencils, crayons, chalks. |
| Music | Provision for activities involving the use of musical instruments, whether commercially manufactured or produced in the nursery. |
| Television | Activities involving either watching a television set, film or slides or listening to a radio, record player or tape recorder. |
| Books | Provision for reading or looking at books or other printed material. |
| Stories | Activities involving the telling or reading of stories by an adult. |
| Physical activity | Provision for play involving gross physical activity, e.g. climbing frame, swing. |
| Vehicle riding | Provision of toys facilitating locomotion, e.g. tricycle, scooter, pedal car. |
| Push–pull | Provision of toys which conventionally require pushing or pulling to produce movement, e.g. prams, wheelbarrows, trolleys. |
| Dressing-up | Provision of clothing not normally worn by children or inappropriate to the setting, whether from a commercial kit or jumble. |
| Representational objects | Provision of representational objects, e.g. toy models of adult objects and real adult objects in conventionally simulated situations other than in the specific context below. |
| Wendy corner | Provision of objects and furniture simulating a home, whether in miniature or of a realistic size, and forming a recognizably separate and distinct part of the nursery. |
| Other fantasy | Provision of other objects, materials or opportunities for the stimulation of fantasy play not elsewhere categorized. |
| Animals | Provision of animals or birds for play or observation. |

CHECKLIST

| | SCAN 1 | | | SCAN 2 | | | SCAN 3 | | | SCAN 4 | | | SCAN 5 | | |
|---|---|---|---|---|---|---|---|---|---|---|---|---|---|---|---|
| | Avail | C | A | Avail | C | A | Avail | C | A | Avail | C | A | Avail | C | A |
| | 1 0 | | | 1 0 | | | 1 0 | | | 1 0 | | | 1 0 | | |
| Wet sand | | | | | | | | | | | | | | | |
| Dry sand | | | | | | | | | | | | | | | |
| Water | | | | | | | | | | | | | | | |
| Clay | | | | | | | | | | | | | | | |
| Brush painting | | | | | | | | | | | | | | | |
| Finger painting | | | | | | | | | | | | | | | |
| Object printing | | | | | | | | | | | | | | | |
| Collage/cutting | | | | | | | | | | | | | | | |
| Large construction | | | | | | | | | | | | | | | |
| Fine construction | | | | | | | | | | | | | | | |
| Modelling | | | | | | | | | | | | | | | |

| Woodwork | | | | | | | | | | | | | | |
|---|---|---|---|---|---|---|---|---|---|---|---|---|---|---|
| Puzzles | | | | | | | | | | | | | | |
| Drawing | | | | | | | | | | | | | | |
| Music | | | | | | | | | | | | | | |
| Television | | | | | | | | | | | | | | |
| Books | | | | | | | | | | | | | | |
| Stories | | | | | | | | | | | | | | |
| Physical activity | | | | | | | | | | | | | | |
| Vehicle riding | | | | | | | | | | | | | | |
| Push-Pull | | | | | | | | | | | | | | |
| Dressing-up | | | | | | | | | | | | | | |
| Representational objects | | | | | | | | | | | | | | |
| Wendy corner | | | | | | | | | | | | | | |
| Other fantasy | | | | | | | | | | | | | | |
| Animals | | | | | | | | | | | | | | |
| Total | | | | | | | | | | | | | | |

Comment

# Appendix B

# Repertory grid analysis: procedure and definitions

Categorization is hierarchical and the constructs are divided into superordinate and subordinate categories. Construct pairs are placed in the category felt to be most appropriate for the given poles. Both poles of the construct are given equal consideration, and constructs placed in the most specific category possible. If a construct (1) is more general than the subordinate categories or (2) contains aspects of two or more subordinate categories it is placed in the most suitable undifferentiated superordinate category.

## Definitions

1  **Child's relationships with children**

    (i)   Ability to mix:
        Constructs which refer to the child's ability to mix well with other children, form friendships or play in groups.
        Examples: plays in group – solitary
                   mixes well     – watches others

    (ii)  Aggression:
        Constructs which describe the degree of aggression displayed by the child, his ability to stand up for himself against other children or his willingness to share toys or materials.
        Examples: competitive – acquiescent
                   aggressive   – tolerant

(iii) Leader–follower
Constructs relating to the child's strength of personality or his tendency to lead or follow others in activities.
Examples: leader            – tags on
          strong personality – weak personality

## 2 Child's personality

(i) Confidence:
Constructs relating to the child's confidence and independence in dealings with other children.
Examples: confident   – shy, introverted
          independent – dependent

(ii) Loquacity:
Constructs describing whether the child is generally talkative and outgoing, or silent and withdrawn.
Examples: chatty   – quiet
          extravert – withdrawn

(iii) Boisterousness:
Constructs describing whether the child is normally noisy and rowdy or quiet.
Examples: noisy      – quiet
          boisterous – shy

(iv) Disposition:
Constructs relating to the child's mood or general demeanour.
Examples: happy     – sullen
          concerned – insensitive
          thoughtful – slap-dash

(v) Emotional adjustment:
Constructs relating to the child's degree of security and emotional stability.
Examples: stable        – insecure
          bounces back  – easily upset
          needs care    – extraverted

## 3 Child's relationship with staff

(i) Independence:
Constructs which refer to the independence of the child from the staff.
Example: clinging – independent of staff

(ii) Conversation:
Constructs which describe the child's willingness to converse with the staff of the nursery.
Examples: talks to teacher     – quiet
            sociable with adults – has difficulty talking to staff

## 4  Attitude to staff

(i) Eagerness:
Constructs describing the child's willingness to enter into activities with the nursery staff.
Examples: eager            – has to be called to activity
           eager to please    – naughty
           approaches adult – waits for attention

(ii) Co-operativeness:
Constructs referring to behaviour problems and the degree of co-operation or compliance shown by the child.
Examples: good       – naughty
           co-operative – unco-operative

## 5  Play

(i) Play ability:
Constructs describing whether the child plays in the nursery or spends his time wandering aimlessly.
Example: plays – wanders about

(ii) Play preference:
Constructs describing in practical detail the kind of play or activity the child prefers (excludes constructs referring to whether the child prefers to play in a group or not).
Example: physical play – table activities

(iii) Play value:
Constructs describing the child's predilection for play as opposed to 'work'.
Example: plays all the time – likes to learn

(iv) Play type:
Constructs which describe the child's play in theoretical terms.
Example: parallel play – co-operative play

## 6 Concentration

Constructs relating to the child's ability to sustain attention or interest in an activity.
Example: concentrates – flits


## 7 Ability

(i) Intelligence:
Constructs referring to the child's overall level of ability or intelligence
Example: bright – dull

(ii) Awareness and comprehension:
Constructs relating to the child's awareness of the nursery environment, her powers of observation and her ability to comprehend.
Examples: observant         – in a world of her own
understands questions – does not comprehend


## 8 Language

(i) Speech:
Constructs which refer to the child's speech production.

(ii) Use:
Constructs which describe aspects of the child's language development other than speech.


## 9 Creativity

Constructs relating to the general degree of creativity or imagination shown by the child without reference to his play preferences.
Example: artistic – unimaginative


## 10 Self-help

Constructs describing the child's ability to assist himself in maintenance activities, e.g. toileting.

## 11 Physical development

Constructs relating to the child's overall physical development and stature, or more specifically to her manipulative abilities or co-ordination.
Example: good manipulation – poor manipulative ability

## 12 Age

(i) Chronological age:
Constructs which refer to the child's age in chronological terms.
Example: old – young

(ii) Maturity:
Constructs referring to the child's overall level of development with respect to his age.
Example: mature – immature

(iii) Rate of development:
Constructs relating to the degree of progress or rate of development made by the child in the nursery.
Example: progressing – regressing

## 13 Sex

Constructs referring to whether the child is a boy or a girl.

## 14 Home background

(i) Stability and security:
Constructs describing the relative security of the home environment.
Example: stable home – unstable home

(ii) Physical care:
Constructs describing the degree of physical care afforded to the child in the home.
Example: clean – dirty

(iii) Care and interest:
Constructs describing the degree of interest in the child shown by the parents and their general relationship with the child.
Examples: caring              – at risk
mother possessive – mother not interested

(iv) Expectations:
Constructs which relate to the parents' interest in the nursery or in education generally and their expectations of the child.
Examples: stimulating     – unstimulating
           high expectations – low expectations

(v) Status:
Aspects of the financial or social position of the family or the employment of the mother.
Examples: middle class   – working class
           mother works – mother at home

(vi) Family:
Constructs which refer to the presence or absence of siblings in the family.

(vii) Parting and separation:
Constructs which relate to the child's behaviour on entering the nursery each day or his need to retain a link with home during the session.
Examples: cries when mother leaves – breezes in
           brings toys from home   – independent

## 15 Settling in

Constructs which describe the child's behaviour when staring at the nursery

## 16 Miscellaneous

Other constructs not defined above.

# Appendix C

# Definitions of categories employed in study of adult activities in the nursery and checklist

## Definitions

*Non-associative activities* (reliability coefficient = 0.69)
1 Independent activity: Adult doing something on own without reference to the children, excluding the more specific categories defined below. Requires a lack of spatial proximity and relevance to children's activity.
2 Tidy up: Clearing and tidying, including the clearing away of toys and putting them on shelves or in cupboards, sweeping the floor, wiping tables.
3 Preparatory activity: Getting materials out of cupboard, store room, etc., and placing on table, etc., without assistance from or the accompaniment of children.
4 Conversation adult: Talking with another adult, where the discussion is the primary focus of the subject's attention.

*Monitorial activities* (reliability coefficient = 0.73)
1 Supervisory activity: Monitoring activity of children with occasional participation. Requires spatial proximity, visual attention and relevance of the subject's behaviour to that of the child.
2 Supervisory watch: Adult is onlooker, observing the activity of the children but not participating. Spatial proximity is not a requirement. Frequently occurs out of doors.
3 Care: Includes all forms of physical care: toileting, adjustment of clothing, provision of food and/or drink, treatment of injuries, blowing of noses, etc.
4 Comfort: Adult comforting or consoling child, either physically or verbally. Includes all forms of cuddling, etc., and holding hands.

*Associative activities* (reliability coefficient = 0.74)

1 Joint activity: Adult doing something with the children which has relevance to the children's activity, but excluding the more specific categories listed below. Usually accompanied by speech and spatial proximity and distinguished by the similarity of the adult's activity to that of the child.
2 Joint activity (E): Where activity has overt educational content subcode (E) is used.
3 Demonstration: Showing children how to do something or to use something.
4 Conversation child: Talking to the child or children without accompanying activity. The content of the conversation should not refer to the preceding activity (if associative) when it should be recorded as being part of that activity.
5 Tidy up (C): Cleaning and tidying, accompanied or assisted by child.
6 Preparatory activity (C): Getting materials out of cupboards, etc., in preparation for an activity, accompanied or assisted by children.

## Out

Subject is out of the room, or out of view of the observer: where possible the reason for absence is noted in the remarks column.

## CHECKLIST

| | 1 | 2 | 3 | 4 | 5 | 6 | 7 | 8 | 9 | 10 | 11 | 12 | 13 | 14 | 15 | 16 | 17 | 18 | 19 | 20 |
|---|---|---|---|---|---|---|---|---|---|---|---|---|---|---|---|---|---|---|---|---|
| Prep. activ. C | | | | | | | | | | | | | | | | | | | | |
| Ind. activ. | | | | | | | | | | | | | | | | | | | | |
| Tidy up C | | | | | | | | | | | | | | | | | | | | |
| Joint activ. | | | | | | | | | | | | | | | | | | | | |
| Demonstration | | | | | | | | | | | | | | | | | | | | |
| Supervisory activ. | | | | | | | | | | | | | | | | | | | | |
| Watch. | | | | | | | | | | | | | | | | | | | | |
| Conversation adult | | | | | | | | | | | | | | | | | | | | |
| Conversation child | | | | | | | | | | | | | | | | | | | | |
| Toileting | | | | | | | | | | | | | | | | | | | | |
| Out | | | | | | | | | | | | | | | | | | | | |
| Conf. | | | | | | | | | | | | | | | | | | | | |
| Elab. | | | | | | | | | | | | | | | | | | | | |
| Init. | | | | | | | | | | | | | | | | | | | | |

Status: ...............

Y / O Date seen: ...............

Establishment

Sheet no.

# Appendix D

# Conventions employed in a study of adult attention spans in the nursery

*Channel 1: Attention to adult activities*
Includes: Non-associative/independent activity; Tidy up; Preparatory activity; Conversation with adult.

*Channel 2: Attention to children and their activities*
Includes: Monitorial/supervisory activity; Care; Comfort; Associative activity; Demonstration; Conversation with child; Tidy up (C); Preparatory activity (C).

*Channel 3: Response*
When an adult responds to a request, comment or physical gesture of a child which was directed at that adult.

*Channel 4: Switch child*
When an adult switches her attention to a different child from the one to whom she was previously attending.

*No channel depressed*
Includes: Supervisory watch; Look/watch; Walk.

# Appendix E

# Definitions of codes and conventions employed in time-sampling study of the play of pre-school children

**Time-sampled behaviour categories**

*Sand*

|   |   |
|---|---|
| | Play with dry or wet sand, soil or any granulated material. |
| Subcoding: | U – Unconventional – note. |
| | D – Desultory. |
| | Conventional sand play assumed unless subcode used. |

*Water*

|   |   |
|---|---|
| | Play requiring liquid as an essential element. |
| Subcoding: | U – Unconventional – note. |
| | D – Desultory. |
| | Conventional water play assumed unless subcode used. |

*Clay*

|   |   |
|---|---|
| | Play with any pliant substance having no predetermined shape. |
| | Modelling – forming a recognizable shape (e.g. man, gun). |
| Subcoding: | M – moulding – manipulating material. |
| | Do – Domestic – using domestic tools (e.g. rolling-pin). |
| | Modelling assumed unless subcode used. |

*Painting*

Brush.

Subcoding:  F – Finger.

O – Object (printing).

Brush painting assumed unless subcode used.

*Collage/Cutting*

Collage – sticking materials onto paper with glue.

Subcoding:  Cu – Cutting – cutting out shapes.

Collage assumed unless subcode used.

*Construction/woodwork*

Construction – large Lego, etc.

Subcoding:  F – Fine movements – Lego, Sticklebricks, etc.

M – Model-making – junk modelling.

W – Woodwork – using woodwork tools and wood (e.g. hammering).

Construction assumed unless subcode used.

*Puzzles*

Puzzles – conventional jig-saws, etc.

Subcoding:  S – Sorting – arranging pieces into pattern, colour matching, etc.

Jig-saws, etc., assumed unless subcode used.

*Colouring/drawing*

Colouring – within predetermined limits.

Subcoding:  D – Drawing – freehand with pencils, crayons, chalk, etc.

Assume colouring unless subcode used.

*Music/noise/TV*

Music-making – making musical noise with instruments.

Subcoding:  N – Noise-making – using instruments but making unmusical noise.

T – TV – watching TV, listening to radio, record player, watching slides or film.

Music-making assumed unless subcode used.

### Books/stories

Books – reading or looking at books, printed material, etc.

Subcoding:   S – Stories – being told stories or being read to.
Books assumed unless subcode used.

### Object manipulate/hold

Manipulate – manipulation of object with look.

Subcoding:   H – Hold – without look.
Manipulate assumed unless subcode used.

### Physical activity

Physical – climbing, sliding, etc.

Subcoding:   R – Repetitive – swing, see-saw, etc.
V – Vehicle ride – pedal toys, etc.
Assume gross physical activity unless subcode used.

Remarks:   'Physical' includes 'rough and tumble play', 'chasing games' and other activities involving gross motor movement. Type of activity to be stated in the object column.

### Push–pull

Active – pushing pram, wheelbarrow, trolley, etc.

Subcoding:   P – Passive – being pushed in pram, wheelbarrow, trolley, etc.
Assume active unless subcode used.

### Walk/run

Walk.

Subcoding:   R – Run.
Assume walk unless subcode used.

Remarks:   Excludes walking and running which is part of a 'physical activity' category.

### Gestures/automanipulation

Gesture – nod, wave, point, etc.

Subcoding:   R – Repetitive – thumb-sucking, nail-biting, fingering clothes, etc.
Assume gesture unless subcode used.

*Dressing up*

Dressing up – in clothes not normally worn by children or inappropriate to occasion, either a commercial kit or jumble, and application of conventional make-up or props (e.g. sunglasses).

Remarks: Note – in object column when child is putting on or taking off clothing.

*Fantasy play*

NB Fantasy play is deduced from the child's overt/vocal behaviour.

*Representational object*

Representational object – use of representational objects, e.g. toy models of adult objects and real adult objects, in conventionally simulated situations, e.g. push mechanical toy (MT) along making motor noises, pointing gun, saying bang.

Note – object in object column.

*Fantasy person play*

Fantasy person – child or other people participating in change of character in the child's imagination, e.g. child becomes cowboy.

Note – imaginative identity in column.

*Immaterial fantasy play*

Immat. fantasy play – includes fantasy people or objects which have no substantive identity in the environment, e.g. child talks to non-existent people such as co-pilot, feeds non-existent horse.

Note – in object column deduced fantasy objects and people.

*Look/watch*

Looking around– general inspection of environment with no apparent focus.

Subcoding: W – Watching        – observing person/people engaging in an activity in which the child is not a constant participant.

V – Visual inspection – of object.

Assume looking around unless subcode is used.

251

*Help/care*

Active       – helping or caring.

Subcoding:      P – passive – receiving assistance from adult or other child.

Assume active helping or caring unless subcode used.

*Tidying up/hanging up pinafore*

Tidying up     – clearing away toys and equipment after play.

Subcoding:      P – pinafore – putting on or hanging up pinafore.

Assume tidying up unless subcode used.

*Vocal*

H – Hum, sing tuneful noise.

M – Moaning, persistent whining, vocal verbalization.

P – Play noises.

R – Recitation – repetition of poem, nursery rhyme, story from memory.

S – Shouting, screaming.

## One-zero sampled and time samples

*Talk to*

Subcoding:      A – Adult.

C – Child.

S – Self.

Assume talk to child unless subcode used.

*Fight/thwart*

Fight – fight, wrestle for toys, pinch, punch, hit, etc.

*Affect*

Laughter.

Subcoding:      W – Weeping.

T – Temper tantrums.

Assume laughter unless subcode used.

## One-zero sampled

*Adult talk*

Subcoding:

Q – Question.
A – Answer to question.
D – Directive.
I – Instructional.
C – Comment.
O – Option (choice).
Assume question unless subcode used.

*Page category*

S – Solitary – no other children within 3 feet, playing alone.
P – Parallel – playing side-by-side but with no interaction.
A – Association – playing side-by-side and lending and borrowing tools and toys, but not fully co-operative.
C – Co-operative – playing together with a common goal.

To be noted when child is performing:

Sand
Water
Clay model
Painting
Collage/cutting
Construction
Puzzles
Colouring/drawing
Music/noise/TV
Books/stories
Physical activity
Push–pull
Dressing up
Representational object
Fantasy object
Fantasy person play
Immaterial fantasy play

*NOT:*

>>> *Object manipulate/hold*
>>> *Walk/run*
>>> *Gesture*
>>> *Look/watch/V*
>>> *Help/care*
>>> *Tidying up/hanging up pinafore*

*Location*

>>> Indoors.
>>> O – Outdoors.
>>> Assume indoors unless subcoded.

# Appendix F

# Behavioural categories employed in analysis of fantasy play

## 1 Environments and props

### (i) Representational

Provision of representational toys and environment usually considered to be conducive to imaginative play. Includes home corner, models of farm, garage, zoo, garden, hospital, and the props used with these such as plates, cutlery, iron, telephone, toy animals, small cars, which are replicas of objects commonly seen in the outside world.

### (ii) Construction

Area where toys are provided for building and construction, often a corner set aside for this purpose in the nursery where materials provided are large wooden or plastic blocks, planks, bricks, etc. Included in this category are small construction toys, such as Lego and Sticklebricks, which are more commonly found on tables.

### (iii) Physical apparatus

Provision of apparatus designed for physical play, e.g. climbing frame, swings, slide, hoops, balls. This category also includes large vehicles, such as cars, trucks, trikes, which could be ridden and pushed or pulled.

### (iv) Materials

This category refers to materials provided to stimulate skills and understanding of raw materials, and includes sand and water, usually provided in troughs, paints at easels or tables, boxes and materials for collage production, clay and dough.

## (v) **General**

This refers to the general play space in a nursery which is not designed for any particular kind of play. In the context of the study it includes such areas as doorways, playground, furniture and any open play space where children were not using any kinds of props in their play.

## 2 Types of fantasy play
## (i) **Representational object play** (RO)

Considered to be the simplest form of fantasy play, this is where a child uses an object in the way for which it was intended, e.g. stirs with a spoon in a bowl, brushes with a broom, drives a car making car noises, dials a telephone and so on.

## (ii) **Fantasy food play** (FF)

Children's reference to food was so frequent that a separate category was included. It refers to food in various ways – e.g. child pretends to stir, cook, eat or drink imaginary food or drink – and occurs in conjunction with RO props such as spoons, plates, bowls, cookers. Where children referred to imaginary food without reference to any props it was considered to be immaterial fantasy play (see below).

## (iii) **Fantasy person play** (FP)

This type of play is sometimes known as role play and is where a child pretends to be someone else, or in a different state, e.g.
  (a) family character: mother, father, baby, sister;
  (b) local character: doctor, teacher, shopkeeper;
  (c) media character: Batman, Goldilocks, dalek;
  (d) different state: 'asleep', 'dead'.

## (iv) **Fantasy object play** (FO)

In this type of play the child uses an object (prop) as if it were something else, e.g. picks up a block and aims it as if it were a gun, or pushes a piece of Lego around making engine noises pretending it is a truck.

## (v) **Immaterial fantasy play** (IF)

Here the child pretends something exists which does not exist, e.g. pretends to pat a dog which is not there, pretends to eat food which doesn't exist, or pretends to sing into an imaginary microphone.

These categories are not mutually exclusive. During a bout of fantasy play more than one kind could occur, and occasionally all of them either simultaneously or closely following one another.

## 3 Time spent at fantasy play
### (i) Brief (Bf)
Events that lasted from a few seconds up to one minute in duration.

### (ii) Medium (Med)
Events lasting from over one minute up to ten minutes in duration.

### (iii) Extended (Ex)
Events that lasted over ten minutes in length, and sometimes through most of the session, which were related to the same theme for the duration, e.g. an extended period of home corner play involving the same children pursuing the same activity over the period, or an extended period of play based on materials such as blocks used as different vehicles. Extended play also included the unfolding of a complex theme where different elements were observed, but where the play was observed to be continuous for a long period of time.

## 4 Themes observed during fantasy play
### (i) Domestic
    (a) Characters: These included fantasy person characters such as father, mother, baby, grandma, brother, sister. Pretending to be asleep was also included in this category.

    (b) Babies: This included reference to babies in play involving fantasy person play, use of dolls, puppets, beds, prams and so on, where the theme of the play was babies.

    (c) Food: Play with cutlery, crockery, bowls, imaginary food, drink, cakes, etc., where the theme of play was food.

    (d) Household objects: Play using familiar household objects, e.g. iron, telephone, taps at sink, crockery (non-food theme, e.g. washing up), cleaning.

    (e) Animals: Play including reference to domestic animals such as cat and dog.

### (ii) Local
    (a) Characters: People who were familiar to nursery children, seen in fantasy person play, such as policemen, firemen, doctors, nurses, teachers, drivers.

    (b) Buildings: Reference to buildings and props associated with them, e.g. house, hospital, syringe, school, fire station, shop, money, roads, railways.

    (c) Vehicles: Play with vehicular themes such as that with cars, trains, fire engines, boats.

(d) Events: Play which centres on a specific event which the children might see, such as fire, accident, robbery, shopping, going to school.

(iii) **Media**
    (a) Characters (specific): Role play of characters seen in books, on television, in films, etc., e.g. Starsky and Hutch, Spiderman, Goldilocks, which are specifically named.
    (b) Characters (non-specific): Role play of characters from the media which are non-specific, e.g. monsters, witches, cowboys, robbers, snakes and 'playing dead'.
    (c) Places: Reference to places referred to in the media, e.g. castles, forts, towers, sea.
    (d) Events: In the context of the study these usually included fights, shooting and weapon use.

These categories are not mutually exclusive. Bouts of fantasy play often included reference to several of these themes.

# Appendix G

# Categorization of activities and behaviour employed in study of how children approach and leave activities

## 1 Categories of free-play activities

### (i) Play with materials

Includes play with sand (wet or dry), water or clay (or other malleable material), woodwork, sorting and rotating tasks, fine construction toys and other miscellaneous materials (e.g. components of clocks available for manipulation).

### (ii) Product-oriented play

Includes brush painting, finger painting, object painting, drawing and colouring (including use of stencils), collage and puppet-making.

### (iii) Representational object play

Includes play in the home corner with domestic objects and toys, play with miniature cars, and with toy animals.

### (iv) Semi-structured activities

Includes various forms of play structured by staff, e.g. games (lotto and dominoes), reading books, playing musical instruments, doing jigsaws puzzles, and a road safety discussion which children could enter freely.

## 2 Categories of approach to activity

(i) **Own initiative**
Child approaches the activity deliberately and without hesitation or reference to an adult. Where appropriate, this category includes approaches which involve the fetching of materials, pinafores or other relevant equipment without assistance.

(ii) **Wander**
The child approaches the activity indecisively often walking slowly, looking briefly in turn at various activities or watching other children, before finally commencing upon the activity.

(iii) **Request**
The child engages in the activity following a request to an adult for permission to do so, or a request to the adult to provide the activity.

(iv) **Adult-initiated**
The child's engagement in an activity follows an adult's suggestion or invitation to do so.

## 3 Categories of departure from an activity

(i) **Spontaneous**
The child leaves the activity spontaneously and decisively, usually to take up another activity immediately.

(ii) **Wander**
The child drifts away from the activity in an indecisive manner, usually looking around or watching other children, and does not engage in another activity immediately.

(iii) **Finish product**
The child finishes the product of an activity in which he has been engaged, frequently making a statement such as, 'I've finished.'

(iv) **Adult intervention**
Child ceases involvement in an activity as a result of the intervention of an adult.

# Appendix H

# Categorization of utterances employed in checklist studies of language usage in the nursery

## 1 Children's speech

| Category | Definition |
| --- | --- |
| **(i) Type of utterance** | |
| Statement | Bald statement or comment, e.g. 'Hands are dirty', 'I'm going to play outside'. |
| Explanation/ elaboration | Elaborated statement, where a principle is implied, e.g. 'I don't like it because it's too wet'. |
| Request | In the form of a question, e.g. 'Can I play in the Wendy House?', asking for permission to do something or go somewhere. |
| Question | E.g. 'What are you doing?' |
| Yes/no | Minimal verbal response to question. |
| **(ii) Antecedents** | |
| Spontaneous | Speech directed at *adult* with no apparent antecedent. |
| Adult-initiated | Speech to adult immediately preceded by the speech or actions of the adult. |
| Child-initiated | Speech to adult or child (noted) immediately preceded by the speech or action of a child. |
| To child | Speech directed at child with no apparent antecedent. |
| Continuo | Utterance, though changed in character, is continuing upon previous response, as when request is followed by explanation without intervening interaction. |

### (iii) **Behavioural responses**

Obey  ⎫
Disobey ⎬  Action complementing utterances.

No response    As when child fails to hear adult's question.

---

## 2 **Adults' speech**

| *Category* | *Definition* |
|---|---|

### (i) **Type of utterance**

| | |
|---|---|
| Statement/ comment | Bald statement or comment, e.g. 'Your hands are dirty'. |
| Explanation | Elaborated statement where principle is implied, e.g. 'This won't stick because it's too wet'. |
| Command | Utterance of imperative nature spoken in forceful tones, e.g. 'Be quiet' or 'Come here', may be disciplinary or otherwise. |
| Request | Takes the form of a question, e.g. 'Will you fetch me the paints?', neutral tones. |
| Question | E.g. 'What are you doing?' |
| Yes/no | Minimal verbal response to question. |
| Approbation | Speech containing explicit approval, e.g. 'That's nice', 'Isn't that clever'. |
| Option | Suggestions offered by adult requiring the child to make a choice, e.g. 'You can make some antlers for the reindeer, or . . .'. |
| Comfort | Verbalization accompanying soothing/cuddling. |

### (ii) **Antecedents**

| | |
|---|---|
| Spontaneous | Speech directed at child with no apparent antecedent. |
| Child-initiated (speech) | Speech to child in response to child's speech. |
| Child-initiated (speech) | Speech to child in response to child's action. |
| To adult | Any speech directed at adult or adults whether spontaneous or initiated by adult. |
| Continuo | Utterance, though changed in character, is continuing upon previous response, as when request is followed by explanation. |

### (iii) **Behavioural responses**

No response    As when adult fails to hear child's question.

---

# Appendix 1

# System of categorization employed in study of children's overtures and adult responses

## 1 Categorization of children's overtures

| Category | Definition |
|---|---|
| Domestic | Comment or request referring to some aspect of toileting or to the adjustment of the child's clothing. |
| Personal | Utterance referring to an aspect of the child's own body (including physical sensations) or clothing, e.g. 'It hurts!', 'Do you like my jumper?' |
| Other children | Utterance referring to the present or past behaviour of peers. |
| Showing | Physical display of an object, e.g. painting or toy. |
| Home | Utterance involving reference to a context outside the nursery, e.g. the home. |
| Intention | Statement of an intention to perform an action, usually in the near future, e.g. 'I'm going to do a painting'. |
| Statement | Utterance referring to the child's present activity, whether to his own actions or to some aspect of the material or toy he is playing with, but not including simple descriptions, e.g. 'I've glued it on'. |
| Observation | Utterances containing a reference to physical properties of the environment, e.g. 'The light's on', 'It's raining'; or of materials used in an activity, e.g. 'That's a white shell'. |
| Request | Utterance seeking adult permission, whether explicit – e.g. 'Can I do a painting?' – or implicit – e.g. 'I haven't had the big bike'. |

| | |
|---|---|
| Question (simple) | Question requiring a simple response, e.g. 'Is it lunch-time?' 'That goes in there, doesn't it?' |
| Question (complex) | Question seeking information and requiring a more detailed response or explanation, e.g. 'What do you use that for?', 'Why don't they put those barrels in there?' |

## 2 Categorization of adult responses to children's overtures

| Category | Definition |
|---|---|
| Question | Utterance in question form seeking to elicit further information, e.g. 'Where are you going?', 'What is that?'; or if adult has misheard, e.g. 'Do what, my love?' |
| Statement/ comment | Statement referring to the child's preceding utterance or current action, excluding statements which are explicitly informative, e.g. 'Yes', 'All right, Richard', 'Yes you can'. |
| Minimal response | |
| Instruction | Utterance instructing the child to perform an action or carry out a task, e.g. 'Give it to her', 'Let's have you round this side, it's safer'. |
| Explanation | Utterance yielding information or an explanation, e.g. 'You have to put these in the oven to cook them and make them tasty to eat'. |
| Approbation | Explicit approval, not elaborated, e.g. 'That's nice', 'Isn't that clever'. |
| Repetition | Utterance incorporating considerable repetition of the child's preceding utterance; includes minor changes in form, e.g. Child: 'I'm going out now.' Adult: 'You're going out now?' |
| Suggestion | Utterance that suggests that the child performs a task or engages in an activity, without the force of an instruction, e.g. 'Are you going to put some little ones in the holes?' |
| Intention | Statement of intention to perform an action or engage in an activity, e.g. 'I'll show you a way to do it', 'I'll go and fetch him'. |
| Negative | Utterance which contradicts a child, e.g. 'No, you're not, you fibber', 'No, it's plasticene isn't it'; or which forbids his action, e.g. 'No you can't go out yet, it's raining'. |

| | |
|---|---|
| Scold | Mild reproval, e.g. 'Nell, you don't have to hit back', 'You haven't been wearing your apron'. |
| Delay | Comment which serves to defer the child's overture, e.g. 'Just a second, darling', 'Yes, but let me take my cup back first'. |
| No response | Apparent failure to respond to the child's opening. |

# References

Abbott, A. L. (1978) 'Views of teachers and parents on nursery provision in education'. Unpublished thesis for the degree of Master of Arts, University of Manchester.

Abbott, A. L., and Fairbrother, R. (eds) (1986) *Education in the Early Years*. Manchester: Didsbury School of Education and E. J. Arnold.

Aitkenhead, A. M. (1978) The structure and dynamics of teachers' perceptions of pupils in the reception class. *British Journal of Educational Psychology*, 48, 354.

Altmann, J. (1974) Observational study of behaviour: sampling methods. *Behaviour*, 49, 227–67.

Anderson, N. (1980) 'The educational potential of imaginative play'. Unpublished MA thesis, University of Keele.

Bate, M., Smith, M., Sumner, R. P., and Sexton, B. (1979) *Manual for Assessment in Nursery Education*. Windsor, Berks.: National Foundation for Educational Research.

Beller, E. K. (1969) The evaluation of effects of early educational intervention on intellectual and social development of lower-class disadvantaged children. In Grotberg, E. (ed.) *Critical Issues in Research Related to Disadvantaged Children*. Princeton, NJ: Educational Testing Service.

Beller, E. K. (1973) Research on organised programs of early education. In Travers, R. M. W. (ed.) *Second Handbook of Research on Teaching*. Chicago: Rand McNally.

Bereiter, C., and Engelmann, S. (1966) *Teaching Disadvantaged Children in the Pre-school*. Englewood Cliffs, NJ: Prentice-Hall.

Berlyne, D. E. (1960) *Conflict, Arousal and Curiosity*. New York: McGraw-Hill.

Berlyne, D. E. (1970) Children's reasoning and thinking. In Mussen, P. H. (ed.) *Carmichael's Manual of Child Psychology* (3rd edn, vol. 1). New York: Wiley.

Bernstein, B. (1961) Social class and linguistic development. In Halsey, A.,

Floyd, J., and Anderson, C. (eds) *Education, Economy and Society*. London: Free Press.

Bernstein, B. (1973) *Class, Codes and Control* (vol. 1): *Theoretical Studies Towards a Sociology of Language*. London: Routledge & Kegan Paul.

Blackstone, T. (1971) *A Fair Start: the Provision of Pre-school Education*. London: Allen Lane.

Blank, M. (1973) *Teaching Learning in the Pre-school: a Dialogue Approach*. Columbus, OH: Merrill.

Blatchford, P., Battle, S., and Mays, J. (1982) *The First Transition: Home to Pre-school*. Windsor, Berks.: National Foundation for Educational Research/Nelson.

Bloom, B. S. (1964) *Stability and Change in Human Characteristics*. New York: Wiley.

Boehm, A. E. (1970) *Boehm Test of Basic Concepts*. New York: Psychological Corporation.

Bolger, A. W. (1975) *Child Study and Guidance in Schools*. London: Constable.

Bradburn, E. (1976) *Margaret McMillan: Framework and Expansion of Nursery Education*. Redhill, Surrey: Denholm House Press.

Brierley, J. K. (1977) *The Growing Brain*. Windsor, Berks.: National Foundation for Educational Research.

Brierley, J. K. (1978) *Growing and Learning*. London: Ward Lock Educational.

Bronfenbrenner, U. (1968) Early deprivation: a cross species analysis. In Levine, S., and Newton, G. (eds) *Early Experience and Behavior*. Springfield, IL: Chas. Thomas.

Bruner, J. S. (1976) Nature and uses of immaturity. In Bruner, J. S., Jolly, A., and Sylva, K. (eds) *Play: Its Role in Development and Evolution*. Harmondsworth, Middx: Penguin.

Bruner, J. (1980) *Under Five in Britain*. London: Grant McIntyre.

Bruner, J. S., Jolly, A., and Sylva, K. (eds) (1976) *Play: Its Role in Development and Evolution*. Harmondsworth, Middx: Penguin.

Caldwell, B. M. (1967) Descriptive evaluations of child development and of developmental settings. *Pediatrics*, 40 (1), 46–54.

Cashdan, A. P., and Philps, J. F. (1975) 'Nursery teachers' classroom behaviour in the light of their constructs of pupils: an exploratory study'. Paper presented to International Society for Study of Behavioural Development, Guildford.

Cass, J. E. (1975a) *The Role of the Teacher in the Nursery School*. Oxford: Pergamon.

Cass, J. E. (1975b) Play. In *State of Play*. London: BBC Publications.

Central Advisory Council for Education (1967) *Children and Their Primary Schools* (Plowden Report). London: Her Majesty's Stationery Office.

Cicirelli, B. (1969) *The Impact of Headstart on Children's Cognitive and Affective Development*. Washington, DC: Office of Economic Opportunity.

Clarke, A. M., and Clarke, A. D. B. (eds) (1976) *Early Experience: Myth and Evidence*. London: Open Books.

# References

Clarke, A. M., and Clarke, A. D. B. (1981) 'Sleeper effects' in development: fact or artifact? *Developmental Review*, 1, 344–60.

Clarke, A. M., and Clarke, A. D. B. (1982) Intervention and sleeper effects: a reply to Victoria Seitz. *Developmental Review*, 2, 76–86.

Clarke, A. M., Wyon, S. M., and Richards, M. P. M. (1969) Free play in nursery school children. *Journal of Child Psychology and Psychiatry*, 10, 205–16.

Cleave, S., Jowett, S., and Bate, M. (1982) *And so to School: a Study of Continuity from Pre-school to Infant School*. Windsor, Berks.: National Foundation for Educational Research/Nelson.

Clift, P., Cleave, S., and Griffin, M. (1980) *The Aims, Role and Deployment of Staff in the Nursery*. Windsor, Berks.: National Foundation for Educational Research/Nelson.

Cobb, J. A. (1972) Relationship of discrete classroom behaviours to fourth-grade academic achievement. *Journal of Educational Psychology*, 63, 74–80.

Connolly, K. J., and Smith, P. J. (1972) Reactions of pre-school children to a strange observer. In Blurton-Jones, N. (ed.) *Ethological Studies of Child Behaviour*. Cambridge: Cambridge University Press.

Consortium for Longitudinal Studies (1983) *As the Twig is Bent . . . Lasting Effects of Pre-school Programs*. Hillsdale, NJ: Erlbaum.

Cooper, J., Moodley, M., and Reynell, J. (1978) *Helping Language Development*. London: Arnold.

Cooper, M. G. (1979) Verbal interaction in nursery school. *British Journal of Educational Psychology*, 49, 214–25.

Crow, L. D., and Crow, A. (1963) *Educational Psychology* (revised edition). New York: Van Nostrand Reinhold.

Curtis, A. M. (1986) *A Curriculum for the Pre-School Child: Learning to Learn*. Windsor, Berks.: National Foundation for Educational Research/Nelson.

Curtis, A. M., and Blatchford, P. (1980) *Meeting the Needs of Socially Handicapped Children*. Windsor, Berks.: National Foundation for Educational Research/Nelson.

Dansky, J. L., and Silverman, I. W. (1973) Play: a general facilitator of verbal fluency. *Developmental Psychology*, 11, 104.

Dash, M. (1980) 'A comparative study of part-time and full-time nursery education'. Unpublished thesis for degree of Master of Arts, University of Keele.

Davie, C., Forrest, B., Hutt, C., Mason, M., Vincent, E., and Ward, T. (1975) 'Play at home and at school'. Paper presented to the 3rd Biennial Congress of the International Society for Study of Behavioural Development, Guildford.

Davie, C., Hutt, S. J., Vincent, E., and Mason, M. (1984) *The Young Child at Home*. Windsor, Berks.: National Foundation for Educational Research/Nelson.

Dearden, R. (1969) The aims of primary education. In Peters, R. D. (ed.) *Perspectives on Plowden*. London: Routledge & Kegan Paul.

Delius, J. (1970) Irrelevant behaviour, information processing and arousal homeostasis. *Psychologische Forschung*, 33, 165–88.

Department of Education and Science (1972) *Education: a Framework for Expansion*. London: Her Majesty's Stationery Office.

Department of Education and Science (1976) *Pre-school Education and Care*. London: Her Majesty's Stationery Office.

Dobbing, J., and Sands, J. (1973) Quantitative growth and development of the human brain. *Archives of the Disabled Child*, 48, 757–67.

Douglas, J. W. B., and Ross, J. M. (1964) The later educational progress and emotional adjustment of children who went to nursery schools or classes. *Educational Research*, 7, 73–80.

Dunn, L. M. (1965) *Expanded Manual for the Peabody Picture Vocabulary Test*. Circle Pines, MN: American Guidance Service.

Eifermann, R. (1971) Social play in childhood. In Herron, R. E., and Sutton-Smith, B. (eds) *Child's Play*. New York: Academic Press.

Fein, G. G. (1975) A transformational analysis of pretending. *Developmental Psychology*, 3, 291–6.

Feitelson, D. (1977) Cross-culture studies. In Tizard, B., and Harvey, D. (eds) *The Biology of Play*. London: Heinemann.

Ferri, E., Birchall, D., Gingell, V., and Gipps, C. (1981) *Combined Nursery Centres*. London: Macmillan.

Foss, B. (1969) Other aspects of child psychology. In Peters, R. S. (ed.) *Perspectives on Plowden*. London: Routledge & Kegan Paul.

Freyberg, J. T. (1973) Increasing the imaginative play of urban disadvantaged children. In Singer, J. (ed.) *The Child's World of Make-Believe*. New York: Academic Press.

Gardner, D. E. M., and Cass, J. E. (1965) *The Role of the Teacher in the Infant and Nursery School*. Oxford: Pergamon Press.

Ginsberg, H. (1972) *The Myth of the Deprived Child: Poor Children's Intellect and Education*. Englewood Cliffs, NJ: Prentice-Hall.

Golomb, C., and Cornelius, C. (1977) Symbolic play and its cognitive significance. *Developmental Psychology*, 13, 246–52.

Goodacre, E. J. (1968) *Teachers and Their Pupils' Home Background*. Slough, Berks.: National Foundation for Educational Research.

Gordon, I. J. (1968) *Parent Involvement in Compensatory Education*. Illinois: University of Illinois Press.

Guilford, J. P. (1971) *The Nature of Human Intelligence*. London: McGraw-Hill.

Gunzburg, H. C. (1972) *Progress Assessment Chart of Social Development*. Birmingham: SEFA (Publications) Ltd.

Guthrie, K., and Hudson, L. (1979) Training conservation through symbolic play: a second look. *Child Development*, 50, 1269–71.

Gutteridge, M. V. (1935) *The Duration of Attention in Young Children*. Melbourne: Melbourne University Press.

Halverson, C. F., and Waldrop, M. F. (1976) Relations between preschool activity and aspects of intellectual and social behaviour at age 7½. *Developmental Psychology*, 12, 107–12.

Harper, L. V., and Sanders, K. M. (1975) Preschool children's use of space: sex differences in outdoor play. *Developmental Psychology*, 11, 119.

# References

Haystead, J., Howarth, V., Strachan, A., and Thompson, H. (1978) *Under-five in Leith: a Study of the Role of Knowledge in the Use or Non-use of Existing Pre-school and Care Facilities*. Interim Report. Leith: Leith Educational Authority.

Herbert, G. W. (1974) Teachers' ratings of classroom behaviour: factorial structure. *British Journal of Educational Psychology*, 44, 223–40.

Hess, R. D., and Shipman, V. C. (1965) Early experience and the socialization of cognitive modes in children. *Child Development*, 36, 869–86.

Hughes, M. M. (1979) Exploration and play revisited: an hierarchical analysis. *International Journal of Behavioural Development*, 2, 215–24.

Hughes, M. M. (1981) 'Motivation and function of play in early childhood'. Unpublished thesis for degree of Doctor of Philosophy, University of Keele.

Hughes, M. M. (1983) Exploration and play in young children. In Archer, J., and Birke, L. *Exploration in Animals and Humans*. New York: Holt, Rinehart & Winston.

Hughes, M. M., and Hutt, C. (1980) Heart-rate correlates of childhood activities: play, exploration, problem solving and daydreaming. *Biological Psychology*, 8, 253–63.

Hutt, C. (1966) Exploration and play in children. In *Play, Exploration and Territory in Mammals*. Symposium of the Zoological Society of London, 18, 61–8.

Hutt, C. (1967) Temporal effects on response decrement and stimulus satiation in exploration. *British Journal of Psychology*, 58, 365–73.

Hutt, C. (1970) Specific and diversive exploration. In Reese, H. W., and Lipsitt, L. P. (eds) *Advances in Child Development and Behavior*, vol. 5. New York: Academic Press.

Hutt, C. (1972) *Males and Females*. Harmondsworth, Middx: Penguin.

Hutt, C. (1979a) Towards a taxonomy of play. In Sutton-Smith, B. (ed.) *Play and Learning*. New York: Gardner Press.

Hutt, C. (1979b) *Play in the Under-Fives: Form, Development and Function*. New York: Brunner/Mazel.

Hutt, C. (1981) Towards a taxonomy and conceptual model of play. In Day, H. I. (ed.) *Advances in Intrinsic Motivation and Aesthetics*. New York: Plenum Press.

Hutt, C., and Hutt, S. J. (1970) Stereotypies and their relation to arousal. In Hutt, S. J., and Hutt, C. (eds) *Behaviour Studies in Psychiatry*. Oxford: Pergamon Press.

Hutt, C., and Hutt, S. J. (1978) Heart-rate variability: the adapative consequences of individual differences and state changes. In Blurton-Jones, N., and Reynolds, V. (eds) *Human Behaviour and Adaptation*. London: Taylor and Francis.

Hutt, S. J., and Hutt, C. (1964) Hyperactivity in a group of epileptic (and some non-epileptic) brain-damaged children. *Epilepsia*, 5, 334–51.

Hutt, S. J., and Hutt, C. (1968) Stereotypy, arousal and autism. *Human Development*, II, 277–86.

Johnson, J. (1974) Fantasy and cognitive representation in culturally disadvantaged children. In Hoffman, M. L., and Pthenakis, W. E. (eds)

*Comparative Studies in a Child's Social Development.* New York: Russell Sage.

Jowett, S., and Sylva, K. (1986) Does kind of pre-school matter? *Educational Research*, 28, 21–31.

Kagan, J. (1971) *Change and Continuity in Infancy.* New York: Wiley.

Kagan, J., and Moss, H. A. (1962) *Birth to Maturity.* New York: Wiley.

Kamii, C., and Devries, R. (1978) *Physical Knowledge in Pre-school Education: Implications of Piaget's Theory.* Englewood Cliffs, NJ: Prentice-Hall.

King, R. (1978) *All Things Bright and Beautiful? A Sociological Study of Infants' Classrooms.* Chichester: Wiley.

Labov, W. (1970) The logic of non-standard English. In Williams, F. (ed.) *Language and Poverty.* Chicago: Markham.

Lahaderne, H. M. (1968) Attitudinal and intellectual correlates of attention: a study of four sixth-grade classrooms. *Journal of Educational Psychology*, 59, 320–4.

Laing, A. F. (1973) Structure in pre-school education. In Chazan, M. (ed.) *Education in the Early Years.* Swansea: Faculty of Education, University College.

Laufer, M. W., Denhoff, E., and Soloman, S. G. (1957) Hyperkinetic impulse disorder in children's behaviour problems. *Psychosomatic Medicine*, 19, 38–49.

Lazar, I., and Darlington, R. (1982) Lasting effects of early education. *Monographs of the Society for Research in Child Development*, 47 (Parts 1–2).

Liebermann, J. N. (1977) *Playfulness: Its Relationship to Imagination and Creativity.* New York: Academic Press.

Loizos, C. (1967) Play behaviour in higher primates: a review. In Morris, D. (ed.) *Primate Ethology.* London: Weidenfeld & Nicolson.

Lomax, C. M. (1977) Interest in books and stories at nursery school. *Educational Research*, 19, 100–13.

Lunzer, E. A. (1958) Intellectual development in the play of young children. *Educational Review*, 11, 205–17.

Makins, V. (1985) High scope: the pre-school curriculum. *Times Educational Supplement*, 5 July.

McCarthy, D. (1982) *Manual for the McCarthy Scales of Children's Abilities.* New York: The Psychological Corporation.

McGrew, W. C. (1972) Aspects of social development in nursery school children with emphasis on introduction to the group. In Blurton-Jones, N. (ed.) *Ethological Studies of Child Behaviour.* London: Cambridge University Press.

Miller, S. (1973) Ends, means and galumphing: some leitmotifs of play. *American Anthropologist*, 75, 87–98.

Money, J., and Ehrhardt, A. A. (1972) *Man and Woman: Boy and Girl.* Baltimore, MD: Johns Hopkins University Press.

Mussen, P. H., Conger, J. J., and Kagan, J. (1974) *Child Development and Personality*, 4th edn. New York: Harper & Row.

Nash, R. (1973) *Classrooms Observed. The Teacher's Perception and the*

*Pupil's Performance*. London: Routledge & Kegan Paul.

Newson, J., and Newson, E. (1968) *Four Years Old in an Urban Community*. London: Allen & Unwin.

O'Connor, M. (1975) The nursery school environment. *Developmental Psychology*, 11 (5), 556–61.

Parry, M., and Archer, H. (1974) *Pre-School Education*. Schools Council Research Studies. London: Macmillan Education Ltd.

Parten, M. (1932) Social participation among pre-school children. *Journal of Abnormal and Social Psychology*, 27, 243–69.

Petersen, I., Sellden, U., and Eeg-Olofsson, O. (1975) The evolution of the EEG in normal children and adolescents from 1 to 21 years. In Remond, A. (ed.) *Handbook of Electroencephalography and Clinical Neurophysiology*, vol. 6B. Amsterdam: Elsevier.

Piaget, J. (1951) *Play, Dreams and Imitation in Childhood*. London: Routledge & Kegan Paul.

Piaget, J. (1952) *The Origins of Intelligence in Children*. New York: International Universities Press.

Plowden, Lady (1982) We didn't know then what we know now. *Times Educational Supplement*, 2 April.

Pre-school Playgroups Association (1987) *Facts and Figures, 1986*. London: PPA.

Pringle, M. K., and Naidoo, S. (1975) *Early Child Care in Britain*. London: Gordon & Breach.

Rabinowicz, T. (1979) The differentiate maturation of the human cerebral cortex. In Falkner, F., and Tanner, J. M. (eds) *Human Growth*, vol. 3: *Neurobiology and Nutrition*. London: Plenum Press.

Reynell, J. (1969) *Reynell Developmental Language Scales: Manual for the Experimental Edition*. Windsor, Berks.: National Foundation for Educational Research.

Riege, W. H. (1971) Environmental influences on brain and behavior of year-old rats. *Developmental Psychobiology*, 4, 157–67.

Roberts, V. (1975) *'I've Made a People'*. London: Black.

Roethlisberger, F. J., and Dickson, W. J. (1939) Management and the worker. *Harvard University Business Research Studies*, 21 (9).

Rolfe, J. M. (1973) Introduction: symposium on heart-rate variability. *Ergonomics*, 16, 1–3.

Rose, G. H., and Ellingson, R. J. (1968) The comparative ontogenesis of visually evoked responses in rat, cat and human infant. *Electroencephalography and Clinical Neurophysiology*, 24, 284–5.

Rosen, C. E. (1974) The effects of sociodramatic play on problem-solving behaviour among culturally disadvantaged pre-school children. *Child Development*, 45, 920–7.

Rubin, K. H., and Maioni, T. L. (1975) Play preference in relationship to egocentrism, popularity and classification skills in pre-school. *Merrill-Palmer Quarterly*, 21, 171–9.

Rubin, K. H., Maioni, T. L., and Hornung, M. (1976) Free play behaviors in middle- and lower-class preschoolers: Parten and Piaget revisited. *Child Development*, 47, 414–19.

Rubin, K. H., Watson, K. S., and Jambar, T. W. (1978) Free play behavior in pre-school and kindergarten children. *Child Development*, 49, 534–6.

Saltz, E., Dixon, D., and Johnson, J. (1977) Training disadvantaged pre-schoolers on various fantasy activities: effects on cognitive functioning and impulse control. *Child Development*, 48, 367–80.

Saltz, E., and Johnson, J. (1974) Training for thematic-fantasy play in culturally disadvantaged children: preliminary results. *Journal of Educational Psychology*, 66, 623–30.

Samuels, S. J., and Turnure, J. E. (1974) Attention and reading achievement in first-grade boys and girls. *Journal of Educational Psychology*, 66, 29–32.

Schwartzman, H. B. (1978) *Transformation: the Anthropology of Play*. New York: Plenum Press.

Schweinhart, L. J., and Weikhart, D. (1983) In Consortium for Longitudinal Studies, *As the Twig is Bent . . . Lasting Effects of Pre-school Programs*. Hillsdale, NJ: Erlbaum.

Sherrod, L., and Singer, J. L. (1977) The development of make-believe play. In Goldstein, J. (ed.) *Sports, Games and Play*. Hillsdale, NJ: Erlbaum.

Shields, M. and Steiner, E. (1973) The language of the three-to-five-year-olds in pre-school education. *Educational Research*, 15, 97–105.

Shinman, S. (1981) *A Chance for Every Child? Access and Response to Pre-school Provision*. London: Tavistock.

Singer, J. L. (1973) *The Child's World of Make-Believe*. New York: Academic Press.

Smilansky, S. (1968) *The Effects of Socio-Dramatic Play on Disadvantaged Pre-school Children*. New York: Wiley.

Smith, P. K. (1970) 'Social and play behaviour of pre-school children'. Unpublished thesis for degree of Doctor of Philosophy, University of Sheffield.

Smith, P. K. (1977) Social and fantasy play in young children. In Tizard, B., and Harvey, D. (eds) *Biology of Play*. London: Heinemann.

Smith, P. K., and Dodsworth, C. (1978) Social class differences in the fantasy play of preschool children. *Journal of Genetic Psychology*, 133, 183–90.

Smith, P. K., and Dutton, S. (1979) Play and training in direct and innovative problem solving. *Child Development*, 50, 830–6.

Smith, P. K., and Syddall, S. (1978) Play and non-play tutoring in pre-school children: is it play or tutoring which matters? *British Journal of Educational Psychology*, 48, 315–25.

Standing, E. M. (1957) *Maria Montessori: her Life and Work*. London: Hollis & Carter.

Stanford-Binet, see Terman, L. M., and Merrill, M. A.

Stodolsky, S. S. (1974) How children find something to do in pre-schools. *Genetic Psychology Monographs*, 90, 245–303.

Sturmey, P., and Crisp, T. (1986) Classroom management. In Coupe, J., and Porter, J. (eds) *The Education of Children with Severe Learning Difficulties*. Beckenham, Kent: Croom Helm.

# References

Sutton-Smith, B. (1966) Piaget on play: a critique. *Psychological Review*, 73, 104–10.

Swift, J. W. (1964) Effects of early group experience: the nursery school and day nursery. In Hoffman, M. L., and Hoffman, L. W. (eds) *Review of Child Development Research*, 1. New York: Russell Sage.

Sylva, K. (1983) Some lasting effects of pre-school. *British Psychological Society Education Review*, 7, 10–16.

Sylva, K., Bruner, J. S., and Genova, P. (1974) The role of play in the problem-solving of children 3–5 years ole. In Bruner, J. S., Jolly, A., and Sylva, K. (eds) *Play: Its Role and Development*. Harmondsworth, Middx: Penguin.

Sylva, K., Roy, C., and Painter, M. (1980) *Childwatching at Playgroups and Nursery School*. London: Grant McIntyre.

Tanner, J. M. (1960) *Education and Physical Growth*. London: University of London Press.

Taylor, M. T. (1976) Teacher's perceptions of their pupils. *Research in Education*, 16, 25–36.

Taylor, P. H., Exon, G., and Holley, B. (1972) *A Study of Nursery Education*. London: Schools Council/Evans/Methuen Educational.

Terman, L. M., and Merrill, M. A. (1960) *The Stanford-Binet Scale of Intelligence* (3rd revision). London: Harrap.

Thomas, V. (1973) Children's use of language in the nursery. *Educational Research*, 15 (3), 209–16.

Thompson, B. (1972) Adjustment to school. *Educational Research*, 17, 128–36.

Tizard, B. (1978) Carry on communicating. *Times Educational Supplement*, 3 February.

Tizard, B. (1979) Language at home and at school. In Cazden, C. B. (ed.) *Language and Early Childhood Education*. Washington, DC: National Association for the Education of Young Children.

Tizard, B., Cooperman, O., Joseph, A., and Tizard, J. (1972) Environmental effects on language development: a study of young children in long-stay residential nurseries. *Child Development*, 43, 337–58.

Tizard, B., Phelps, J. P., and Plewis, I. (1976a) Staff behavior in pre-school centres. *Journal of Child Psychology and Psychiatry*, 17, 21–33.

Tizard, B., Phelps, J. P., and Plewis, I. (1976b) Play in pre-school centres – I. Play resources and their relation to age, sex and I.Q. *Journal of Child Psychology and Psychiatry*, 17, 251–64.

Tizard, J., Moss, P., and Perry, J. (1976c) *All Our Children*. London: Temple Smith.

Tough, J. (1973) *Focus on Meaning*. London: Allen & Unwin.

Tough, J. (1976) *Listening to Children Talking*. London: Ward Lock.

Tough, J. (1979) *The Development of Meaning*. London: Allen & Unwin.

Turner, I. F., and Green, R. V. (1977) Stated intention and executive practice in a traditional pre-school programme. *Research in Education*, 18, 35–44.

Tyler, S. (1979) Time sampling: a matter of convention. *Animal Behaviour*, 27, 801–10.

274

Tyler, S. (1985) *Keele Pre-School Assessment Guide*. Windsor, Berks.: National Foundation for Educational Research/Nelson.

Van Alstyne, D. (1932) *Play Behavior and Choice of Materials of Pre-school Children*. Chicago: University of Chicago Press.

Van der Eyken, W. (1974) *The Pre-school Years*, 3rd edition. Harmondsworth, Middx: Penguin.

Wallach, M. A., and Kogan, N. (1965) A new look at the creativity–intelligence distinction. *Journal of Personality*, 33, 348–69.

Ward, P. (1982) 'Pre-school provision and parental involvement: the views of staff and parents of children attending nursery schools and playgroups'. Unpublished thesis for the degree of Master of Arts, University of Keele.

Watt, J. S. (1977) *Cooperation in Pre-school Education*. Research Report. London: Social Science Research Council.

Webb, E. (1963) From full-time to part-time in a nursery school. *The New Era*, 44, 193–4.

Weisner, A., and McCall, R. B. (1976) Exploration and play: résumé and redirection. *American Psychologist*, 31, 492–508.

Wellman, B. L. (1943) The effects of pre-school attendance upon intellectual development. In Barker, R. G., Kounin, J. S., and Wright, H. F. (eds) *Child Behavior and Development*. New York: McGraw-Hill.

Wilson, G. (1980) 'The effects of fantasy play intervention upon cognition in under-fives'. Unpublished manuscript, University of Keele.

Wood, D., McMahon, I., and Cranstoun, Y. (1980) *Working with Under Fives*. London: Grant McIntyre.

Wood, H., and Wood, D. (1983) Questioning the pre-school child. *Educational Review*, 35, 149–62.

Woodhead, M. (1976) *Intervening in Disadvantage: a Challenge for Nursery Education*. Slough, Berks.: National Foundation for Educational Research.

Woodhead, M. (1985) Pre-school education has long-term effects: but can they be generalised? *Oxford Review of Education*, 11, 133–55.

Yakovlev, P. I., and Lecours, A. R. (1967) The myologenetic cycles of regional maturation of the brain. In Minkowski, A. (ed.) *Regional Development of the Brain in Early Life*. Oxford: Blackwell.

Yardley, A. (1973) *Young Children Thinking*. London: Evans.

Zigler, E., and Trickett, P. (1978) IQ, social competence and evaluation of early childhood intervention programs. *American Psychologist*, 2, 789–98.

# Author index

277

# Subject index

activities in pre-school provisions 70ff.
activity spans: defined 118–19; for
free-play in different pre-school
provisions 119; in intervention study
184; of staff in different pre-school
provisions 58–60; staff effects upon
126
Adjustment to School Scale 202
adults in pre-schools: activities in the
pre-school 55, 63, 210, 212–13,
218, 230, 254–6; attention to
children 257; bids for by children
in reception class 202; categorisation
of children's approaches to 273–5;
children's overtures to 139ff.;
characteristics 209; deployment of
their attention 60; dialogues with
children 148ff.; effects upon
children's attention spans 217;
expenditure of their time 57, 213;
managerial style of 227, 230;
opaque versus transparent structure
in styles 230; repertory grid analysis
of pre-school benefits 248–53;
responses to bids of children from
different pre-school background 200;
responses to childrens' overtures
142ff, 202–3; styles of speech 216;
training of 219–20
attention spans: approach to play
opportunities, and 124, 269–70;
defined 120; effects of adults upon
197–8; in reception class according

to pre-school experience 198; in
tutored and untutored groups 183,
184; of adults in nursery 257; of
children in different pre-school
provisions 120; of pre-school
children 217; of staff in different
pre-school provisions 60–3; play
with materials in intervention study
184; with adult present in reception
class 202–3

Boehm, Test of Basic Concepts 202
Bondi, Sir Herman 187
British Association for Early Childhood
Education (BAECE) 5, 33

Central Advisory Council for Education
3, 4, 5, 10; *see also* Plowden
childhood: innocence of 228
concrete operations 188
conservation skills 189, 190
creativity: measures of 173–4
critical periods: brain development 7;
EEG changes 7; effects of early
education during 9, 10; evoked
potentials 7; imprinting in animals
7, 10; in child development 7;
somatic growth 7

day dreaming: physiological correlates
of 12
Department of Education and Science
3, 17, 18, 218

280